Life After Kes

An anthology of the film - Kes

by

Simon W. Golding

Life After Kes

An anthology of the film

by

Simon W. Golding

ISBN 0-9548793-3-3

Published by GET Publishing, Bridgnorth , Shropshire WV15 5DG

info@get-publishing.co.uk

First published 2005

Printed in the United Kingdom by Taws Printers Ltd., Telford, Shropshire TF17GN

* * *

Dedication

I thank my wonderful partner, Gabrielle, for her full support and guidance during my writing career. I also thank her for our lovely daughter, Summer and stepchildren Oliver and Goldie. Without my parents help, who gave me everything, but never spoilt me, who shaped me and made me what I am, I would be hollow and shapeless. For Harry, who has passed on, his memory lives within me. All participated in my character. Who I am and whatever I become belongs to them.

Finally, my thanks to the people of Barnsley, for sharing with us the amazing story of the making of *Kes*.

* * *

Foreword

Life After Kes is an anthology of one of the greatest British movies ever made. I am an immense admirer of Ken Loach. We met in 1966 when I employed Carol White in a film with Orson Welles and Oliver Reed just before he used her in *Poor Cow*. We served together on various matters for the Director's Guild of Great Britain. Ken is completely unique. *Kes* is one of the most moving films ever. I cried during it. It deeply affected me with its humanity and revelation of life as it is really lived by many people in our country. I'm sure it is little different today. Ken's insights into a young man growing up in a hostile environment were simply brilliant. Ken has ploughed his own furrow. One of the best things you can say about Ken is that his films are like no one else's. He is a truly great innovator, creator and director.

Michael Winner

Introduction

Firstly, why a book about a film that was made over 35 years ago? Actually 30 years ago I was offered either *Cider With Rosie* by Laurie Lee or *A Kestrel for a Knave* by Barry Hines – for my O-level exam. Glancing at the dust jackets I immediately opted for the latter. Those two fingers defiantly dominating the picture in grainy symbolism clinched it for me. I somehow realised that Churchill's salute; so many decades before, bore no resemblance to this act of defiance. Although this striking effigy on the front cover was taken from the movie, some five years previous, I had not seen or heard of either book or film.

My initial response was negative – I wanted to study *Billy Liar* by Keith Waterhouse. I had watched the film and related to the main character Billy Fisher. Of course I had not yet met Hines's literary protagonist, Billy Casper, and had the future treat of immersing my mind in the adventures of his central character. A character that faced the world without the luxury of a grammar school education; unlike the other Billy. They did share a certain similar escapism. For Fisher it was his imaginary Walter Mitty world – for Casper it was a very harsh world with only his hawk, Kes, to eliminate the very real threat of a dangerous life down the pit or a menial job for a low wage. When I read the book I was totally hooked. It was a baptism that spawned my insatiable thirst for reading. I truly believe for every great book you read your capacity and endurance on the less rewarding volumes increases. I once read *Fly Away* by Desmond Bagley, and loved every page. I subsequently read nearly all Bagley's books, around fifteen, before giving up and realising I had read, in my opinion, his best work first. My insatiable thirst would never be quenched no matter how many of his books I devoured.

A Kestrel for a Knave, as a historical document, mirrored perfectly the feelings and attitudes towards the end of the sixties. Incredibly the actors all carried a strong relationship with their screen characters. Apart from Colin Welland – none of the cast were professional. Not that that would make any difference, *'You don't treat them any differently than professionals,'* explains the director, Ken Loach. Mr Gryce (Bob Bowes) who was Billy's screen principal was a real headmaster. Barry Hines, the author and scriptwriter, had taught physical education at St Helen's. David Bradley who played Billy was a pupil at the school as were most of his screen friends. So were most of the teachers in the film. Trevor Hesketh, who played Casper's form teacher; was David Bradley's form teacher. Ken Loach, the director, even insisted that Welland teach his screen class a couple of weeks prior to filming. The actor, a former teacher himself, actually followed the national curriculum; teaching his screen pupils, with most insisting they finish the projects he had set them.

Billy Casper, unlike the author, was a victim of the eleven-plus. A government directive that turned out, who passed the exam, prospective white-collar workers, fresh from grammar schools, into jobs that were safe and well paid. The failures, housed in secondary modern schools, could only look forward to unskilled manual labour or the dangers of the coal face. *Kes* protests at this educational void that does not take into account individual skills, and suggests this is a consequence of a capitalist society which demands a steady supply of unskilled labour. At the age of 11 years the governing power, teachers, pupils, and in some cases parents – viewed these latter Easter school leavers as total failures. With some teachers fighting over jobs that sent them to grammar schools, although, as often the case, their money would not increase. A badge of failure, that might haunt the most determined child through to adulthood – destined for a boring working life of under-paid and under-skilled drudgery. It was all down to a government who failed to realise individual talent. Billy Casper, like so many young boys and girls joining adulthood – carried the stamp of failure. But Billy was a survivor.

When I was handed the book in the mid seventies I had not yet viewed the film, *Kes*. The movie premiere in March 1970 seemed a million miles away from the dimly lit library, after our teacher Mr Collicott had drawn the awful lime and green coloured curtains. It was winter 1975 and a huge dusty metal and wood contraption was wheeled into the library. A television set sat on top and underneath, the size of a family suitcase, was a state-of-the-art VCR. From the opening credits; with John Cameron's haunting musical score, I watched in silence and amazement. The film even ran over the school bell, but nobody minded or certainly no-one showed the normal signs of fidgeting or the early symptoms of St. Vitus Dance. I knew then, as most of us did, that we had experienced cinematic history.

With the tradition of these harsh lessons to carry around in our consciousness have we turned a complete circle? Have we possibly as a nation learnt nothing from Casper's experiences? Are the teachers in a better position now – 35 years on? They said about the film at the time *'Bad teachers hated it and good teachers loved it!'* I wonder how many teachers hate it or love it today?

Children spend around 15,000 hours of their lives in the classroom. What they get out of it matters for the rest of their lives. I always thought good teachers were the most important factor in whether children benefit from school and it's teachers who determine whether children get a quality education. Not the curriculum, not class size, not funding, not computers and the internet, these are all secondary to having quality teachers. Barry Hines, author of *A Kestrel For A Knave*, said in 1970, *'Schools usually fit children to them instead of fitting themselves to the children, part of a system which conditions the ruling classes to superiority, lower classes to inferiority. Teachers are cynical or frustrated, and leave the job at a high rate.'* How true is the statement today?

Three wise men initially gave us *Kes,* in the shape of author Barry Hines, director Ken Loach and producer Tony Garnett. All three chiselled out a superbly adapted screenplay and built an ensemble cast and crew which was both daring and courageous. In 2001 *Kes* was voted, by the British Film Institute, the 7th greatest British film ever made.

This book not only pays homage to the vision and extraordinary talent that was involved in front and behind the camera, but also compares and probes the changes in the educational system. Are we any better off today? Have we advanced? Have we learnt anything? Has it all gone round in a circle like a merry-go-round and where and when we ever get off – it's really only a few feet away from where we got on? Has the government learnt anything? Have the teachers forgotten anything? After 35 years is Loach's gritty Northern drama as important a message today as it was then?

We can only turn to our experts of today and ask? People who were working in the profession then in 1968 and have experienced nearly four decades of change up till the present day. The children of the 1960's, like Billy Casper and peers of his day, are the fathers and mothers of the new millennium.

It is said *Nobody likes change* – but if we are making mistakes or returning to problems of yesteryear I believe it is time to get off the merry-go-round and play another game. Preferably one that does not have us going round in ever decreasing circles.

The truth of the film as a snapshot of time, pre-comprehensive schooling, pre-miners strike, as agreed by most – was extremely accurate. The right ingredients were all present. Great raw performances, a cracking story by Hines, men of vision like Loach and Garnett, a first class crew, and cinematographer Chris Menges's use of washed-out tones, add to the grim feeling of a very political and intense film. Loach said of his powerful movie, *'It should be dedicated to all the lads who fail their 11-plus. There's a colossal waste of people and talent, often through schools where full potential is not brought out.'*

The question we are left with after the film - will Billy Casper ever have the chance to develop his potential or will he leave the stagnation of the school for the stagnation of some mundane blind-alley job? And this should be a question aimed at all school leavers who have failed to find their potential. It's inherent beneath the surface of every young mind, if only adults can bother to look for it.

It was a tremendous honour to speak to the men and women, actors and crew I spoke to while compiling this book. Everyone I talked to, without exception, offered boundless enthusiasm and unfailing co-operation. They all had stories to tell – fascinating, entertaining, sad, funny, educational, and ironic, the list goes on. The crew was young and ambitious and the actors - a mixed bunch of amateurs, cabaret and variety entertainers, and the odd professional.

It took nearly two years of research to compile this journal and a worrying harmful legacy was unfolding. It would appear that this long-odds British classic, *Kes*, had somehow scarred South Yorkshire. A blackened, tainted view of the North was emerging, a powerful image portrayed ingeniously by real Yorkshire folk, had left negative impressions some thirty five years on. Similar to a great classic role, where the actor gets typecast – Barnsley was left with an overwhelming inheritance of stereotypical Northern gloom.

Building up to the millennium, with a passionate breed the likes of Steve Houghton (Leader of the Borough Council) breathing new life back into Barnsley, the ghost of *Kes* still hovers unnervingly over the town, casting the odd dark cloud. It appears that some members, a mixed international breed of movie goers, do not always view *Kes* as a frozen moment in time - a series of pictures emanating from Loach's, and his team's, inner eye. Long after the arc lamps had popped off; Barnsley was left with a calling card that the world could see and comment on. Who ultimately is responsible – the filmmaker for producing a credible job or the odd gullible viewer who watches and believes - and believes what he or she watches?

I would dig around Barnsley and see if I could find, together with the skeletal remains of *Kes*, any evidence of this unnerving legacy. It appears the *Billy Casper Syndrome*, cultured by successive governments, was still alive and kicking, as relevant today as it was when Kes flew high above the town of Barnsley.

Thanks to important initiatives like The Dickie Bird Foundation who assist financially disadvantaged young people to participate in sport. This inspirational organisation gives a few Billy Caspers the rare chance to shine.

There was always a danger that I might somehow destroy my feelings for the movie, by dissecting it and speaking intimately to the people who made it. I am pleased to say it has only intensified my passion for the film, knowing how many individual stories were creeping in and out of the lives of the cast and crew. All the people I met and spoke to helped me a great deal and offered boundless energy and vivid memories.

The Seed of an Idea – Life before *Kes*

A Kestrel For A Knave was published by Michael Joseph Limited, and later in paperback by Penguin, in 1968. Shortly afterwards followed the film – but what about life before *Kes*?

The elements that make up the story are quite simple. There is no complexity of a tangled dynamic power struggle – with fortunes and supremacy switching backwards and forwards – and neither should there be.

Billy Casper is a troubled teenager growing up in a Yorkshire mining town. Treated as a failure at school, having been labelled such after failing the eleven-plus, and unhappy at home; with an uncaring mother and bullying older brother, Billy discovers a new passion in his life when he acquires a kestrel hawk, which he names Kes. The young lad identifies with her silent strength, and she inspires in him, as he develops into a patient and skilled falconer, the trust and love nothing else can.

On the surface the educated and sporty author Hines appears to be far removed from Casper, who lacked any educational attributes and certainly no prowess on the soccer field. You also felt that Billy, the undernourished, scrawny weed, would not stray from his birthplace – again distance was placed between character and creator.

Author Barry Hines was born in 1939 in the mining village of Hoyland Common near Barnsley, where his father was a miner. He played football for the England Grammar School team and, after leaving school, for a short time for Barnsley whilst working there as an apprentice mining surveyor. He studied Physical Education for three years at Loughborough Training College and taught for two years in a London comprehensive school, before returning to the North. Inspiration had visited the author, Hines, a few years before.

His first novel was called *The Blinder* and published in 1966. It was loosely based, to a certain extent, on himself and his aspirations; an extremely academic footballer with 4 'A' levels and the chance of playing for Manchester United. Not bad timing to put a soccer oriented novel on the bookshelves with all the euphoria surrounding England winning the 1966 world cup. Good timing and a bit of luck.

Barry Hines started to write, he says, because he read and wanted to read novels that, like Allan Sillitoe and Stan Barstow's work, had real working class men and women as their main characters. When you look at *Kes* I wondered about the female roles. St Helen's, location for the film, almost appears like a boys school, with very few female parts representing the teachers, the odd bible reader or story telling pupil, a librarian, and of course – the uncaring Mrs Casper. The girls never really moved the story along, just validated the narration. Whether this was a reflection of the author's experiences or the simple fact that the spotlight fell on Billy, as a 14 year-old boy, just was not interested in girls – the birds and the bees or certainly the bees did not interest him.

Hines based his characters in *Kes* on stereotypical characters around him at the time and admits that he sympathises more with the character of Mrs Casper, the struggling mother trying to raise two boys and hold down a full-time job.

Although he claims the character of Billy is not him, he hints at a relatively wide knowledge of kestrels and their habits as is evident from the novel. '*The original Billy Casper was a famous American golfer whom I had read about in the sports pages. Later, after the book was published, I saw Billy Casper on television. He was a big burly type, the exact opposite of my skinny little character. But it didn't matter then, my Billy Casper had been born.*'

Often it seems that a name sticks in the mind of an author and is suddenly brought forward hidden in some dark recess of the mind – you just hope it is at the right time.

'*Curiously, there was another American golfer, called Tom Kite, whose name I would have liked to use. He sounded like a straight arrow, a brave, upright sort of fellow, but unfortunately I had seen him playing on television so I was never able to use the name.*' It would have been interesting if the book's main character for *Kes* had the surname of a bird of prey - Kite? Perhaps the film could then have starred George Segal, Peter Finch or Gregory Peck! Perhaps not.

Geographically Hines was living in an ideal place to almost watch *Kes* being played out in front of his own eyes – almost through his front window in Hoyland. '*In the village where I lived, the miners walked to work across meadows, with sky larks singing overhead, before crowding into the cage at the pit top and plunging into the darkness.*'

Barry even walked the same paths in the forest as Billy would do in the book and film. *'Like Billy Casper, the main character in* A Kestrel for a Knave, *I spent much of my childhood exploring the countryside, but unlike Billy I was no academic failure. I had passed the eleven-plus and went to grammar school. Most of my friends however had failed and gone to the local secondary modern – the model for the school in the film.'*

The biggest single feature and strongest message in the book, which was evident in the film, was the total criticism of the system. *'…Those children who had failed the eleven-plus had effectively been told that they were unintelligent and many of them continued to believe it for the rest of their lives,'* states Barry, seriously. *'Teachers were similarly affected. I remember one secondary modern schoolteacher telling me he had obtained a post in a grammar school and even though his salary would remain the same, he still regarded it as promotion. The eleven-plus system was ruinously divisive at all levels.'*

In a way I was snatched from the jaws of failure by the comprehensive system. When I sat my eleven-plus in 1973, I was at private school, Haden Hill, in Netherton, West Midlands. It was all black gowns, quails eggs and flicking each other with wet towels.

I had previously been to a school that placed more emphasis on religion than on any educational needs. By the age of eight I knew the names of all the apostles but not the capital of England. My parents whisked me away to Haden Hill, with a more intimate educational approach, to try and prepare me for the eleven-plus. It failed and so did I. Luckily in Kinver, Edgecliff School was now a comprehensive – so I was now no longer a failure. The new system of enlightenment was streaming – although I was in the bottom stream – a puddle really, casting my mind back looking around at the rest of my dishevelled group. I wondered what I had got myself into. I often wonder where the others are now and how well or poorly they have done. Of course it was much easier to climb down the ladder into our class, but I do not remember many of that first branded lot making any moves upwards – which was the general idea. In fact five years on, although we had swapped and changed subjects – I did see an awful lot of very familiar faces. Eventually, when I grew up physically and emotionally, I had to go back to school and re-sit all my exams. It was unpleasant and hard work – just to get to a standard most average 16 year olds took for granted.

One evening I was drinking in the Bellman's Cross, in Shatterford, near my family home, it's a trendy restaurant now – with a couple of hyphens and a French chef in bright clothes, and in walked a familiar face. It took a few minutes to work out a fellow classmate from the puddle. I was about to go over and introduce myself but the ex-pupil I remembered had ordered a large pizza from behind the bar. The landlady, being helpful, shouted over that she would cut it into slices for him. *'Do you want me to cut it into six pieces or ten?'* she asked. His brow furrowed like all puddleonians do, *'Six pieces – I wouldn't be able to eat ten!'* Once a puddle man always a puddle man. I walked away in disgust.

Even if the people around the author Hines, ceased to perform in his future book, some told stories that would eventually end up on the page. *'I used some of the incidents my friends told me about, in* A Kestrel for a Knave. *For example, the boy who was caned when he took a massage to the headmaster, the big brother roaming the corridors seeking vengeance because his brother had failed to place a bet on a winning horse, and the boy falling asleep in assembly. These anecdotes – and many more which weren't included in the novel – were told to me with great amusement and relish.'*

In the novel and ultimately the film, Billy Casper has to find his passion in a world of abuse - a nemesis of rage that encircles his every move. Barry Hines chose a kestrel, a very special kind of bird, to elevate his hero, a means of escape from his working class shackles and environmental depression that was all around him.

Hines kept baby magpies as a child and humorously related his experiences of stealing them from their nests (something he regrets now), fattening them up on scraps of food and having them flying around the house until they were strong enough to be set free, which would roughly coincide with the time his mother shouted, *'that magpie has to go!'* *'The bird would always sit on the window sill outside and look in,'* Barry reminisces, *'before it finally flew away.'*

Although I do not think a magpie would have had the same dramatic effect – although, if there was only one, it could have been called *Sorrow* – or *Maggie?* It gets even better with the latter as a film score; a title song in 1968, Honeybus released a chorus,

> *She fly's like a bird in the sky*
> *She fly's like a bird and I wish that she was mine*
> *She fly's like a bird, ho me, ho my*
> *I see, I sigh, now I know*
> *I just can't let Maggie go*

But it would have probably been a very different movie. Any producers out there can have that one on me!

We know that Barry and his brother, Richard used to watch the kestrels nesting every year and they always wanting one. 'We knew a kestrel's nest, high up in the wall of a crumbling medieval hall. Generations of kestrels had nested in the same spot, and we used to stand out of sight at the edge of an adjacent wood watching the parents return with mice and small birds for the ravenous fledglings.'

Eventually a young hawk did enter the Hines household. 'My interest in falconry was increased further by reading The Goshawk by T. H. White, a classic text about a battle of wills between a novice falconer and a young goshawk. Then, more importantly, watching my brother train a young kestrel which had been given to him by a friend.'

So Barry Hines looked out of his window at the common in Hoyland watching his brother fly his kestrel. Following his dad to work across the meadow before he dropped towards the centre of the earth, en-route to the coal face. He remembered early years spent listening to his mates regale tales of their secondary modern school exploits and much later swapped stories in the staff room when he was a teacher. It was all just another day in the life of A Kestrel for a Knave.

2

The Beginning – From Book to Screen

'I think that it's a kind of pride, and as you say independence. It's like an awareness, a satisfaction with its own beauty and prowess. It seems to look you in the eye and say, "Who the hell are you anyway?"' Billy Casper describing Kes, From the novel *A Kestrel for a Knave*, by BARRY HINES (Penguin Books).

Producer Tony Garnett had been alerted to the talents of Barry Hines by Alfred Bradley, a legendary radio producer at BBC North in Leeds, and read the writer's first novel, *The Blinder*. Garnett arranged a meeting in London and asked the author if he wanted to do a *Wednesday Play*? Hines said he would very much like to, but he had a book going round in his head and felt that was what he should write next.

'That immediately showed his integrity,' remembers Garnett, *'because the advance on a literary novel was very small compared with the money for a Wednesday Play.'*

'He was a teacher with a couple of young kids, a mortgage and so on, he didn't have much money. Literary novels only earned a few hundred quid in those days. He would have got a few thousand for a TV play so I said the offer was still open, but when he finished the book would he let me have a look at it.'

Barry's agent was true to his word and sent Garnett a typed manuscript. *'I mean I read it in one gulp,'* laughs Tony. *'And I knew straight away it had to be made into a film. I think Ken was editing Poor Cow (1967) at the time – and I handed him the novel and said – I got a great one here Ken. And I knew, I knew it was right. I mean politically it was right and the characters just leapt off the page. You do have to look for truthfulness in writing. In fact there wasn't a lot of screenwriting to do because it was all there. It was a very simple and strong narrative – just what you need for a film.'*

Loach was in total agreement, impressed by the story, and both men joined Hines in adapting the book for the screen, although the original narrative was written in such a simple, visual way that, according to Garnett, this amounted to little more than *'a cut-and-paste job.'*

Hines found like minds in fellow former grammar school boys Garnett and Loach. *'Tony and Ken came up to Hoyland Common,'* Hines recalled, *'and went on a walk around the woods at the Old Hall Farm, which was actually used in the film as Monastery Farm, where the boy finds the hawk, and just chatted to make sure we were on the same wavelength – it wasn't a story about falconry! The book was political, saying that the Billy Caspers of the world were regarded as washouts and failures and no good at anything. I was trying to show that, in different circumstances, Billy was a clever boy. He wasn't an academic, but he wasn't thick; it was more to do with motivation.'*

In 1968, the regime of Hugh Greene at the BBC was in its death throes, signalling the end of the Corporation's liberal era, in which radical ideas had found a voice, Loach and Garnett left to set up their own production company, along with talent agent Clive Goodwin and Garnett's friend and solicitor, Irving Teitelbaum. With the decision to adapt Barry Hines's book as their first project, Kestrel Films was chosen as the company's name and Loach was guaranteed to have Garnett as his producer, ensuring that he would never again have to accede to the demands of an outsider, as in *Poor Cow.* A small amount of money from the National Film Finance Corporation enabled Kestrel to set up and run an office.

Once the location was agreed upon, St Helen's school in Barnsley, it was Tony Garnett's job to liaise with the school. Mr Hirst, the headmaster passed on the entire enquiry to one of his teachers Trevor Hesketh. Trevor, who was David Bradley's form teacher, said at the time, *'Questions flowed across the staff room. What effect would filming have on the children? Would the building suffer? Would the film create a good or bad impression of the school to the audiences? Who would be in it? Would the local authority approve? Would the majority of staff co-operate? Who were these filmmakers anyway?'* When Tony Garnett Productions showed their hand, any fears were quickly dispelled. With television plays like *Up the Junction* and *Cathy Come Home* added to their CV, reputation was respected. *'The atmosphere in the staff room gradually changed to one of servility in some,'* remembers, Hesketh, *'and of active co-operation in others.'*

Everything was not straightforward. Some of the teachers had read the novel. *'Yes, some had reservations, as the story involved a boy, with an unsatisfactory home background, whose sole interest in life was training a kestrel hawk,'* adds, Trevor. *'School life was boring, indeed painful to the boy, and he was a misfit in every way. Only one teacher managed to discover his knowledge of birds, but, by the other teachers, he was treated as an outcast.'* Not the sort of subject matter that would naturally be courted by the teaching profession as a whole.

Although St Helen's Secondary Modern was the antithesis in character of the school in the novel, faith was placed in the hands of the film's director, the blessing of the authority, and the benediction of the headmaster. Boys, girls and staff all auditioned for leading roles. It was always the policy of Garnett and Loach to use real people wherever possible. Teachers would play teachers and pupils would play pupils and so on. Through Loach's lens the public were witnessing the stepping-stone from movie drama to what we now call *reality TV.* You never felt you were watching actors in a play, but eaves dropping on true life.

Raising money for a film is always difficult, but for a film of this nature - low budget, no sex, little violence and no stars; Loach and Garnett found it particularly daunting. But they secured a deal and began building the cast and crew that would project Hines's novel onto the silver screen.

With the cast and crew assembled in South Yorkshire, disaster struck: the film backers pulled out. National General, a Hollywood production and cinema-owning company keen to break into the British market, had agreed a £165,000 budget in a deal with Tony Garnett through its London subsidiary, Cathy Centre Productions. *'The money just fell away,'* explains Garnett, *'So Ken and I went up and down Wardour Street* (capital of Britain's film industry) *trying to raise cash. People just sniggered and said it was about the wrong kind of bird. It was getting desperate because the chicks were about to fly the nest and we couldn't do the movie without the kestrels. Also, we had a conscience about the crew because they would have been out of work, so I called a meeting at my house and told all the heads of department that the money had fallen away, we weren't sure whether we could put the film together and they were free to take other work. Every one of them said: "We want to do this and we'll stick with it."'*

Eventually, a fairy godfather arrived in the shape of Tony Richardson, a British film legend who had directed classics such as *The Entertainer, The Loneliness of the Long Distance Runner* and *Tom Jones.* The latter had made a fortune for United Artists and they were reluctant to say no to the director. Also, $400,000, the budget to make *Kes,* to an organisation like them was of no consequence.

17

Richardson had heard about Loach and Garnett's predicament and, through his association with United Artists across the Atlantic, used his reputation to pick up the telephone and get an instant deal. The deal was even more impressive as United Artists London branch had already turned down *Kes*.

'Tony (Richardson) *heard about our plight and asked to see us,'* remembers Garnett. 'We *went on to the West End offices of his company, Woodfall Films in Curzon Street, and he asked us how much we wanted. I told him £165,000 and he said: "All right. Come back this afternoon." We returned at five-thirty and he was in the middle of trying to set up his movie,* Laughter in the Dark *staring Nicol Williamson, and was having problems with that.'*

Eventually they acquiesced, with one stipulation. United Artists made Richardson agree a cross-collateralisation deal for *Kes* and *Laughter in the Dark* under which, if either film went over budget, would have to be paid for from the profits of the other.

Richardson left the two men to make the film without interference, even though Woodfall Films was one of the production companies for the movie. It was also Richardson who came up with the title, *Kes* (the name Billy gives to his hawk). The original working titles were *A Kestrel for a Knave* and *A Pocket of Silence* – the latter a reference Mr Farthing (Colin Welland) makes about the bird.

Apart from the children who were drafted in from near-by schools, other actors came from the local variety and revue circuits. Hines recommended a local English teacher he knew, enter the ebullient Brian Glover, to play the PE teacher and one of the funniest and most memorable scenes in British cinematic history was burnt on to celluloid and would be enjoyed by generations of cinemagoers all over the world.

37 years on and the film is still shown on FilmFour most months as a classic of the British cinema, and the original book, *A Kestrel for a Knave,* is still a cornerstone of the school curriculum. Long after the pits that threatened Casper have closed down, new versions of the play are appearing on the stage. Some believe the film to be as relevant now as it was when the credits first rolled at the premier at the ABC Cinema in Doncaster in 1969. If this is true we have served a tremendous injustice to our future – the pupils of today. Returning to St Helen's (now Edward Sheerien), location for the film – for the launch of the book, gave us a great chance to find out. In fact as I am penning my third draft of the novel in late March of 2005 – the school is still waiting to be granted Arts Status and give funds to possibly

encourage the odd Casper in the class. After all St. Helen's has been in the spotlight not only for *Kes*, but also when the director Ken Loach returned to the school to let the pupils audition for the movie *Black Jack*, which was released in 1979.

3

The Search – Tracking Down the Credits

It wasn't easy tracking down the cast and crew of a movie that had been shot over 37 years ago. I really didn't know where to start. I decided upon David Bradley, who played the lead; Billy Casper, as my focal point. I thought this would be an easy start, how wrong I was.

Firstly I contacted Equity and assumed the efficient voice on the other end of the telephone would simply give me an agent's number. I was curtly informed that *Dai* Bradley, his name whilst in Equity – there was already a David Bradley registered, was no longer a member. For the purposes of this novel I also adopted the name Dai, from this point onwards, and began my extraordinary journey.

After trying several exhausting dead ends – journalists, former colleagues and repertory companies etc. I placed an advert in the Stage. A week later I received a call from an actor, Dave Brown, who had worked with Bradley. I rang the number he gave me and spoke to a charming helpful girl called Lula who informed me Dai had moved out a year ago and she had no number or knowledge of his movements since. I even tried to find his sister, who Lula informed me owned a cab company in Barnsley – I telephoned everyone – nothing came up. I had already rung every Bradley in Yorkshire. The trail didn't quite die there as Lula mentioned, in passing, a chiropracticioner that Dai's agent and friend used to go to, but she couldn't remember his name. She remembered it was somewhere in Manwood Road, London, but not the business name. Onward to directory enquiries on-line and, eventually, I found a name.

A bubbly Jamaican voice (Cynthia Dunne), emanating from the receiver, informed me that she remembered the gentleman, he was an agent and he used to come to her practise, but she could not quite remember his name. But added, he had a deep voice, he was an actor, a radio presenter who was married and helped the charity raising money for Aids victims. She also mentioned that she was sure he was in a Carry On, oh and suffered problems with his third and fourth lumbar discs. I then went through my video collection of Carry On's to see if a name would jump out at me. It didn't.

Then, one Monday morning I received a call from Akin Ajumo from the Guardian who gave me an address of Dai's agent; MakDee Management, which he knew was hot about three years ago. Back to Directory enquires on-line – it was ex-directory. I wondered how many agents are ex-directory – only very big and successful ones I thought. I telephoned the 118118 and it was confirmed, but the girl did let me have the name of the person living at that address – Don McCorkindale – clang! I did remember seeing that name down the credits of *Carry On Cabby*; he played Tubby. Unfortunately, I was informed, that Tubby no longer represented Mr Bradley and that was the end of that. I had a month's worth of wasted telephone calls and a bill which was as long as some of the telephone numbers I had been calling and still no nearer to finding Bradley.

As I was about to give up I received another call from Lula. She had been talking to a mutual friend and had heard that Dai was working, behind the scenes, in a West End theatre production – something ...*Nights*. I tried Arabian Nights, Boogey Nights, Forty Days and Forty Nights, Phoenix Nights... here we go again I thought. Actually, it did not take long before I was ringing the Apollo Theatre, West End, where they were putting on *Bombay Nights*. Yes, Dai Bradley was working for them for nearly a year, as a dresser, and they gave me the number to the stage door. I nervously fingered the buttons and waited for an answer. The male middle-aged voice, it always is, then informed me that Dai Bradley had left the company two weeks ago. There was a beat, before the voice said, '*He used to be very friendly with Paul – the security guard, he's on tonight; after around 1:00 am. You could try him?*' I could handle the failure, but the hope was getting me down. I rang back at 1:01 am and Paul answered on the third ring. He did not have or would not give me a forwarding address, although he said he was working somewhere in Wolverhampton. Which was ironic as this was only 20 miles from my office, although without a contact number he may as well have been on safari in Whipsnade Zoo. I replaced the telephone totally dejected.

The end of my journey to track down the lad who had played Billy Casper all those years ago was quite unremarkable. I had been contacted by Ethan Hardcastle from the Daily Mail, he had seen the advert asking for Bradley in the Stage, and wanted to do a piece on it – he did not know where the actor was either. Following the publication of Hardcastle's article I had a call from a young girl called Nicky Blackman; or Spilly as she was known to Dai (she informed me she was a little accident prone), offered me his contact number. Although, she pointed out, she had not spoken to him in several months. With all what I had been through I dialled the number quite nonchalantly. A voice answered immediately, '*Hi, can I help you?*' It was a long way from the scruffy urchin character of Billy Casper's course Yorkshire brogue, but I knew it was Dai. We spoke briefly and he gave me his agent's telephone number. It appears *Tubby* was back on the scene. I fully understood Dai's reluctance to go into detail during that initial chat. He wanted to keep it as formal as possible and conduct his business through his rejuvenated friendship with former agent, Don McCorkindale. Bradley was contemplating his own biography and feared my work may possibly detract from his. To me it was like I was the first man to climb Everest and at the final summit I discovered someone had built a restaurant. A few months later he contacted me and informed me McCorkindale was no longer representing him – although I believe they are still very good friends. We have had much correspondence back and forth. The last time I heard from him he gave me a full curriculum vitae which I have found most helpful.

Strangely, all the other cast and crew members fell into place. In one afternoon I had arranged meetings, over the next few months, with the director, Ken Loach, the producer, Tony Garnett, the writer Barry Hines, even tough cookie Freddie Fletcher who played Jud and Colin Welland; who played the kindly Mr Farthing. Subsequently I arranged to see John Cameron who wrote the evocative score and the brilliant cinematographer of *Kes*, Chris Menges. Also Joey Kaye, the club comedian, and Trevor Hesketh; Bradley's form teacher, The 4D Jones band who played during Mrs Casper's and Jud's night out, and most of the football team (Manchester United and Spurs), returned my calls and other meetings were set up. I even tracked down the young lad, Martin Harley, who was innocently caned in Gryce's office – he certainly had a story to tell.

I reached a lot of the extras through Friends United; visiting the school where the film was made; St Helen's Secondary Modern, in Barnsley. www.ayup.co.uk - a tremendous site – the real voice of Yorkshire, ran a great piece and invited members of the cast and crew or anybody who was connected to the film, to get in touch with me. I had a tremendous response and filled in many of the cast and crew up and down the credits. I was also greatly assisted by The Yorkshire Post (Andrew Robinson) and The Barnsley Chronicle (Ian Thompson), they both ran pieces for me.

Jim Ryder (*Billy's friend*), Anne Goulding (*extra – playground scene*), Zoë Sunderland (*librarian*), Eric Bolderson (*Farmer*), Les Stringer (butcher), John Grayson *(Jud's best friend)* etc. and many many more came forward through the different media channels and shared their experiences with me.

A truly sad loss was the death of Brian Glover who passed away on 24th July 1997 aged 63. His portrayal of the tyrannical PE instructor, Mr Sugden, was one of the greatest, funniest, bitterest support performances in British film history. Brian Glover is sadly missed. I thank Brian's widow, Tara, for all her help.

I really wanted and tried to be truthful to everyone as well as myself. Dialogue offered without thought can sometimes be not very user friendly. People repeat words and can contradict themselves. If people said it, and it was relevant to the book – good or bad – it was included.

In my experience, when reading some novelist's words of non-fiction, an inaccurate or ill perceived phrase or even a word in the wrong place – I can become dissociated from the author. Four pages into reading Goldie Hawn's (big hero of mine) autobiography, the actress describes at around the age of two, with brand new skin, placing her feet in her mouth and they tasted sweet. Putting aside the very young age, personally, apart from the odd member of the Royal Family (yes Fergie), I do not think people generally recognize feet taste sweet. Not even the hooves of a Spanish Cava grape treader!

I was also let down by another hero of mine, ex-SAS and explorer extraordinaire; author Ranulph Fiennes. He wrote a true story, as it was told to him, called *The Sett*. It was actually cantered around my old school village of Kinver. Ranulph, if I remember correctly, described one character's mental thoughts a few seconds before he died instantly by a single shot. As he had no chance to communicate those last inner feelings, I can only assume this was creative writing – a treasured instrument for the fictionist but has no place in fact.

It is my profession, as a non-fiction novelist, to deliver an accurate account of events as I see them or they are told to me. You have fiction, faction and fact – the latter being my greatest tool. I have genuinely tried not to misrepresent anyone. Ninety-nine percent of all my interviews were recoded on state-of-the-art mini disc. The other one percent – well, that was down to my memory. Read on with faith...

The Genre – School Films – By John Cunningham

4

PET SUBJECT

Britain used to make great films about schools. But nowadays, argues John Cunningham, we could learn a few lessons from the US. His article in the Guardian, Friday 24 September 1999 compares the two systems..............

In the middle of the mayhem that passes for normal in the current crop of US high-school movies - zitty geeks lusting after their teachers, pushy kids fixing the school elections, would-be prom queens killing their rivals, space aliens invading the minds and bodies of teachers - along comes a British film with nothing so deranged going on in the classroom: just the usual bullies and sadists, and a stand-out teacher with a heart of gold.

One UK offering among a glut of US high-school movies is hardly a counter-offensive. It isn't even new; it's the re-launch of a film made over 20 years ago. Kes is among the best-remembered films about childhood and classroom. The main character is the deprived Barnsley boy, Billy Casper, unloved at home and tormented at school, who forges a relationship with a fledgling kestrel he finds and rears as a pet.

Kes is very much about education: the new-built secondary modern might seem like a shiny palace for the kids from the dead-end council estate it serves, but it's run with Victorian harshness and has failed Billy from day one. The director, Ken Loach, takes a hard look at the teaching profession: the bullish head, the seriously nasty PE teacher (Brian Glover) and the altruistic English master, Mr Farthing (Colin Welland) who discovers and encourages Billy's passionate concern for the falcon.

Kes was part of a small cluster of British school films made at the end of the 60s - the angry decade. Lindsay Anderson's If... and James Clavell's To Sir, With Love show the range: from revolution in a public school to the role of a black teacher in London's East End. The Prime *of Miss Jean Brodie*, directed by Ronald Neame and set in the crème de la crème world of a girls' academy in 30s Edinburgh, belongs to the same fecund batch: it was made in 1968.

However, there has been no comparable bunch of movies on the same theme since then. It's interesting to speculate why. There were plenty of other social realist subjects around in the grainy 60s, class, sex and race among them. There were many other professions that writers such as John Braine, John Osborne, Alan Sillitoe and David Storey (whose works were adapted for the screen) could select for their heroes and anti-heroes; teachers were soon eclipsed by liars, layabouts, petty criminals and seedy seaside entertainers as emblems of 60s realism.

Yet, as film-makers in many cultures have recognised, schools are obvious subjects: they can be legitimately portrayed as microcosms of the larger world into which pupils are debauched; their hierarchies invite conflict as well as consensus; the way teachers use or abuse their unique power is intriguing; their treatment of youngsters who assert their personalities - either as rebels or geniuses - is the essence of drama. With such possibilities, it's not surprising that both the US and Britain have a long history of teacher/school films. But while directors here seem pretty much to have given up the theme it's had a resurgence in America since the 80s. Cynics say US studios are interested largely because teenagers form a big, powerful and growing block of movie-goers, and they're simply catering to that sector. But there's more to it than that. British directors, while not treating education as an hermetically-sealed activity, have usually addressed only the social and emotional territory that lies close to teachers and their charges. Directors in the US, by contrast, have thrown off these restrictions. Any fad or trend that Americans go for - sexual, criminal, occult, power-driven, or just plain wacky - can be played out on a campus setting.

It's as if we in the UK are too concerned with playing by the rules of what we imagine a school movie to be about. Or perhaps filmmakers are turned off by teachers, because they're seen as endlessly whingeing, or because education issues are perceived as too bureaucratic to put on screen. Yet just as many dramatic calamities befall the profession here as in America, though they might be in different categories. While the US has real-life dramas involving the mass slaying of teachers and pupils, we wring our hands when it's revealed that sir (or miss) gets into bed with a busty (or priapic) pupil. But, while the media is full of such scandals, we don't make films about them

This wasn't always the case. A rough analysis of several teacher/ school films shows that they fall broadly into three groups. First, comedy/farce: schools, particularly boarding, single-sex and fee-paying, have long been a sure-fire target, with larger than life teachers in the firing line. From *The Happiest Days of Your Life* (a farce made in 1950, about the wartime evacuation of a girl's school to a boy college), through the *St Trinian's series* (usually Alastair Sim in drag) to *Carry On Teacher* (Hattie Jacques as a battleaxe in the form-room; Kenneth Williams as a literature teacher), the tables were turned - those who once controlled us could be subjected to every humiliation in the book.

The second group, the altruistic/role model teacher had if anything a more enduring appeal. Even more revealing than Colin Welland as Billy's "enabler" in *Kes* is Sidney Poitier in *To Sir, With Love* (1967). Set in a sink school, Poitier is under siege by Cockney kids. But he manages to prove to his rebellious charges that education has some point when he scraps the prescribed timetable and substitutes his own programme of what he calls "survival training". The warm glow audiences felt for Poitier can't be dismissed as sentimental fiction because the script was based on a novel by the Caribbean writer ER Braithwaite, who came to London in the 50s and taught at a state school.

There's a mixture of triumph and temptation in the third group. We are introduced to teachers who appear to live for their jobs; they have altruism no surrogate parent could ever attain; but then a dark personal hinterland is gradually revealed. These well-rounded films are often adaptations of novels and plays - so their worth has already been proven, and it's a type of film British directors used to do amazingly well. Hard to go wrong with material by Terence Rattigan (The Browning Version) and Muriel Spark (The Prime of Miss Jean Brodie), but both show the terrible power that teachers have to construct personas in the classroom, to manipulate their pasts and reinvent themselves. The torment that such an exercise can conceal was dazzlingly demonstrated in Term of Trial, directed in 1962 by Peter Glenville. Laurence Olivier is an idealistic but disillusioned teacher in a mixed school in the north. He's an alcoholic driven to drink by a nagging wife and a sense of failure: teaching is the only job he could get after a prison sentence for his pacifist stance in the war. He's already on the edge, but there's worse to come. One of his pupils, Sarah Miles, appears anxious for extra lessons but he, naively, doesn't see that this conceals a crush on him. On a school trip to Paris, she alleges he's sexually assaulted her. He's cleared of the charge, but we're left wondering what there is to salvage of his career and his marriage.

Powerful stuff, and you can't help wondering if there wasn't some way even an occasional film still couldn't draw on the same fecund themes. After all, re-defining permissible behaviour between teachers and adolescents in their care continues to cause explosions. It's not an area which American directors have avoided. Sure, even 10 years ago, Peter Weir made a good old-fashioned picture about an inspiring teacher - *Dead Poets Society* - but themes have moved on. The sports fields of even privileged campuses are seeing different kinds of battles. And US directors have since allowed the wider world to invade the classrooms. In *Rushmore*, the contestants vying for a young widowed teacher, Miss Cross (played by Olivia Williams) are a spotty, specs-wearing pupil (academic duffer but brilliant organiser) and the middle-aged father of two of his classmates.

In *Election* the venom and chicanery of a national presidential election is compressed into a fight for the student presidency, throwing in adultery, seduction and lesbianism as well. The ruthless chief contender, Tracy Flick, has a past: an affair with one of her teachers. There's no way she's going to let that damage her election chances; she even airbrushes the guy (who was sacked) out of the school group photograph.

In fact, high schools are just like any adult workplace; the full range of feuds, fanaticisms and fantasies is played out. Childhood isn't ring fenced by school rules. It's an ugly world in there. US movies are exploiting it for all it's worth. Maybe the Brits should have another bash at something they used to do rather well.

5

The Film - Kes

It was the summer of '68. The wireless blurted out *Lady Madonna* by The Beatles, Cliff Richard had *Celebrations* and Louis Armstrong thought *What A Wonderful World*. *Dad's Army* began its fine run on television, as did *Hawaii Five-O*. The big screen boasted *Funny Girl* with Barbra Streisand and *Oliver!*, with the angelic Mark Lester asking for more. Jack Lemmon and Walter Matthau were the *Odd Couple* and Steve McQueen starred in the *Thomas Crown Affair* while the Beatles also had a *Yellow Submarine*.

It was during this time that a Hollywood movie was being made in Barnsley. At the heart of it all was a scrawny kid from St Helens Secondary Modern who had acted in a few school pantomimes and was pretty good at football. His name was Dai Bradley. With only one actor of note (Colin Welland), a few local cabaret people (Lynne Perrie, Duggie Brown, Joey Kaye etc.), and a whole heap of raw school kids, cinematic history was about to be made. Loach disregarded the inner city intimacy and chose the exposed countryside and perfectly caught the moment. Menges captured the extraordinary juxtaposition of heavy industry and open scenery. Shots of coal-miners walking to work, of workingmen's club entertainers, of blackened factories spewing smoke, of lush woodlands, and of red brick streets punctuate the film's central theme of a working class waif with no prospects finding escape through training a kestrel.

The movie would be a low-budget, sexless, starless and relatively un-violent. With what appeared to be both hands tied behind their backs; Loach, Garnett and Hines started trawling for talent. Barry Hines had brought in a friend of his, an English teacher called Brian Glover, to play the games teacher Mr Sugden, and one of the most memorable scenes in English film history was born. Sugden, strutting around the football pitch as Bobby Charlton surrounded by bored and miserable boys struck a chord with any young lad forced to play footie on a cold rainy school day.

There is no Hollywood pretence when looking at a Loach film

set, usually on location, amongst the people. Geoffrey Mather, for the Daily Express, visited one of the locations for Kes, at Monastery farm. They were filming Casper's first sight of the hawk as it flies and returns to its nest. *'A dozen of us have stood now for two hours on a dirt path dividing fields from woods,'* says Mather, *'and it has seemed like a thousand years. It is mid-morning, with much cloud and the camera has a filter to enhance the illusion. The boy, local lad David Bradley, runs across the rough field towards a gaunt ruin of a wall. High in the wall — and these shots come later — he will discover the kestrel nest.'* With the seriousness of film-making, Mather lightens the day with an incident off camera. *'The attractive girl assistant, in yellow mini-mac, is hugging her typewriter. It has accompanied her through bog and boggart, clough and fold and this morning she created a welcome diversion when she tried to climb backwards from the top of the equipment van without losing her dignity. She failed miserably.'*

One method that Loach instituted to heighten the reality for those appearing in front of the camera was to move the film crew as far away from the action as possible. *'The priority is to get a performance that people will believe, that has originality and spontaneity,'* he explained. *'If you put the technical apparatus too close to the actors, they will find that a distraction. So, if you can remove the lights and the boom from being in the eye-line and set the camera back, it gives them the freedom to relate to the other people in the scene.'* With a long focus lens, usually about seventy millimetres, the camera discovers its subject and frames it in medium shot. The camera is totally unobtrusive. It might have seemed impossible to do this when one scene with Dai Bradley, Colin Welland and the kestrel had to be filmed in the garden shed where Billy keeps the bird, but Loach simply found a small hole through which to shoot, leaving the performers alone in their own space. When Dennis Wicks and his brother, Eric, built the shed, they were not film scene builders, but were domestic craftsman — which is exactly what Loach wanted. *'We were in total silence,'* said Welland, *'and you couldn't help but respond to it and feel the awe that was described in Barry's book. A lesser director would have had the camera there, sat behind it and taken one wall out, but Ken allowed the reality to unfold, totally undisturbed by the camera.'*

Often Loach has left reply dialogue off a script so the actor is unsure of the other character's response. As in everyday life — we respond to others, absorbing what they say and reacting to it. He has indulged many tricks to get the performance he desires — the realism he knows is there. *'It's always a matter of judgment on the day,'* he explains, *'what you tell them, how you prepare the ground, how you set it up. I think I have tried to refine the methods and, in the end, take more chances. In a way, the more reckless you are, the more extraordinary the results you get, provided you assess the risks. I've been very lucky with the people we've cast, but I think what has become clearer over the years is that you have to direct for them. You not only have to guide their performances by talking to them, you actually have to create events for them to respond to. A lot of effort has to go into the circumstances in which they can work, and you find that most of your directing goes into creating something off-camera.'*

Loach developed his Realist approach by using non-professional actors wherever possible and believes that people, in general, have great potential. Therefore for each project, he spends his time searching for the right talent in order to produce the necessary level of naturalism, for example, who could forget ex-wrestler Brian Glover in *Kes* as the sadistic sports teacher, who believed he was Bobby Charlton's natural successor. Indeed it was pure comedy sharpened on the knife of tragedy. This method of working with semi-professionals or people, who had little or no performance experience, was a theme that runs throughout Loach's work. The total opposite procedure to big budget movies here and abroad. First you get a script and marry that to a box-office actor, often the actor may be in the running first; then go looking for a suitable script. In some cases the studio knows a big bucks actor can carry a weak script and they can still make money.

To get the documentary-style pictures of the streets of Barnsley – such as small boys seen wearing pyjamas on the doorstep – Loach would send the film crew off for a coffee and roam around in a van, with just the cameraman and sound recordist in the back. Using children, however, meant taking risks and many, many takes of each scene. Loach would try and surprise the kids to get the genuine reactions he required. During an assembly scene he wanted the children to appear distracted, so one of the crew did a striptease outside the window.

There is sadness to the end of the movie, that Billy is trapped in his world with no real hope of improvement. *'In the film,'* says Loach, *'through the story, you see a whole side to life that the world cannot afford to see, that it can't afford to acknowledge. At the time, in the North of England, boys like Billy were needed for unskilled labour. People who saw the film said to us, "Couldn't he get a job in a zoo?", which misses the entire point, because if it's not Billy who's going to be exploited as unskilled labour, it's going to be someone else who's in that predicament; the world requires him and people like him to fill that role. The world just isn't prepared to take on board the fact that he has this talent and imagination, because he's expected to work down the pit all his life, like his brother, and that's if he's lucky.'*

Cleverly, Loach proved his fundamental belief to be correct. *'One of the ideas of the film,'* he explained, *'is that every boy and girl has huge potential without space to develop and there are pre-arranged slots ready for them as manual labourers. We thought that, if our thesis was correct, within this group of boys, there would be one who could bring Billy Casper to life.'* And of course he was right. Dai Bradley was an extraordinary talent. He was whittled down from 2000 boys, over three Barnsley schools, all who were very good and many making it into the film.

Almost all the key players involved in the movie went on to bigger things. Ken Loach went on to direct a series of uncompromising films. Tony Garnett would produce more award winning dramas. Colin Welland got a Best Screenplay Academy Award for *Chariots Of Fire.* Chris Menges, as cinematographer, would receive one Oscar nomination (Neil Jordan's *Michael Collins*) and take two Oscars home (Puttnam's *Killing Fields, and The Mission,*) and would direct five movies himself, including *A World Apart* and *Crisscross* starring Goldie Hawn. But the young lad, Dai Bradley, whose marvellous performance made the movie so touching, did not find things quite so easy.

Kes the movie was not an immediate success and it took time to get it released. In America it was over dubbed to help audiences comprehend the film, but apart from a showing at the New York Film Festival it had no impact at all. Now though it is widely regarded as a film classic. It was recently voted No.7 in the top ten British films of all time, alongside *The Third Man, Laurence of Arabia,* and *The Thirty-nine Steps.*

A local journalist summed up the feeling of the day, *'To those of us who were bought up in Yorkshire, it's an incredible towering achievement. It put our voices, our people, our struggles, our aspirations up on the big screen and for that it will always be number one. Looking around our schools there are hundreds of Billy Caspers running around, full of frustration and pent-up energy, and in the old mining areas there's precious little to look forward to for lads like this. In the movie young Billy is sliding into a world of manual labour and a dead end job. Now, his young equivalents will be signing on when they leave school at Easter. In this sense, Kes still flies uncomfortably close to home. Casper's ghost still haunts the land.'*

With great literature, music and films, it can evoke strong images of previously lived experience. Mike Tomkies, for Show Page, wandered down memory lane. Mike had often disappeared alone in his beloved woods and stretching fields of his home town. He had tried to tame many birds, jackdaws, magpies and jays. He even tried a wild wood pigeon and a baby tawny owl he fed on mice and dead birds. *'Then there was the sparrowhawk. I found him slightly injured in a lane one day and nursed him back to health. I remember when he flew for pieces of cheap red beef or dead birds on my lure. There always seemed to be an eerie silence around us. In the glades when the sparrowhawk flew, the birds ceased to sing.'*

'He was the true arrogant aristocrat. I could never tame him or master him; merely for the time he needed me, be his man. When he finally flew away, there were tears in my eyes but joy in my heart. For he seemed to me then to be the symbol of possible attainable freedom.'

'But all this was many years ago and had faded into the blur of memory — until I viewed Kes at the Premier. Once again I was alone in the green of a Yorkshire field, while around and above me flew my hawk.'

I think originally when Barry Hines wrote the book, *A Kestrel for a Knave* and subsequently went on to adapt the screenplay with Loach and Garnett — it was mainly about the working class. I think it more likely reflects the human spirit. Another common misconception about *Kes* is that it was a criticism of all aspects of the educational system. It is not a sociological film and is not concerned with the size of classes, teacher's salaries, or problems of classroom technique. Everyone knows, of course, now, as in 1970, there are plenty of dedicated and highly skilled teachers who maintain close and affectionate relationships with most of the children in their care. But what is the general picture?

Kes is a criticism of society as a whole from the point of view of one undersized and wretchedly unhappy member of it.

Often when *Kes* is broadcast over the years, in the early days; BBC2 and more recently Channel 4, there always is some outcry. Typical criticism is that it should be repeated every year; like *The Great Escape,* and should be on early — so kids Billy Casper's age (14) and below are around to watch it. Although I think in a typical household, these days, parents excuse themselves for bed before their teen-something offspring. Bel Monney from the Daily Mirror, in 1979 commented, *'I think all ages should watch the film. Why? To remind us what we do to many children when we send them to school. And to* confirm to our kids what many of them already know — that school can be a sad waste of time.' This was not some journalist spinning words for her column, Mooney when the film was released — was a teacher. 'I knew how it felt to be faced by a sea of blank looks — and to want to murder the 15-year-old joker at the back of the class. But Kes put me on the other side of the gulf. Yes, it's hard for the teachers in a tough school, but it's terrible for the pupils.'

In 1978, Mooney, while conducting research for a book, visited a number of secondary schools around Britain. To her dismay — nothing had changed since the movie. In fact all the places visited could have been swapped for the school in Kes. 'Same dreary routine,' emphasises Mooney. 'Same bored or bullying teachers. Same useless facilities. Same inadequate headmaster masquerading as a figure of authority. And the same hopeless future for the kids.' It seems no school is without a responsibility and even now educational opportunities are not equal. It is probably a sad fact that a young boy or girl attending a small school in Devon has a better chance than those sent to a huge inner-city comprehensive. 'Can you imagine Billy Casper at Harrow?' says Mooney, 'He would be looked on as a strange genius, who would go on to study birds at Oxford. For that matter can you imagine Prince Charles at Toughtown Comprehensive? The teachers would see him as an opinionated trouble-maker who should be caned into submission. Even the most difficult individual can achieve dignity — but ONLY if he or she feels involved and ONLY if he or she is shown respect. Until that happens in all our schools the Billy Caspers of this world haven't got a chance.'

Ken Loach told United Artists he could bring the film in for a staggeringly low budget of £100,000. They offered him £160,000, but held some of Loach's fee until Kes had made a certain amount of money. In February 1970 they were still holding the money. The film was made in early summer 1968. Loach professionally stuck to his seven-week schedule and brought the picture in under budget at £155,000. Due to this marginally small figure, the filming style adopted by Loach arose partly out of the logistics. 'Although the budget for Kes was quite small for a feature film,' explained Tony Garnett, 'there were no expensive stars and we were able to shoot for seven weeks, in locations that were close together, and shoot a quarter of a million feet of 35mm film; that was a huge luxury.'

During the actual filming United Artists were extremely helpful and did not let the director, cast and crew go without anything. Then the film was edited and finished and things spiralled downwards as United Artists started to distance themselves from the finished project.

Rank would not touch it. Typical comments fired from both the distributors and the exhibitors were, *'I understood Ancient Latin better'* and *'We got a foreign-language film here.'* Ken always said he believed the investors were fighting shy of it because they do not know how to sell it.

'It does not belong to a category they can recognise,' said the director adding, *'It's about an adolescent and yet there's no sex in it. It's about a boy and his pet bird and yet it's far too bleak for kiddies. It's about the working classes and yet there are no cheerful cheeky low-life characters in it.'* He finished by saying there should be some nationalisation of some kind, not necessarily the contemporary model, this would be the only way to break the big-circuit stranglehold.

Beyond this he believed the only deals the film-maker should be involved in are agreements between him and the public about what films they want him to make; films, Loach hopes, like *Kes*, which offer a general audience an experience in which they can recognise something from their own lives. By way of some kind of continuing dialogue, the film-maker should be accountable to the audience and not the entrepreneur.

This was an exciting time for all concerned. New techniques were being used. Old formats were brought back into practise as experience sometimes won over technology.

Using natural light, another change in direction, as far as possible became another Loach filming method and, as with *Poor Cow*, he would have preferred to cement the realism by shooting *Kes* in black and white, but United Artists stipulated that it must be made in colour. So, to avoid ending up with picturesque scenes of the Yorkshire countryside, the film stock was preflashed to de-saturate and take some of the colours out. Ken knew what he was doing from the very start, the true distinction of any great artist – defying any outside influences and single mindedly pursuing a goal that is a vision that he and his trusted colleagues share. Garnett and Loach were of one mind and they were ready to take on anyone.

Making *Kes* was one hurdle overcome – and Loach trimmed £10,000 off the budget supplied by United Artists – but getting it screened in cinemas was another. Tony Garnett's own initial reaction to the broad Yorkshire accents in the film and some incidents of swearing provided a warning of what was to come. *'We went to see the rushes in a cinema in Barnsley,'* said Richard Hines. *'As we walked back to the hotel afterwards, Tony Garnett had a face like thunder, so my* brother, Barry, asked him what was wrong. "We are going to end up with an X-certificate film that's not understood five miles outside Barnsley." he said.'

Garnett himself faced the wrath of the film's backer. 'United Artists weren't interested at all,' he recalled. 'I showed it to one of their executives, Eric Pleskow, who was in London as part of a visit to Europe, just him in the viewing theatre and me biting my finger nails at the back. When it finished and the lights came up, he got up, walked down the aisle and, as he passed me, he didn't even break his stride. "I would have preferred it in Hungarian."'

The publicity surrounding the movie also hit opposition. When the movie was released in Yorkshire there was concern about the publicity photos that promoted the film. The streamer poster which was 14ft long, depicted a grainy image of the schoolboy star, Dai Bradley, defiantly raising two fingers with the caption '....to you, mate'. It all became too much for Geoffrey Hilditch, Halifax's Passenger Transport Manager who banned the image from all buses in his area. He said at the time, 'This sort of thing is not acceptable in polite circles and I find it distasteful. I have some responsibility for what is shown on buses and have had no complaint whatever up to now.'

Maurice Jagger, Halifax Passenger Transport committee chairman said, 'Adverts for our buses are vetted by the manager. If there were an appeal it would be dealt with by the committee.'

A spokesman for United Artists, the films distributors, who had done little to promote their movie, defended the symbolic image, stating, 'Mr Hilditch's views were apparently not shared by other transport companies. Advertising had been accepted by nine other towns in Yorkshire.'

In the movie Billy says quite a lot more than this act of defiance. But anyone who has any feelings for children, and can still feel the heart thump of picked-upon schooldays, must see this extraordinary depiction of working class life, any life, for the truth it portrays. In prison life they do not all say 'you're a terrible rotter, Henry, for using my soap.' The same as school kids do not all converse like the Famous Five!

Regarding Casper's 'V' sign and the comment that went with it, some satirical journalist from The Yorkshire Post, pointed out at the time, 'The peerless Kes is at the ABC for a third week, a fact that entitles us, I think, to make the same gesture that David Bradley can be observed making on the posters to the gentleman in the circuit booking department who had doubts about it because it had "the wrong kind of bird." To you, *too, mate.'*

One of the posters was on a display at the side of a house in Mottram Street, and according to Eldon Street hairdresser Malcolm Brown it has been stopping people in their tracks. *'It's certainly had more impact than a Guinness advert,'* said Mr Brown. *'But whether people like it or not is a different matter.'* A retired miner confessed, *'I knew what the sign meant before I was eight, and I don't think children today are any different. It doesn't offend me.'*

There was another negative that had to be addressed, although the film makers acted impeccably towards the caring and training of all three hawks that appeared in the movie. I suppose quite understandably there was concern about the adverse effects the film would have on birds of prey. The Times, in 1970, ran a piece suggesting that it might tempt young people to keep birds of prey when they are not able to do so properly. This fear was highlighted by Mr Peter Conder, director of the Royal Society for the Protection of Birds, in the November issue of the society's magazine called *Birds*. *'Falcons exert a strange fascination,'* he says. *'By its skill in depicting so this fascination, the film may have had unfortunate effects…'*

'We had over 250 letters from young people during the summer asking how falcons or hawks can be obtained. How many birds have actually been taken we cannot guess. How many of these have survived? All birds of prey are protected by law,' Mr Conder says, adding, *'but the lad shinning up a tree to a kestrel's nest probably does not know this.'*

If there were any undue concerns around this time, it settled down very quickly. The one element that comes across in the film, and the message is quite powerful, the extraordinary lengths one has to go to when training a hawk. It requires constant attention, technique, intelligence, and extreme patience. And finally, together with all the equipment required and technical knowledge, if you have managed to man the bird – there is little back in return. Most children would shy away from such a task and possibly prefer a more conventional pet.

It was decided quite early on that the director, producer and author would pen the screenplay. They also agreed, within reason, to be faithful to the book. All appreciated the powerful message it contained and although they were dealing with a different media, a much more powerful tool, they would not sentimentalise the story. Although it was about a boy and his pet bird – it was not one for Disney.

The three scriptwriters were all ex-grammar school boys, who had obviously all passed the eleven-plus, but this was not a foreign world to them. They were all politically aware. They were all great studiers of the human race. They all knew a three-dimensional character and could have placed Casper in any school, in any county and given him another bird or skill that requires the same patience and intelligence – and it still would have been a hit. In any era the film was symbolic, though without the slightest trace of art symbolism.

After weeks and weeks and numerous discussions on what is in and what is out - the film is in the can. Hours have passed drinking stale coffee in a smoke filled editing suite. The final touches are completed and like a master artist; Loach the director with the help of his producer, Tony Garnett, and cinematographer, Menges, knows instinctively when to stop adding brush strokes. There is no time for self-congratulations – a custom Loach never wallows in. For him it is another piece of cinematic history for whoever ends up watching it.

If Ken Loach lived in a world of blindness and deafness he would have made films. He is a moviemaker who makes movies for himself. He is not interested in safe genre friendly films for the masses or for the numerous critics to indulge their words in. In *Kes* he had all the ingredients he wanted – a strong social message attacking political policies and attitudes and pointing an accusing finger at the teaching profession. This was not just another sentimental child-and-pet film. Margaret Hinxman, from the Sunday Telegraph, observed, *'Every frame of the film is a telling comment on an over-burdened mass educational system which has only the time and patience to cope with stereotypes, be right little villains or conscientious scholars.'*

The heart of the idea, the eleven-plus and all that went with it, was launched in 1944 with the Education Act (known as the Butler Act). The LEA directive was to encourage and establish grammar schools, secondary modern schools and technical schools with pupils allocated by academic selection. It was a tri-partite education system – grammar, secondary and technical, although the latter did not really develop and ended up educating less than 2% of children. It was decided that the sifting of the children would occur through the '11-plus' examination. A white paper preceding the act criticised the system, stating, *'There is nothing to be said about a system that subjects children at the age of 11 to the strain of competitive examination in which not only their schooling but also their future careers depend.'*

This was not so much, *'give a dog a bad name – but give a puppy a bad name.'* To make matters worse secondary schools received inferior levels of funding and some staff was of a lower calibre. It was a two horse race and one of the horses had only three legs.

The governing power at the time and the pre-government all

shared in the system of the eleven-plus, a system that may brandish you a failure by 11, and a system that refused to recognise individual talent. In the North, for Billy Casper, and many boys and girls like him, who ended up in secondary modern schools after failing the eleven-plus, the choice was either low paid un-skilled jobs or an alternative of a dangerous job down the pit for the boys or the noisy weaving sheds for the girls. Alas, the eleven-plus examination proved to be an ideal tool for the government where the unlucky candidates were streamlined for manual labour. With regards the teaching profession, as was stated at the time; when commenting about the film, good teachers loved it and bad teachers hated it.

David Robinson, from The Financial Times, stated, '*The film mercilessly counts the odds, with realistic fatalism; the inescapable pressures of background; the inadequacy of a school which has fine buildings and facilities but few real human contacts; the irrelevancy to a boy of Billy's wretched attainments of the bureaucratic style of the Youth Employment Officer.*'

It is true that few films have displayed these enfeebling effects of the classroom situation, in which teachers are not only cleverer and superior to everyone else in the room; but a whole head taller. We all know from watching a court case where the judge's raised platform gives him or her an air of superiority, albeit only 18 inches.

In James Clavell's *To Sir with Love* (1967), we see Sydney Poitier's character running along the lines of *Kes's* Mr Farthing (Colin Welland) figure with more in common with the children in the class rather than his colleagues in the staff room. *To Sir With Love* the conflict here appears to be with the other teachers and how they interact with the central protagonist rather than their indifference with the pupils. *The Blackboard Jungle* (1955) was another film that underlined the liberal schoolmaster. *Kes* the portrays of the teachers – the blustery headmaster who hears no voice but his own; the fat, pink, show-off bully of a games master are immensely funny and accurate. The other side is shown as well; the sympathetic teacher and the difficulty of making contact with a suspicious child. As Billy complains to Mr Farthing, '*They don't care about us nor do we care about them.*' This statement is ironically underlined during the films assembly reading, '*Do not despise these little ones, I say...*' but the adults lack of respect for their miniature human beings contrasts cruelly with Billy's honour for his bird.

There is a richness and earthiness to *Kes* that takes the movie away from other films, in this genre, such as *Ring of Bright Water*.

Ken Loach and his collaborators steered away from showing the picturesque side of the boy-bird relationship, but only in the effect it has on the boy. Regarding this refreshing angle on pet films, John Russell Taylor from The Times, wrote, 'They depict this with a remarkable lack of sentimentality; Billy is not transformed and ennobled by it; he remains awkward and ungovernable as ever – a born victim. If one feels that this interest of his in animals may signal the birth of a private man, there is no reason to suppose that it will improve his relationship with the world around him, in school or after.'

The ensemble was magnificent and Chris Menges with his diverse years of experience in documentary television and powerful movie drama gave Loach the colours and shades to complete the canvas. The highly trained and motivated crew all worked together like a precision piece of machinery. The cast was mainly a group, with the exception of Colin Welland, a mixture of cabaret stars, comedians and school kids. All played their part and some memorable performances were born and standards set.

No one in the film, even the frantic and frightening headmaster (Bob Bowes), is shown without sympathy – as he romances about previous generations of kids who have stood in his office. Jud (Freddie Fletcher), Billy's elder brother, is a cocky, over-powering bully, but when we see him at the pit-head, and at the local club, we understand why. To Ken Loach everything finds its reason in environment, in the injustice of society. Mrs Casper, fading, tarty, an abandoned wife, really tries to do her best – 'Billy, I've left two bob on the mantelpiece,' she says, ' for a bottle of pop and some crisps' – but her best is just not good enough. One can even sympathise a little with the over zealous egotistical sadistic PT instructor, Sugden. Those kids must, after all, be hell?

It is often screened on Channel 4 and FilmFour and there apt words about the film are both indulgent and flattering – 'A deeply affecting film that is gripping all the way from drab start to shattering climax. Loach's cinematic style is already fully formed here, with the film's naturalistic, semi-improvisatory feel, a profoundly humanist attitude, and a pervading sense of doom leavened by flashes of wit, principally the wonderful football sequence in which PE teacher Glover fulfils his Bobby Charlton fantasy.'

New generations are viewing the film for the first time. Often dads and moms will place it infront of their siblings. As playwright Willy Russell explained to me, 'I've seen it a number of times since, I've been through the thing of watching it with my own kids which is great, and seeing the same kind of impact on them – and they weren't kids *who had been brought up with the kind of probations that Billy Casper and my generation of working class kids had. My kids were absolutely captivated and knocked out by it — reduced to tears but with singing hearts in moments of it.'*

The last word on the film I will leave to Alexander Walker of the Evening Standard, who sums up the poetry of the film by writing, *'Kes pictures the boy in his world — and it's not one to reassure you about his future. Kes leaves it an open question whether the flicker of fulfilment that the boy has found will have the energy to go on feeding itself — or be snuffed out by the life others will make for him.'*

6

The Premier – The Best Kept Secret

The theatrical trailer to Kes; the movie's calling card was powerful and direct. The voiceover was the prominent Burton-esque jut-jawed Patrick Allen, famous for voiceovers of the James Bond movies, Carry On films and most famously provided the voiceover for the *Protect and Survive* civil nuclear defence series (1975). With the skilful Kes soundtrack present in the background Allen builds the story, *'This is Billy Casper. Billy Casper cheats, steals, lies, fights, because well because he has to. You see if you're not like the others, if you simply don't belong, then you have to manage alone. Alone... unless, unless you have a friend – like Kes. A very special friend who doesn't mind that you're different... What makes Billy Casper the way he is? What's wrong with the boy? Perhaps, perhaps it's a secret. A secret shared only with Kes... You might think it's funny. You might think he gets what's coming to him. You might be wrong.'*

In an unusual version of role reversal the distributors and exhibitors seem to shy away from any publicity surrounding Kes; their film. They appeared not to want to talk about it and the only muffled leaks from tensions in the various boardrooms – were all negative. The critics, even the ones who normally played it safe and chipped in with glossy praise; after a movie had been heaped in warm words and broken all box-office records – gave early congratulations to the film-makers and condemned anyone who blocked its path.

Patrick Gibbs, from the Daily Telegraph, described Kes in one notice as, *'one of the most accomplished films of its kind in the whole of British post-war production.'* It seems most critics offered only praise for the film, and scathing indignation for the back peddling distributors and exhibitors.

American critic Howard Schumann summed it up: *'Kes is gritty, sad, funny, and very moving, a film that avoids maudlin sentimentality to tell a simple story with an authenticity you will long remember.'*

One of the early champions for Kes was John Russell Taylor of the Times, *'Since it was first shown to the press I have urged all sorts of people, with all sorts of tastes, to see it, and they have all come away enraptured.'*

Apart from a special screening at the private cinema at Bowater House, Knightsbridge and two airings at the London Film Festival the movie did not go on general release until late 1970. So there was no grand showbiz West End opening. It was treated like there was something indecent about the movie – stifling its progress as not to infect innocent watchers. The real truth for caution was the distributors who were apparently alarmed by the strong Yorkshire accent which they felt would be incomprehensible to the remainder of the English speaking world.

The Sun's Fergus Cashin explained the feeling of most of the critics of the day by writing; '*Kes is a beautiful, gritty, heart-shredding film about the North. My tears will turn to anger if this delicate, sensitive and deliciously wry masterpiece by Ken Loach is not given a full release throughout the country.*'

The critics loved it and the public who were lucky enough to see it; loved it. So what was the problem? It would appear that *Kes*, made in the summer of 1968, would simply be released and the rest would be history, but its main premier had a strangled start. The Rank Organisation, the exhibitors, had little confidence and were only prepared to dip a single toe into the water. The baptising pool was at the ABC Cinema in Doncaster. The Yorkshire site is actually 150 miles from London – the fare in 1969 was £2.8s quite a bit to add to a cinema ticket. But that was the distance you had to go and the price you had to pay to see a film that the British Film Institute ranked 7th greatest British film ever.

The special guests and dignitaries, apart from the actors, crew etc. who trod the red carpet included; Lord Goodman, Chairman of the arts Council: the Rt. Hon. Jennie Lee, Minister of Education and Science with special responsibilities for the Arts; and the Rt. Hon. Edward Short, Secretary of State for Education and Science. Charles Berman, a director of United Artists, represented the distributors. The sprinkle of celebrities included Freddie Truman, Len Hutton, Jackie Charlton, Billy Bremner, Doncaster Rovers football team, Don Revie and Leeds United football team, Brian Close, Stan Barstow, Wilfred Pickles (and Mabel) and John Braine. Four days later, on 29th March 1970, the film would have premier openings in ten cinemas in South Yorkshire. Lights - camera, but NO action.

The movie business is soaked in individual expertise and obsessional crusades that expand ordinary minds and attitudes. The pure nature of the film industry breeds pioneers not always attuned to average thinking. I do believe it is an honourable profession – although some members may be less honourable than others. The respectful and influential banner the trade sales under attracts great funds – but some projects, like *Kes*, are less attractive than others. From the other side of the fence – *you pays your money and you takes your choice*.

Sometimes what appears to be money in the bank can lead to financial ruin – the movie business was never designed to be an exact science. United Artists were as nervous about *Kes* as a teetotaller would be at Oliver Reed's stag do.

I have often, in a small way, experienced the feelings of loss when everything appeared to be shouting at a bargain. An un-named charity shop, with two old entrepreneurial dears serving behind a donated counter, beckoned me towards a new line they had received that day. Action trousers or combat fatigues were fetching good money at the top high street stores in the nineties. As I perused this unlikely oasis of fashion, they had every size, the stock impressed me at well below market value. A huge sign stated that every garment contained a blemish – with added message – NO goods will be replaced after purchase. Every pair of trouser carried a bright sticker reinforcing the warning. In between smiling at the period staff I meticulously studied every pair with little or no success – they seemed to be all perfects. I handed over my garment, paid my money and left. When I got home, smug with my purchase, I removed the warning sticker – underneath was a jagged hole. I can still hear the old dears clinking their sherry glasses in triumph. If you can not trust elderly volunteer charity workers – who can you trust?

In two days, at the ABC, Sheffield, it smashed box office records – the cinema had been running for nearly ten years. In fact Huddersfield, Harrogate and Halifax cinema managers reported *'fantastic audiences,'* another said, *'I've never known anything like it.'* The final result was the picture broke house records at seven out of the ten Northern cinemas where it opened in March 1970. Ian Sainsbury, a journalist, said at the time, *'It's rare for a cinema audience to clap – but Kes got a round of applause after the last performance on Sunday night.'* An uncharitable, tongue-in-cheek explanation of this extraordinary phenomenon was offered by the producer, Tony Garnett, *'The house was full of Barry Hines's aunties.'*

The business of general release in Britain, certainly at the beginning of the 70s, was quite simple. There were two major exhibitors, Rank and ABC. They owned most of the cinema seats in Britain between them. If you could not persuade one or the other that your film was worth putting on general release at their cinemas throughout the country, you will not begin to get your money back on your backer's investment. To get a booking on the art house circuit, or have your name in lights at the Curzon, or have a distinguished run at the Academy, will not even keep you in cigars. In fact a poker player with a nervous twitch takes home more cash.

This sort of turn-over is not worth a bean in terms of film money. During the 70's the identity of the few men – perhaps only two effectively – who make the crucial decisions, the life-or-death decisions, at Rank and ABC is not a secret but they rarely talk to the press, and will not give reasons for their decisions.

Rightly so, much blame for all the despondency and negativity was directed at the distributors, United Artists, who were unwilling to give the public the chance to make their own choice of films, which do not conform to the prevailing commercial conventions. One executive explained his reasons for blocking the movie, *'It's a very nice family picture, but quite spoilt by having a sad ending.'* Hollywood speaks.

Again the men in suits harp back to the strong accents used in the movie, although it would appear that the difference from the Barnsley dialect to BBC grade announcers English is not that far removed from Brooklyn to New York. Up till then radio 4 had broadcast rather modulated Northern accents, even for Barnsley, that parents and teachers used, as opposed to the raw South Yorkshire kids used for each other. But here in the UK we are quite used to dealing with regional accents up and down the country. Counties who border each other can have a diverse distraction in accents – but we all seem to manage quite well.

Willy Russell, playwright, knew instinctively that the dialect was right in *Kes*. *'It walked that terribly precarious ledge that so many fall off and end up wallowing in bathos,'* explained Willy. *'But again the hardness of the language, the accuracy of the language, kept it away from just acting. It's when you get that kind of stuff done* (mocking) *'North Country' accent on – and they go into this nonsensical romantic idea what being Northern's about. It's so insulting and patronising.'*

Different countries, even in the English-speaking world, do differ considerably and there may be some consideration for this. There may also be some justification for sub-titles when the film did travel across the pond to America. The two scenes the Americans had a problem with was the early morning opening scene between Billy and his brother, and the conversation between Billy and his schoolmates before they go into the headmaster's study to be caned.

Garnett commented at the time, *'Because of the quaint convention that American people speak the same language as we do, we have to make it intelligible to them. I think they speak a foreign language – and they only understand posh English and phoney Cockney. So I wanted it sub-titled. But, quite reasonably, United Artists objected to this because American audiences have resistance to subtitles, except in the art houses. And to think I've spent most of my life watching Marlon Brando in films and not understanding a word he said.'*

Bob Bowes, who plays the headmaster in *Kes*, offered some advice with regards understanding Barnsley brogue. *'I suppose it would be difficult for American audiences to understand that when a Yorkshire lad, says, "Purremineer," he means "Put them in here," or that, "Astagorratanner" means, "Have you got sixpence."'*

The Yorkshire Post joined in by adding, *'With the original dialogue, it would have at least convinced the Americans that all British people don't use cockney accents. And United Artists, about forcing accent changes, say it isn't really there fault, "burraberritiz," (But I bet it is).'*

Whether it was embarrassment on behalf of United Artists or with the fragmented premier, they simply forgot about the enthusiastic notices and excellent box office receipts, they refused to let it be selected for the official Cannes Festival entry. They had already given up on the film and wrote off the money. As far as they were concerned, *Kes* did not exist; it had flown the nest.

The Rank Organisation exhibits United Artists films in Britain through its chain of Odeon cinemas. It appears unfathomable to understand why *Kes* did not automatically receive a booking in view of the strong feelings of Mr John Davis, the Rank chairman, has about family entertainment. On many occasions Davis has publicly attacked the growing numbers of X-rated films although at the time, in 1969, 26% of Rank's releases were X category.

A Bill Tidy cartoon summed up the attitude to *Kes* on its release. At the time of it's premier in Doncaster, Tidy drew a cartoon showing a cinema manager wearing an immaculate dinner jacket, bow tie – and scruffy flat cap. Clearly, the outside world was still not ready for a film about life in the raw in Barnsley.

Barry Hines, presented the original Tidy cartoon to his publisher. The butt of the joke belonged to the distributors – who thought *Kes* would fade away into obscurity and treated it accordingly. Barry Hines says, *'United Artists were very derogatory about it. It was nice when*

Kes *did so well.'*

During this stagnant period for *Kes* it was shown in Sheffield, Halifax, York, Barnsley, Hull, Harrogate, Chesterfield and Grimsby. I'm sure as far as the distributors, United Artists, were concerned these were the main cities throughout the United Kingdom. The men in grey suits, the powerhouses of the organisation certainly collectively had not heard of Barnsley – the film's location. Mr M. Young, the sales director of United Artists, who financed *Kes* stated openly in 1968 that it would be given a restricted Northern release in about 12 cinemas. With this tentative start, and no actual release date, he added, *'It may coincide with school holidays.'* He suggested March or possibly August or September.

When it was glimpsed briefly at the London Film Festival premier is was described by the Festival Committee as the outstanding film of the year. Praise indeed when you view the cinematic releases of that year – *Funny Girl, Chitty, Chitty, Bang, Bang, The Battle of Britain* and Carry On feature; *Follow That Camel.* In fact there were 92 feature films produced in 1969. The Festival opened on November 18th 1969, and seat reservations were swallowed up almost immediately for the 19th and 22nd performances. Rank were not available to comment on their subdued availability of *Kes* and declined to comment on the interest shown in sales – there was a lot of bums on seats.

There was a tremendous uproar at the timidity of the distributors and exhibitors, whose fears were proven to be weightless. The Yorkshire accent was not as foreign as all that, though some southern ears may find it takes a bit of getting used to.

Eventually Ken Loach's *Kes* was lured to London in June, with its U certificate, at the distinguished art house; Academy One in Oxford Street. With its new home, in the first weekend in London it broke all box office records for Academy One. In fact the response was so great that enthusiasm spilled in Academy Three; filling it to capacity. It would have completed an unheard of hat-trick by filling Academy Two, had it not been pre-booked for the gruff charmer with Tetsuo Abe in *Boy* (1969), the latest film of the much-acclaimed young Japanese director, Nagisa Oshima.

Barry Hines recalls being in London when the film was being screened at the Academy, *'The queue was hundreds of yards long. It seemed to go on forever.'*

There was a rumour going around that between the ABC Doncaster premier and its eventual launch at Academy One in London that the film had been seriously dubbed. There may have been some slight re-recording but that was all. Some of the re-dubbing was a single word others were a re-worked phrase here or there – which took a morning's studio time.

The producer, Tony Garnett takes up the story, *'There was a serious suggestion that there should be subtitles south of Nottingham. I mean me and Ken fell about laughing – but it was a genuine suggestion. Me and Ken have never liked the process ADR, what was post syncing then, it's very difficult to get a natural performance through this method.'*

During those early days, in one sense *Kes* might have been in a better position if it were less comprehensible. Maybe in a foreign language, fitted with subtitles, it would have had no problem in getting a general showing. The conflict of art against popular cinema seemed to have dogged *Kes* in its early life. This misjudgement caused it to fall into that awkward category which causes mistrust in the establishment.

Willy Russell remembered it well. *'I was about twenty-one and I'd just got married,'* he explained. *'I was in London for my honeymoon and I read somewhere about the stupid hoo-hahh with some people saying it needed sub-titles. That made me interested immediately because I had and still have very good friends in and around the Barnsley area. A couple of these were Ann and Steve Rusby, who are the parents of the singer Kate Rusby. She's huge in the folk music scene. I knew Steve knew Brian Glover – so that was the connection there. So I knew Barnsley language. I kind of understood the problems and knew if they had got it right; the filmmakers had got it right – it would work.'*

Apart from Clive Goodwin, one of the directors at Kestrel Films, whipping up press interest in the movie, it was simply public pressure and reassurance that had taken the film from its original release in selected Northern cinemas, to its 60 ABC cinema run and finally a full circuit release. **Hallelujah!** Class will tell in the end. The press had consistently praised the movie – but now the public had to leave their sofas and go and see it.

The Hollywood industry boys were forced to give the film a wider distribution than they intended, which they maintained was the plan from the start. I am sure the faceless suits at United Artists and Rank were rubbing their hands together at the over riding success at the Academy, booking it for an indefinite run. Their conflict of interest was handling *Kes* as art cinema and not tarnishing the happidrome image of popular cinema which they lay down their dollars to protect. Nina Hibbin, from the Morning Star, said at the time, *'I'm willing to bet that thousands of filmgoers who have never been inside an art cinema will be queuing up for Kes, and once old habits are broken, new ones are easily acquired.'*

The 1970 New York Film Festival was in its eighth year when *Kes* was included in there fresh works of hand picked prodigies. Although I think even they would agree it has, at times, displayed a babble of indifferent talent with a lack of originality. The actual lists of films put in front of the festival officers are quite sparse. To a degree many Eastern European pictures were not available and American companies prefer to release their films without any festival foreplay.

Stefan Kanfer from Time Magazine, in a slightly bad mood, commented on the overall presentation of the New York Film Festival, *'This year we have a selection of solemn bores and hedged experiments that mark the 1970 festival. Presented with inconsistent aesthetic standards and promoted with hyperthyroid jargon.'*

It fell to Jay Cocks to review *Kes's* inclusion, who wrote, *'Kes suffers from the somewhat shop-worn metaphor that forms its core, but director Ken Loach still conjures up some forceful moments. The casual sadism of schoolmasters, the brutality of one child to another are rendered with outstanding empathy.'*

Although attitudes would change, it appears the American premier of *Kes* was harangued by their press in the same way the American distributors and exhibitors had treated its release in the United Kingdom. They wanted to bury the film in the same grave as Casper had buried his dead hawk.

7

The Director – Ken Loach

'One leap forwards, two leaps back, will politics get me the sack?'
Billy Bragg, on Ken Loach - *'Waiting For The Great Leap Forwards'*

The director Jean Renoir, son of famous painter Pierre Auguste Renoir, once said, *'A director only makes one film in his life. Then he breaks it into pieces and makes it again.'* The legacy of Loach's most famous work is that some of the people of Barnsley may have wanted to break it into pieces, but not necessarily have it put back together again – certainly not in South Yorkshire. What Ken Loach set out to do, with the help of Tony Garnett, was to bring Barry Hines's book to life using sound and moving pictures. The movie had to be true to the spirit of the novel, with its criticising political teeth bared. The result was a British classic that brought the critics and public to their feet applauding, but the implications of such a movie cast the whole of Barnsley in shadow. The world cared very little what was really happening in the close-knit mining town and some thirty-five years on the film is still being held up by some as an accurate depiction of South Yorkshire.

Who ultimately has to take responsibility for this? Whether a certain amount of criticism can be levelled at the uneducated and uninformed cinemagoer, Ken Loach, as a filmmaker, must acknowledge that he went a long way to freeze the lives and times of the local people. Real teachers and real kids playing out their lives on screen was dangerous – nearly everything Loach has produced is dangerous; he is that sort of filmmaker.

The question should not be about apportioning blame – but what can be done to address the balance. Steve Houghton, leader of Barnsley council, stands firm, proud of his Yorkshire, over-seeing the advanced metropolis what is emerging. The new Barnsley will be as far removed from Loach's sixties vision of the town as

Casper was from most of his teachers, friends and family. Putting a book of this type together draws a lot of patience from everyone concerned. Often details have to be cross-checked as anecdotes and stories unfold. It is time consuming, and as I have fully experienced in writing *Life After Kes*, full cooperation from everybody involved is paramount.

When I telephoned Sixteen Films Ltd, Ken Loach's production company, his PA, Camilla Bray, answered. We had already batted a few e-mails back and forth so I already knew Ken was on board and fully behind the project. I was calling to get the producer's number, Tony Garnett. I was sitting in my office; lounging in my effect-leather swivel chair, when Camilla said, *'Hold on a minute, I'll just get Ken.'* This completely threw me – I was not ready to talk to the great man yet – I would liked to have washed, shaved and probably do something I rarely do – put on a tie; if I can find one. I did one thing – I stood up to talk to Mr Loach. Such is the effect the man has – and yet he is an honest fellow with no pretence, ego or any of that Hollywood nonsense.

He is also one of the most modest of directors, would probably say he had a lot to be modest about - that his team deserves as much praise as he does. What he finds is the truth of any given situation through good casting, scripts that often seem totally improvised but are not, and the courage of his strong and unwavering left-leaning convictions. In his best movies, Loach is able to turn the particular into the universal and to appeal to audiences the world over. *Kes* was such a film.

My first face to face introduction to Ken Loach, was totally unexpected and was not connected with this novel, although it did happen while I was writing the book. Originally I had been granted time to interview Ken during September 2004. I meticulously planned a succession of meetings to capitalise on Mr Loach's generosity and also afford me time to rebound comments and stories from other willing participants.

Following a full page article in the Yorkshire Post about the book, a production team contacted us about filming a documentary. The day I received a call from Simone, from True North Productions, based in Television Centre (Leeds), the project was gratefully doomed to be delayed to fit the stringent requirements of television broadcasting schedules. After myself and my publisher met head of development; Anna Hall (I kept calling her Annie Hall – I am a big Woody Allen fan), we both knew the project would be packed in ice for a while. *Life After Kes,* designed to be in the shops by Christmas 2004 was now looking at a national launch of late 2005. I would now have plenty of time to conclude my research and interviews; and my bank manager would age ten years. As is often the case, mine and my publisher's vision of what the documentary should say was different from True North's. We felt, politically, it should have the same teeth as the original book and the film. By the time we had conducted many discussions, Anna Hall had been snapped up by Channel 4. We parted on good terms, convinced we would find a production company, this time after the release of the book, which would carry the story forward. So production companies, on your marks, get set - go!

We had lost time, but a few wonderful opportunities came out of this postponement, which bore some wonderful friendships and a couple of books. With an unusual amount of freedom for a freelance writer I embarked on a chapter for the book called; The Peers - The Industry Salutes (end of book). It gave me the chance to contact certain people in the entertainment business, who I had greatly admired, and offered them the chance to comment on the movie *Kes*. Of course some had little knowledge of Ken's work, others felt unqualified to contribute and a small minority disagreed with Loach's views and one, a British, double Oscar winning actress; and now a Labour politician, claimed not to know any of his work — if you are still unsure I do name her.

The first significant contact was Iciar Bollain an established and famous Spanish director, writer and actress, who Ken Loach was fortunate to cast in *Land and Freedom* (1995). I initially contacted Iciar to let me have a quote for this book — what it was like working with Ken Loach. It turned out that Iciar had written a book about Loach's *Carla's Song* (1996), starring Robert Carlyle, called *Un Observador Solidario* (A Quixotic Observer) published by El Pais Aguilar in 1997 - a best seller in Spain. Some chapters had already been translated by a friend, Roger Mortimore. I found the book totally absorbing and wanted to put it in front of an English market. Iciar was delighted and we decided to work on the book together — her English is better than mine and my Spanish is failed O-level standard. We are currently working on a translation, from Spanish to English, for the UK national market. Together with my publisher's idea of a book covering all of Loach's work (working title Real To Reel), I was rapidly becoming his official biographer. At this point, due to the national postponement of the book launch, I had not met Ken Loach.

On September 1st 2004, after scooping 7 Goyas, and many more prestigious awards, *Take My Eyes* (Te Doy Mis Ojos) had its British premier at the UGC Haymarket Theatre. Iciar Bollain had directed and co-wrote (with Alicia Luna) this magnificent, powerful film about spousal abuse. Iciar invited me to my first premier and very excited I was.

I met Iciar at the Rathbone Hotel and travelled with Georgia; the publicist, to the Haymarket. The first person I met was of course Ken Loach, which was all very casual, and although my face was unfamiliar to him, thankfully my name was not. If he had found my calls to his office at Sixteen Films, requesting films, documentaries, articles etc. obtrusive and time consuming – he showed none of it to me. Ken Loach was exactly like everyone had described – a totally genuine, gentle man and quietly spoken. I thought of the films Ken Loach has made over the years, the documentaries and the teleplays, all the controversy with their intrusive social and political thrusts. The feelings and outrage most of his work has established. Some of his programmes are still locked away – too sensitive and powerful for the various governing bodies to stomach. Ken's rapier mind that battles injustices and will take on delicate issues, governmental procedures and even countries if he feels the authoritative system has let the people down – the common man, the ordinary man. All this power and strong will cocooned inside such a fragile frame and warm manner. A contrast I found even more inquisitive.

It was extra thrilling when Ken came and sat next to me for the screening and we both shared our admiration for Bollain's dramatic 90 minutes of sheer realism. The movie was dirty, funny, inspirational, passionate, shameful and moving – just like life can be. Ken Loach's words in the Observer, the week after, praising her work as director and co-writer, was totally justified.

I made only one slip up, which is pretty good for me, at a drinks party afterwards. This was no grand affair, with starched waiters, steaming silver domes and a round of 'well done darling'. We just sort of drifted over the road to the local pub; I can't even remember the name of it. The small entourage of film-makers, friends and associates – we numbered around twenty, stood at the bar all honoured to be sharing Iciar's time. I mingled happily meeting new faces and swapping our mutual appreciation for the movie. We were all contented critics that night. I had briefly been introduced to the distributor, following a question and answer session after the screening; he had actually introduced Iciar Bollain. I shook his hand and thanked him for the drink he had just bought me – after my Barry Norman or should I say Jonathan Ross film 2004 critique – I then asked him if this was his first viewing of the film. He was very polite and explained that he had seen the movie a few times. I would imagine that that is the first thing they teach you at Distribution School: *'Remember boys and girls – if you want to be a good distributor for the movie business – you must see the movie first, before you start distributing it!'* He wandered off and joined the publicist.

Ken Loach, socially conscious, dealing mainly with British socio-economic order and the problems of the working class, a member of the British *Free Cinema* movement of the 1950s and 60s, it is easy to see Loach as something of a miserabilist, but his films have always been shot through with humour. On *Desert Island Discs,* he said that, *'during the making of* Kes, *we were all holding our sides. We all regarded it as a comedy.'*

Just as Loach had effectively created his own Everton supporters club in *The Golden Vision* (1968), he established a family feel during the shooting of *Kes* that would become one of his trademarks, alongside his reputation for maintaining a calm set and never shouting *'Action!'* or *'Cut!',* preferring to let events establish themselves naturally before the camera. *'All the people involved came from within a few miles of each other,'* comments Loach, *'so there was a strong sense of community. That most of the cast was untrained as actors proved to be a great advantage because they were drawing on their own experiences. This meant they had a remarkable ability to make a fictional situation believable in front of the camera.'*

Jacob Leigh, author of *The Cinema of Ken Loach,* points out, *'Words matter for Loach, but the performances and his ability to use his actors personalities matter more.'* Loach, summing up this whole fascination with working with real people, says, *'The most extraordinary location is someone's face and what's happening on it. That's the stuff of drama and it doesn't change. It relies on instinct, not intellect. The actor must have a gut reaction.'*

Actor Garry Lammin, who played the cockney charge-hand, Mick, in Loach's *Riff-Raff* (1990) explained some of the intricacies of film making, *'To me, Ken Loach was more like a psychotherapist than a director. He never tells you what he thinks, but, instead, is more interested in what you think. He asks you questions. He might ask you, for instance, how you thought the subtext of a scene might affect your response, if, say, two hours earlier, you had received news that your house had burned down and that you were not insured.'*

I found myself remembering something that Sir Michael Caine

said when he first met Woody Allen - that he was not really funny, but waited for you to say something funny — which he could use and exploit at a later date. Loach, the power-house of British cinema, who you could easily see directing a movie similar to a dictator ruling a country.

Loach is fully aware that if you point the equivalent of a gun at an actor and tell him to act — this strain will show up in the performance. 'He understands that actors are creative people,' explains Lammin, 'who are capable of bringing their own resonance and perceptions to a scene and the story. But, what I really like about Ken Loach, is the fact that, in a very gentle and dignified way, he successfully blends and camouflages the actor/director boundaries, and, because of this approach, you subconsciously reflect back to Ken something very close to what he was searching for in the scene.'

A film with similar poignancy, as Alexander Walker points out, to Kes is Francois Truffaut's The 400 Blows, which allowed its boy hero-victim to look questioningly at the audience; breaking the fourth wall, from the pathos of his frozen face in the culminating shot. 'Loach and Garnett typically avoid this dramatic full stop in favour of an oblique anticlimax. Something I feel encapsulates the whole feel of the movie. Life only ends in death and the experiences along the way are usually a random tableau of scenes with no real end or full stop. Each experience falling short or overlapping another. Unlike the kestrel's, Billy's life has not ended and the burial scene finishes that experience and the audience is left with many questions. Human spirit is very strong and it's certainly in abundance with Casper, but we all ask after each crushing disappointment how long can hope remain?'

The South Yorkshire countryside was where Ken Loach discovered a hive of political awareness that would feature in many of his films and television documentary-dramas. He also developed a new style of detached, observational film-making, in sharp contrast to the in-your-face, handheld-camera-on-the-run mode that had become a trademark of his Wednesday Plays. In the summer of 1968, making what became one of the British cinema's finest masterpieces, Loach shot the gentle but essentially tragic Kes in and around Barnsley, where the idyllic Yorkshire landscape was tempered by scenes of coal mines and industrial activity.

Struggle, tragedy and censorship, all of which might suggest that his potential remains unfulfilled, have surrounded the career of humanist film-maker Ken Loach. However, I think it is fair to say that Loach has ultimately given the world of cinema a distinct canon of work that is enjoyed and respected by peers, critics and audiences alike.

This is not to downgrade the serious - some say over-earnest - side of Loach's work, which invariably deals with the injustice of uncaring capitalism and invokes a properly socialist alternative. It's just to emphasise what a very good film-maker he is when encouraged by good writers such as Barry Hines.

Loach was born in Nuneaton, England on the 17th June 1936. His early childhood was lived out around the relocations demanded of his family by the onset of war. By the age of 25, he had completed two years of National Service in the Royal Air Force, going on to read law at St. Peter's Hall, Oxford. Here he involved himself with the University's drama group leading to, upon completing his course, working as an actor in repertory theatre. Parallax pictures, where many of Ken's films have been nurtured, mainly by producer Sally Hibbin, states on their web page, '*Ken Loach started work as an actor – and was probably the worst actor in Britain.*'

This may have been the case and Loach receiving his director's ticket may have saved the world from his acting. Although at the start of the sixties decade Loach was incongruously under-studying Kenneth Williams in Peter Cooke's *One Over the Eight* at the Duke of York Theatre in London. '*I found him very intimidating, at first sight,*' remembered Loach. '*He was very mercurial and waspish and a very strong personality. He could reduce you to shreds with a look. We did have a friendship as we both liked reading history books, especially ancient history. But then you would start again where you left off and he would cut you dead. There was always a constant uncertainty of how you would be received.*'

In 1961, Loach received a sponsorship from ABC TV, to become an assistant director at the Northampton Repertory Theatre before, in 1963, joining the BBC as a trainee television director. His first undertaking was to direct *Catherine* in 1964, which starred Tony Garnett who was to play a large part in Loach's career. He was then assigned to direct three episodes of the popular, gritty police series *Z Cars*, where he would meet and befriend Colin Welland.

Following this, he directed the TV movie *Diary of a Young Man* (1964). It is interesting to note that his approach to *Diary...* is quite the antithesis of *naturalism,* a term that is often applied to Loach's work, mainly due to the series being written by Troy Kennedy Martin, author of the polemical essay *Nat's Go Home,* published in 1964. The subsequent period was one of extreme significance in Loach's career, as he directed his first Wednesday Play for the BBC. He would direct a further nine between 1965 and 1971, arguably finding, during this time, the vision and voice that has defined his later career. Amongst these were two raw industrial dramas written by Jim Allen, an ex-coalminer, *The Big Flame* (1971) and *Rank and File* (1971).

Even before *Kes* was filmed, Ken Loach had made his mark at the BBC. After several directional pieces, his first major notice came with *Cathy Come Home* (1966), which addressed the issues of homelessness and led to questions being asked in parliament on the topic. During an interview in 1993 with the director, Melvin Bragg said, '*The end of it when the two children are taken away from Cathy, which is a heartrending scene that triggered quite a tremendous reaction. As big as a reaction as I have ever seen while working in television.*' It was obvious that Loach and his team had grabbed the headlines; probably by the throat, but as Loach is quick to comment, '...*clearly we didn't change anything. That in itself was quite a politicising experience. People started talking about the Cathy's of this world and so on. We were seen by politicians of various hues; to what a valuable contribution this was to understanding the problem. And we asked what changes do you envisage? And of course they didn't envisage any.*' The establishment absorbed all the cries of anguish, the protests and demonstrations − recognised there was a problem − but did absolutely nothing about it.

Regarding the issue of homelessness, the teleplay was latched onto by various political institutions upon transmission, and this eventually led to the advent of the charity, Shelter, something Loach refuses to take any credit for. Some have described *Cathy Come Home*, and especially the train station scene where Cathy's children are taken away, as gut wrenching and harrowing. '*It was so powerful, probably one of the most extraordinary things I have ever experienced watching film,*' commented the established director Alan Parker.

Loach's *Cathy Come Home* and *Up The Junction* (1965) were the first *Wednesday Plays* to escape the trappings of a studio set-up and, using genuine vox-pop interviews and statistics, was a ground-breaking piece of cinéma vérité-esque documentary fiction, which was to cause great debate over the very nature of television drama.

Also during this period, Loach had time to put his hand to the direction of his first feature film, *Poor Cow* , although he felt that this film highlighted, if nothing else, his cinematic immaturity. But he was about to strike back. The mannered handling of his first feature was about to change. Czech cinema was to open eyes and enlighten. This crop of sharp-edged humanist films from Czechoslovakia, bought a cool, crisp perspective to *Kes*. Chris Menges had been working on the classic; Lindsay Anderson's *If...* (1968) arrived fresh from the influences of the Czech cameraman, Miroslav Ondricek. It had a profound effect on Menges on how light should be photographed, about which lenses were sympathetic and which were not, and about how to contain the action. Loach was fully behind his cinematographer, 'We *talked a lot about that,*' adds Loach, '*and decided that the effort shouldn't be to make the camera do all the work, but should be to make what is in front of the camera as authentic and truthful as possible. The camera's job was to record it in a sympathetic way and to be unobtrusive, not to be slick. So when we came to do Kes, there was a conscious move away from newsreely, chasing kind of photography to a more reflective, observed, sympathetically lit style of photography. I tend not to use the wider lenses, just a narrow range that corresponds to your eye's range. You get frames that are more pleasing.*'

The idea of lighting a scene in such a way that the space they were shooting would be lit rather than the shot itself. '*That was very important,*' explained Loach, '*because it meant we could dispense with the idea of actors having to hit their marks and that liberated them to move about at will.*' A great advantage when working with inexperienced actors who tended to wander off target. The less any actor has to think about, and one of the fundamental principles of everyday life, and Loach was trying to create realism at its highest level, we move about totally free of imaginary boundaries. '*We also wouldn't be concerned about bathing them in a pool of light or catching a light in their eyes, which is the traditional way of shooting someone. We wanted to light the space so that the light fell democratically but unostentatiously on everyone. Not only is it more pleasing that way, but the lighting isn't then saying, "This is the leading actor in the scene or the film and these actors aren't so important." This is what we did on Kes and it became a central tenet of how we worked.*' Again it was the natural way. Life does not throw light in the faces of important people, central protagonists or the person who is speaking. People rise above their situation and get noticed by movement or oration or an amalgamation of the two. This was not the birth of some artistic invention – but it was in its infancy in the 60's and the men and women who grasped this were pioneers.

Czech was the New Wave of cinema, some looked on and mocked, because it was different, others copied, and others, like

Loach and Menges, adopted and fashioned these new ideas and made them work for themselves. These extrovert Czech directors, people like Milos Forman and Jiri Menzel and others, mainly in the sixties, were humanists, making compassionate films. *'They weren't soft in any way,'* says Loach, *'but had a very sharp, dry wit. At times they were quite savage but still with that strong humanist streak. That's what we took from them anyway. They made us feel that they were the kinds of films we wanted to make.'*

Troubled by his first foray into the cinematic world, Loach and Tony Garnett, with whom he had worked with on many of the *Wednesday Plays*, set up Kestrel Productions to actualise some low-key independent work. *'Both politically and aesthetically we had the same attitudes and agenda.'* says Garnett about Ken Loach.

Their first film was *Kes*, which many acknowledge as a pivotal film in the late 60's period of British cinema. The issue of hope, destiny and struggle in working class communities that is intrinsic to *Kes* has become the benchmark of Loach's cinema, what some have called social-conscience realism. Loach uses the camera as plainly as possible and employing a deliberately unemphatic cutting technique, explores the boy's background with great affection, honesty, and understanding. And he has inspired many directors: Mike Leigh, Roland Joffè and Stephen Frears; the latter stating, *'Without Ken Loach, I wouldn't be here.'*

There were a couple of questions I asked both the producer and director. Totally different perspectives – two professions with one common goal, certainly during the making of *Kes*, to create and develop a piece of work that is both true to the book and themselves. I wondered, nearly forty years on, with as many films under their belt; looking back, with what they know now, would they have made the film any differently? Taking slightly less time than his former producer, Tony Garnett, the answer was the same; a confident, unequivocal no. *'It was very much of it's time, really, both in the style and the stage we were all at,'* says Loach thoughtfully, *'I was very influenced, cinematically, by Chris (Menges) – and we both had a collective view on where we wanted to go.'*

With regards whether Loach would make the film today – if the book landed on his desk, he duplicated his old friend Garnett and let out a residing – yes! *'I just hope I would have the bottle to cast the kids from the local schools in Barnsley,'* laughs Ken, *'instead of searching the whole of South Yorkshire. We decided just to make simple choices, which worked out Ok. And of course it was hugely enjoyable. I mean all films are a bit of a sweat from time to time, but this was a total delight - I mean meeting those lads from Barnsley. It was a huge privilege to be able to work on Kes.'*

When Ken learned I had tracked most of the credits down he was immensely excited and asked how a few of them were getting on, referring to them either by their real names or their character names. When I explained about the national launch and if he would be able to come along, he is currently locked in the cutting room working on *The Wind That Shakes The Barley.* Loach's answer was unlike a busy director with a thousand thoughts on his mind and as many tasks to achieve, *'I'll be there like a shot,'* he said, without a beat.

All concerned are quick to point out the merits in Barry Hines's classic, *A Kestrel For A Knave,* and Ken is no exception. *'The prime credit has to go to Barry for writing it, it was clearly a very important book,'* comments Loach seriously, *'a simple story, it told you a great deal about how the world was working. The book, and hopefully the film, transcends the narrow issue of educational opportunities at that time. I think it has more profound things to say about growing up, family relationships and a lad who's excluded in one sphere; finding escape in something else. Of course if it works it has timeless qualities as well as specifics and social points.'*

Following the box-office success of *Kes,* Loach briefly returned to the *Wednesday Play,* re-inventing *In Two Minds* as a film; *Family Life.* However, this was commercially unsuccessful, which hit the Kestrel finances extremely hard. This failure has been blamed mainly on poor distribution. A further set-back occurred when a Loach-directed film made for London Weekend Television (LWT); to explain the work of the Save The Children Fund was refused by the charity, with LWT distancing themselves from their financing of the film. You can not buy an answer from Ken Loach — he may take your money, but he delivers a film or documentary he and his immediate colleagues totally believe in. Things were to get steadily worse. After a family tragedy, Loach was to take an understandably extended sabbatical from direction, returning in 1975 with *Days Of Hope,* a four-part television series looking at the British Labour movement between 1916 and 1926. The series was chastised for being avowedly partisan, a criticism that had dogged Loach since the success of *Cathy Come Home,* and has continued to do so since, seemingly indicative of the problems of the documentary-drama mode.

Grittier TV films followed with *Rank and File* (1976) and *The Price of Coal* (1976), both highlighted the harsh life of the mining communities. *The Gamekeeper* (1979) concerned a steelworker turned gamekeeper for the duke's estate. Then came *Looks and Smiles* (1981), which could almost be seen as the follow-up to *Kes,* as it dealt with unemployment and dissatisfied youth, whose only way out was to join the Army and see the world. It should be noted that these projects (excepting *Rank and File*) were all written by Barry Hines. It seems to me that the kitchen soap dramas of the 60's had given way to a 70's, full of Yorkshire grit.

Family Life's failure led to a period in the wilderness for Loach, parting company with Garnett in the late 1970's, as his long-time associate tried to find work outside of England.

A 3 million rise in unemployment, the crushing of the miner's union strike, a significant cut in arts subsidy, as well as successful defence of the Falklands were seen during Thatcher's first two terms of office. By this time she had gained many enemies in the creative community, for instance; community theatre groups, the avant-garde film work of Peter Greenaway and Derek Jarman, the poetry of Adrian Mitchell and the Red Wedge music and comedy tours fronted by Paul Weller and Billy Bragg.

Not surprisingly Ken has joined a small band of revolutionaries who have snubbed the royal awards. *'I turned down the OBE because it's not a club you want to join when you look at the villains who've got it. It's all the things I think are despicable: patronage, deferring to the monarchy and the name of the British Empire, which is a monument of exploitation and conquest.'* You can not please all the people all the time – but you can give them something to think about.

Almost as a comfort blanket, Loach returned to his former hunting ground, and from the same pool as Dai Bradley came from, tried to pluck out another star turn. During 1978, Loach, when searching for young actors with natural Yorkshire accents, returned to the 700-pupil St Helen's and found twelve-year-old Louise Cooper. Louise played Belle and was so good that when Leon Garfield, the author of *Black Jack*, visited the film set he presented her with a book inscribed, *'Thank you for being my perfect Belle.'*

It was the end for Tony Garnett and the double-act. While the newspaper reviews of *Black Jack* had been turned into fish and chip papers, Garnett jetted off to the United States. The eighties were about to start.

With everything else happening at St Helen's, on the back of the success of *Kes* and trawling for untapped talent for *Black Jack*, the secondary modern was rapidly turning into a stage school. Mr

Hesketh, teacher and actor, said at the time, 'We are a community school and only those living in the catchment area can come – that's fairly rigidly applied. Children are not transferred here for dramatic reasons.' It is quite ironic, twenty-five years after that statement was made St Helen's; now Edward Sheerien, has still not been granted Performing Arts Status, although it might change this year.

However, this spiralling decay and relative stagnation, combined with his lack of any meaningful creative outlet since *Days Of Hope*, merely strengthened Loach's militancy. To combat the prevalence of Thatcherism, Loach embarked on a series of documentaries.

It was also at this point that Loach's career began its extended low, tellingly coinciding with the election of the Conservative Party to a government under the leadership of Margaret Thatcher, who embodied the very antithesis of Loach's ideology. '*I think the style we started in Kes hadn't progressed enough,*' explained the director, '*I was in a bit of a rut, in the way of working. I didn't find the right ideas to suggest films to raise money on. But at the time what was happening in the country was so extreme – like being knocked over by a tidal wave; of the first Thatcherite onslaught when unemployment shot through the roof and factories were closing – the attack was overwhelming.*'

Margaret Thatcher would not be one of the top ten people Loach would have on his dinner list. Or maybe she would, so he could personally challenge her. Certainly trying to find a voice through cinema was a slow business, sometimes taking 3 to 5 years from conception to screen, issues by then would have changed and new more pressing matters would be in place. Through some of Ken's friends at Central, the old ATV studios, in the documentary department, he was able to start making an impact in that genre. '*A documentary can be like a pamphlet. It can be made and shown very quickly. It to me seemed the appropriate form, at that time, to capture what was happening.*'

In 1993 Ken Loach was the subject of *The South Bank Show*. Melvin Bragg, who has clashed swords with Loach over *Which Side Are You On* (1984), introduced the director thus, '*...He's a quiet survivor. His unashamedly political work whether for the cinema or television, in the form of drama or documentary is distinguished by qualities of consistency and single mindedness. Rare in an industry, where more often guided by commercial rather than political consideration... His body of work is beginning to be seen for what it is – an uncompromising and impressive testimony to our times.*' Praise indeed from a former sparring partner.

The broadcast was frank and unforgiving as well as praising and intelligent. Both men obviously respected each other – the gloves were off, but there was no hitting below the belt. Bragg was relaxed and Loach was natural and fluent. The last quarter of the show dealt with Loach's documentary career.

In true Orwellian style, in 1984 his voice was squeezed off the TV screens, when two main projects were cancelled; those of *Questions of Leadership* (1984), and *Which Side Are You On* (1984). The former, his first foray into documentary, was commissioned and put together for ITV's *The South Bank Show,* but Editor Melvyn Bragg stepped in and refused to authorise the broadcast. During the 1993 interview Bragg explained to the director why he had withdrawn the piece, *'I thought* Which Side Are You On *was a very powerful piece of work. But what I thought as editor of* The South Bank Show *it was more of a political film than an arts film.'* Both men did not fall out seriously over the piece, but there were many heated discussions in the cutting room. Not only was Loach's harrowing depiction of violence on and around the picket line, while the music and poetry was being played by the miner's – certain allegations were being banded about surrounding the police and their actions. Loach staunchly maintained to Bragg that these allegations came straight from the front line. As the songs and poetry depicted – of miner's getting beaten up in the cells, shins being kicked in on the picket line and of others being brutalised for little reason. It is clear to see on his film of police not wearing their obligatory numbers. Were they hiding their identity or were they not official members of the constabulary, but hired thugs in blue suits. Which side are you on?

However, *Which Side Are You On?* was eventually shown on Channel 4, three months after the heat of Thatcher's overpowering of the strikers had subsided. Loach returned to these themes in his 1983 four-part Channel 4 programme, which extended the themes of the original broadcast but concerned the miner's strike. Having spent two years on the programmes, the final films were banned and even today, cannot be legally shown outside of a film club. Is it not it time that these programmes were now aired for all to see?

This was not new ground for Ken Loach, in 1971 he made The Save the Children Fund Film. The Save the Children Fund, which had commissioned the film, was so displeased with the final product that they allegedly tried to destroy the negative. They failed at this and the film is still preserved, but it has yet to be shown publicly.

Between 1983 and 1990, Loach's focus and confidence would appear to have wavered, in the face of his inability to find finance. Backers were afraid to put faith in a man notorious for making unbroadcastable material. However, in 1986, he did manage to direct the feature *Fatherland*, written by Trevor Griffith, his first foray into a working relationship with FilmFour. It was this alliance that was to pay dividends in the future, and as the 80's came to a close, Loach renewed his partnership with his former writer, Jim Allen.

As Loach himself describes, '*It took years of walking up and down Wardour Street, briefcase in hand, desperately seeking finance, before things started to happen.*' He directed, in 1990, Allen's typically polemical screenplay film *Hidden Agenda*, which won Loach the Jury Prize at the Cannes Film Festival of that year. Described by Conservative MP, Ivor Stanbrook, as '*the official IRA entry*', this tag proved worrying to exhibitors but, nevertheless, received critical acclaim and relative box-office success. You cannot please all the people all the time. The only person Loach is interested in pleasing is the punter sitting in the seat with his or her popcorn in their lap. They validate his existence as a film-maker. Make them think, make them respond, do not pull any punches and tell it how it is. Warts and all. Show the warts, name them and finish with a close up.

During the 1990s, Loach made six very successful films, certainly at a critical level and virtually all have dealt with a social evil as Loach might describe it. His creative renaissance would seem to begin with the working-class triumvirate of *Riff-Raff* (1991), *Raining Stones* (1993) and *Ladybird Ladybird* (1994). The latter film, based on a true story, was criticised by Carol Sarler in the Sunday Times for, as she alleged, that Loach had '*distorted the facts of the case*' and '*exploiting a families unhappiness*', for his own end, an attack which particularly angered Loach, who disputed the claims but his right to reply was denied by the paper's editors.

His subsequent films have seen Loach travel to Spain and Nicaragua to pursue stories of social struggle with *Land And Freedom* (1995) and *Carla's Song* (1996) respectively. Following the successful film, *My Name Is Joe* (1998) Loach returned to the themes of the working-class struggle familiar from his television, and early 90's film work. This particular project certainly gave rise to a distinct resurgence of interest in his work. Loach's career has been subject to many fits and starts, but his reputation at the end of the Nineties, after a 35-year career, remains relatively intact.

The millennium saw Loach's career steadily flourishing with *Bread and Roses* (2000) followed with very respectful reviews and

4 prestigious awards. *The Navigators* (2001), saw the writer Rob Dawber picking up a BAFTA. Loach enjoyed a tremendous response for his next feature, *Sweet Sixteen* (2002), the production received 21 nominations and eventually picked up 9 wins. These included a BAFTA Scotland Award, Best British Independent Film Award and at the Cannes Film Festival 2002 won Best Screenplay. September 11 (2002), it follows the effects of the 9/11 terrorist attacks told from different points of view around the world. The eleven short clips were shot by 11 directors. The BBCi reviewed the contributions and stated, *'Best of all is Ken Loach's segment, in which a Chilean refugee offers his condolences to the American victims.'*

For Ken's latest work he has returned to Scotland for, *A Fond Kiss...,*(2004) although it is still early days it has already been recognised by the Berlin International Film Festival taking the Ecumenical Jury Prize and the Guild of German Art House Cinemas. *Ticket,* an ensemble direction, will be released in December 2005 as Ken works hard on his latest project, another Paul Laverty script, *The Wind That Shakes the Barley.* Filmed in and around County Cork in Ireland. Even though filming has finished and the exhausting hours in the cutting room have begun, Ken was unsure or reluctant to offer any clues about the finished work.

Since *Cathy Come Home* in 1966, Loach has been making powerful films with a political point, and the fact that he frequently casts people who are new to acting - people spotted at schools or community groups or open auditions - almost always works to his advantage, trapping a fierce, unencumbered realism in every frame. In order to extract a freshness of reaction from his cast, he releases the script scene by scene, engineering on-set surprises and relying on improvisation, so that the performers are as close to living through events as possible. *'The key thing is finding the right people,'* explains Loach. *'It's not the director telling them, "This is what you should do." It's them telling me.'*

'The director's technique quickly became apparent during Kes,' explains Trevor Hesketh, *'he was extremely patient, coaxing, unruffled, even-tempered and on friendly terms with everyone. The script of the film was to be only a vehicle for the expression of the personalities of the actors. Situations were suggested and speech became spontaneous, with some electrifying results. Staff interested in drama realised immediately that the film was being created by the actors, within the confines of the plot, but inspired by the genius of the director.'*

Loach argues that professional film actors, no matter how skilled, will always find it difficult to disguise their regional and class origins.

'If a part has to carry a lot of information,' says Loach, 'then you need someone who can learn the lines well, yet deliver them with spontaneity. If it is a part which involves a primarily emotional exchange with somebody, then you want someone whose emotions are very available, and who can respond in that way. You also cast for authenticity of age, class or region.' Loach has strong views on this subject of a theme of not using professional actors and drawing on the talents of a local community. 'There are simply some things you can't act in film, you can do it in the theatre, but film looks right into your eyes. It can see you think. I think it is very hard to disguise your class and very hard to disguise where you are from. I think it's very hard to do all those things we do unselfconsciously. It is a level of authenticity.' Loach is adamant about his technique for film. 'There are really only two types of acting,' explains Loach. 'There is theatre acting and film acting. The latter can be something different. Someone can be taken through a story and experience the story and put themselves in that position and respond as they would respond. So you are really experiencing that person in that story and I guess that's what we have tried to do over the years and it has developed into a way of working.'

If it is a slice-of-life film someone is after they cannot do better than send for Ken Loach. Although he is unconventional in his approach, he knows when it is right, realism seems to emit from every soul who plays in front of him, but he takes this all in his stride. Loach says, 'There's a lot of mystique about film directing. It doesn't call for large caravans and your name on the backs of chairs. All that gets in the way.'

So what comes to mind when you hear the name Ken Loach? I guess that it all depends on your age. If you are one of our younger readers then you maybe familiar with his most recent International successes; those of *Land and Freedom*, *Carla's Song*, and *Bread and Roses*. Or more recently the film *The Navigators* and *Sweet Sixteen*. And for the older generation it is all about one wonderful movie, (one central to Loach's fascination for all-things-Yorkshire) the film *Kes*. It's a landscape that he's made so familiar by detailing issues of hope, destiny and struggle within working communities, filled with natural characters that breathe life into celluloid.

Loach's outspoken way, his calm honest powerful words when attacking an organisation or even a super power, lingers on and usually end up in text. His criticism, more than once, has travelled across the pond to the USA. His American experiences whilst making one film left him with the need to cleanse himself forever of their grasp: 'Hollywood has to be the most difficult place in the world to make *films.'* He has since turned his back on the Hollywood dollar. He endeared himself further to that insulated community in Cannes last year (during a special screening of *Kes*), when he asked British film-makers to stop allowing themselves to be colonised so ruthlessly by US ideas and its market potential. He has strong views and equally strong convictions. He will keep poking the stick into the hornets nest to see what happens? Loach's films are not always viewer friendly, and his artistic style is something he will not comment on, saying, *'It's just boring and self-indulgent when directors go on about how they work and their cinematic style.'*

Ken Loach doesn't necessarily portray the working class as heroic, but, above all, he seems interested in exploring the complexity of their dilemmas. *'There's a kind of fun about working-class characters,'* explains Loach, *'and their stories work on a very primal level. I also work with memories of still photographs and documentaries, which convinced me that working-class experience was where drama, the raw material of drama, was.'*

In the meantime, whatever he turns his attention to next, be it local or of an international flavour, one thing you can be certain of is that it will not be Hollywood friendly. For me, it's good to know that his grip on social realism has not softened and that there is still a voice that does not shy away from the phrase working class.

Derek Malcolm summed up the feelings at the Cannes Film Festival 2000, *'He is a director admired, and often loved, all over the world. I remember once presiding over the International Critics' Jury at Cannes and, as the British representative, gingerly suggesting that one of Loach's films should at least be on the shortlist. "What?" said several members of the jury in unison. "On the shortlist? He's got to win!" One of them, a Latin American, added, "Who else can make you laugh and then cry in the space of two minutes?"'*

They say the greatest risk of all - is never to take a risk. Ken Loach continues to take risks. He continues to give us thought provoking drama. Often his work is offensive to individuals or organisations. Sometimes his work is banned and never gets aired. Occasionally he bites the hand that feeds him, usually the faceless bureaucratic figures that have put up the money for a film. But he never shies away from his responsibility of boundary-stretching film-maker. An angry voice that speaks out for the common people, people you meet in the street, working class people — people who work. He uses the powerful media of the big screen to paint his message in images. He will continue to thrill, entertain and of course — enrage. A savage humanist with the ability to make you laugh and then cry in the space of two minutes.

8

The Producer – Tony Garnett

Tony Garnett was born in 1935 in Birmingham, England, where he spent his youth. His parents were born in Aston and lived in the Black Country. As a boy Tony used to explore the region on his bike, *'I spent my free time,'* comments Garnett, *'scrumping apples in Evesham, racing over Cannock Chase, and bathing in the River Severn. My Uncle Fred had a milk round in the City Centre. I helped him on Saturdays and spent my wages on all the Shakespeare productions at Stratford.'* He was then and still is an avid supporter of Aston Villa Football Club. When I spoke to him to ask if he would contribute to my book – he asked first where I was from, he knew it was not far from Birmingham. He was right; I was actually born in Dudley, in the West Midlands. And I think of all those wasted elocution lessons, after school, at Haden Hill. Tony still did not offer his support, but wryly asked what football team I supported? Luckily (and a bit of research) I gave him the right answer, this was mainly due to the fact that my partner's father used to play for the Villa. If I had said Wolverhampton Wanderers or West Bromwich Albion I have no idea how much co-operation I would have received. But I guess Tony's chapter would have been a lot briefer.

By 1954 Tony was studying psychology at the University of London. At the university, he began acting and after graduation he worked for a while as an actor including appearances in BBC television productions. Then Garnett gave up acting to become an assistant to Roger Smith, a script editor at the BBC. Shortly afterwards Garnett became a producer at the BBC and directed the film *Prostitute*. At the beginning of the sixties, following this brief career as an actor, (*Incident at Echo Six, Z Cars*) his career began to take shape when he was recruited by Sidney Newman, Head of BBC drama, as a script editor for a new BBC series; *The Wednesday Play.*

British television drama in the 1950s had been dominated by classic theatrical texts produced in the studio, normally live, with occasional 35mm film inserts. The arrival of videotape meant only that these productions were done live-to-tape. *The Wednesday Play,* with a commitment to new talent and new techniques, changed all that. 'At the time,' says Garnett, 'you were allowed about four days filming, with cumbersome 35mm equipment, just to show a car pulling up or driving away. So we used those four days to whizz round and shoot half the script with a hand-held 16mm camera - about 35 to 40 minutes screen time.'

Having met on the set of *Catherine*, as actor and director (Loach's directional debut), it was in 1964, while Tony, from the BBC Drama Department, producer of *The Wednesday Play*, that their friendship was cemented. It was the birth of a collaboration that would last many years. The marriage was a fruitful one and although they have not worked together for some time, it was actually Garnett's move to the USA that finished the partnership, both keep in contact. 'Yes, I'm meeting him when he gets back from filming in Ireland,' explained Tony, recently. 'We are actually very close — our families as well.'

Unlike some business break-ups; neither has lost their admiration or respect for the other. Each have gone off and carved deeper reputations in their chosen fields.

Tony Garnett's long association with the BBC is flavoured with wry speculative awareness rather than tired bitter cynicism. 'I don't work in documentaries — I think they're too difficult; we work in fiction. Just like I used to argue with the BBC in the sixties that news and current affairs deal in what they mendaciously call fact, and often lie — we deal in fiction and try to tell the truth.'

One of their early collaborations with Garnett as producer and Loach as director was the powerful *Cathy Come Home*. In a Britain complacent that its welfare system was among the best in the world, this documentary-style film of the devastating effects of homelessness on one young family had enormous impact. Never before or since has one single piece of drama had such an effect on an entire nation.

In the early years with *Cathy*... having been broadcast – headlines screamed and politicians were, as usual, outraged. In fact, rare in politics - a world of sound bites and backbites, governing power and opposing condemnation; they, as a group, were incongruously unified. As usual, when the men and women in and around power had pontificated their individual disgust — everything went back to normal. Tony Garnett philosophically reviewed his early years in television, 'In those days I had this naïve idea that we could make a film and change the world. In fact there were marginal changes (after *Cathy Come Home*) in legislation for the treatment of the homeless. I have to say that now the problems of the homeless is infinitely worse and most of *the people responsible for it live in nice houses.'*

The stark realism of *Cathy...* led to angry calls for action to prevent such circumstances from happening – but little was achieved. The changes in social attitudes and awareness were limited, and the issues addressed were discussed in Parliament and promptly forgotten. The real positive move to combat this most disturbing situation was born from the people. The charity, Shelter, was founded a week later - as a national campaign for the homeless, and quickly became an important voice in housing matters.

They were both 32-year-old graduates from television making their way into the movie business. They had made their reputations with emotive BBC productions as *Cathy...* and *Up The Junction*. *Kes* was their first feature film together, which they shot on location in Barnsley for the ludicrous sum of £155,000. At the time Garnett commented, rather doubtfully, *'I think we've got a percentage of it. Our lawyer says so anyhow. But I'm not bothered. I'd been happy to make it just for the wages.'*

There was quite a lot of publicity before filming began and the production team feared that audiences of well-wishers, autograph hunters, friends and family, may descend on St Helen's and possibly spoil shots and performances. Tony Garnett put out a plea, *'The whole concept and substance of our film depends on being able to capture the normal and the natural reactions of children. And this will be impossible if they are surrounded by crowds of sightseers. If people will only wait to see the finished product at the cinema then it would be a great help.'*

After all, they were not making the film in the studios and had the comfort of a controlled set. The entire film was being shot on location, in a school and surrounding locations – all public places. Trevor Hesketh, says, *'It was amazing. Take the football match and some of the other scenes – nobody turned up! Everybody new about the film – but everybody stayed away.'* It seems a great testimony to the people of Barnsley and surrounding areas. That they took all this in their stride and made their attendance at the right time - at the cinemas. If I knew a film was being made in my area, you could not have kept me away. I would have been in every shot. Juggling, trick cycling, singing and dancing, reciting Shakespeare and playing the spoons!

Although Tony was the producer of a movie, financed by a huge USA movie house, both him and Ken were happy to muck in with the cast and crew. Often they would be spotted at Finney's fish and chip shop in the town, dining each for 1s. 10d. Tony Garnett comments, *'It was actually David (Bradley) who took us there, he's a connoisseur of fish* and chips – *talks about them like an Oxford don talks about claret.'* Jim Ryder, they used his proper name in the film, remembers Tony Garnett taking a bunch of young actors to the sweet shop. It appears the cast and crew, including the director, producer and writer, all shared their world, with no egos or anyone pulling rank. This was a professional team, everyone was important, similar to a great painting, every brush stroke, however miniscule or seemingly insignificant – contributed towards the finished masterpiece.

This was their calling card. Everyone knows you are judged by your last film – make a bad one and you might never get finance again, produce a classic and they will never forget it. Everyone who watches a movie has a rock in their hand, critics, backers, producers, peers, the public etc. Of course some people have got bigger rocks than others – but all can potentially hurt you. It is no good if the critics love it but the public hate it. If it is the other way round it may take so long for a film to get recognised – your movie career may already have ended. I remember my second book I had published, a fictional novel called *Tally* – it was struggling to sell. My agent at the time, obviously trying to be diplomatic, said, '...*everybody loved it – but nobody bought it!*' Ego one – bank balance nil.

Garnett need not have worried as nearly all the critics raved about it and shunted the men in suits, from United Artists and Rank, who seriously delayed the success of the movie by not giving it a general release for nearly two and a half years after it was completed. *Kes* also shook up the government and as usual rustled a few feathers (pun intended). The educational system hit back meekly, but voices were drowned out by praise. Garnett, commenting about *Kes*, and the enormous impact and criticism from the teaching profession, 'We *were not attacking individual teachers, but a system which is geared to produce factory fodder rather than helping to facilitate the enrichment of personalities of our children.'*

Like all intelligent men – when you ask a question they have to ponder, dead air is not a recipe for vague speech. I asked Tony, with what he knows now, would he have wished the film to be made any differently? Time stood still as he reviewed his experienced and varied career. '...*I think it's one of the few pieces of work,'* Tony eventually commented, '*I have been involved with, where I can truly say there wouldn't be anything substantially different and that's nearly forty years down the line. And I can't say that about anything else I've done. Because as soon as you finish a film and see it – you say, oh I know how we should have made it,* (laughing) *and of course then it's too late!'*

There were many mountains to climb just to get *Kes* made, and then came the promotional side of the arrangement. 'Although there was enormous problems putting it together,' Tony explained, 'particularly financially, and then an enormous amount of problems getting it released – the actual making of Kes, and particularly the harmonious collaboration between Barry, Ken and me and finding that cast in Barnsley and Chris Menges coming through for the first time as a camera operator; he was just terrific, terrific – it was all just so wonderful and right.'

It all came together beautifully for Kes, like the workings of the complicated Patek Philippe's Caliber 89 clock. 'Once or twice in life – everything just comes together,' says the producer. 'And the other thing is we were all too young to realise just how difficult it was to get right. And of course under-pinning it all was Barry's honest narrative. It's another testament to – if the material isn't right – just don't do it, why bother. At the end of the day it was all... serendipity. I can't emphasise enough all the elements that came together – we were just very very lucky.'

Nearly forty years later, like I asked Loach, I wondered if the book were offered to the producer today – would he still make it? 'Oh I would do it tomorrow, if I could get the funding, I just don't think I could get the money to make it,' says Tony. 'I probably couldn't get it made now, and it was very difficult to get it made then. Oh yes, I would do it like a shot. One of the sad reasons why is that we are still throwing a shameful proportion of our young people onto the scrap heap. It was happening forty years ago and it's still happening today. So much for progress! And so much for Tony Blair's education, education, education! So it's just as relevant, unfortunately and it deeply saddens me to say that.'

It was around the time of the release of Kes, in 1970, that Garnett and Loach, who had practically invented the Wednesday Play, completed their last for London Weekend Television. It was about the death of an old Liverpool man. Garnett said of this sad end to some marvellous thought-provoking plays, 'Regards the Wednesday Plays, it's time for us to walk off into the sunset.'

Tony Garnett never believed in leaving television behind, regardless of the success Kes eventually enjoyed. He said at the time the movie premiered, 'For some subjects, TV is better than the cinema. You can get 12 million people at once on the telly. It's ideal for immediate social propaganda. Western art is obsessed with form. TV is not a form, it's a means. Film is a form; it can be moulded, sculpted. The TV image is impoverished beside the cinema. No one seems to have done any research on the psychological differences between television and film audiences, which is surprising, because most feature films are now made with an eye to eventual TV sales in five years.' Although these were comments made in 1970 – it mirrors the feelings of today and shows Garnett to be a forward thinking guru of his art. Tony is also very modest. When discussing his role as producer, which in the cinema can mean anything from glorified accountant to a creative entrepreneur, he says, *'It's a bit embarrassing being the mouth for 40 or 50 people. But power and responsibility must reside in the same place. As Nye Bevan used to say: "A good producer is someone who's made a smashing film and everyone thinks he's done nothing." If I have to put my foot down, I feel I've failed. The film should make itself.'*

Journalist, Ian Sainsbury described Garnett when he met him while filming *Kes, 'He is a small, wiry young man dressed, when I met him, in denim shirt, jacket and trousers. He wears spectacles and has a smile that both somehow seem too big for him and he has more ideas than a dog has fleas.'*

In the 1970s Garnett's pace slowed somewhat but not the combative quality of the work. In 1975 *Days of Hope* emerged, a Jim Allen mini-series, he rewrote the history of the decade before the 1926 General Strike as a betrayal of the working class by its own leaders. 1978 saw another Allen mini-series, *Law and Order*, which caused uproar by treating professional criminals as just another group of capitalist entrepreneurs trying to turn a profit and in 1980 Garnett enjoyed his directorial debut with *Prostitute*.

The next decade 1980 to 1990 saw the end of the partnership for Garnett and Loach. The move across the water to the United States quashed any further projects materializing. Garnett, like Loach, the reason they got on so well, was very socially aware. He now felt that artistically and politically out of place in Britain. He joined Universal and wrote and directed *Deep In The Heart* (1983), although Universal thought the project un-commercial and deferred its release. Although this was familiar territory for the producer turned director, and must have mirrored the attitudes that had surrounded *Kes's* release – he marched on and forced Hollywood to sit up and listen – if not sit up and beg. Undeterred Tony went on to produce and show off his varied skills with *Earth Girls Are Easy* (1988), the *Seasame Street Presents: Follow The Bird* (1985) and *Fat man and Little Boy* (1989), which starred Paul Newman.

Tony Garnett returned to English shores at the beginning of the nineties and formed Island World Productions, with John Haymen. Garnett was obviously in a very business like mood as his new production company would be a forerunner for British television. It continues to produce a number of successful TV shows. There brief during this exciting time was to create a production company making dramatic fiction for television. And they did just that. 1992 spawned *Between the Lines* and *Cardiac Arrest*. In 1996 came the birth of *This Life* an aspirational, non-political drama series about twenty-somethings which had the nation hooked by the end of its second and final series. This was also the year *Ballykissangel* began its long run. This was followed up, passing over the millennium with hard hitting police series, *The Cops* (1998) and *Attachments* (2000/1). Impressed by the run of dramatic hits and award winning TV, Reading University recognised his talents by making Garnett a Doctor of Letters.

Tony Garnett marches onwards and upwards and is still a big name associated with quality drama – although his inexhaustible energy is directed at the small screen. *'We've got a lot of television at the moment,'* comments Tony. *'In fact I've got some shooting in Leeds. It's the channel 4 series about nurses. There's also another* Singles *about to start for channel 5* (laughing) *that's North Yorkshire funnily enough. And a whole lot of other stuff. In a way I would sooner work on the telly – you reach people quickly and this is a television country not a cinema country.'*

Garnett comments now, *'If I were 30 years younger, I would probably be working on the Web now. It has the excitement to me that going to the BBC had in 1963, the feeling that we don't know what's possible, but anything might be.'* I am sure whatever Tony Garnett turned his hand to he would make a success of it. But it would have to quench his artistic and political bent. It would have to be thought provoking and be a voice of the people for the people. With this criteria realised, whatever else – it would be entertaining.

9

The Writer – Barry Hines

Whatever is written about *Kes* and the deserving praise given to its director and producer, Barry Hines not only provided the colours for Loach to paint his masterpiece, but the subject matter. Without Hines's contribution, his literary work, his vision and total skill of his craft – there would be a void in British cinema history. You must have a beginning and the genesis was *A Kestrel for a Knave*.

Barry Hines says about penning his most famous novel, *'Most of it is stories that were told to me by my brother and my mates, about the Secondary Modern in Sheffield.'* We all hear great stories in youth as we do in adult life – it is very rare to weave them into a powerful, moving social document that can then be turned into a classic British movie. *'I had been a teacher in several schools in south Yorkshire so it was familiar ground,'* offered Hines, *'I had taught plenty of pupils like Billy Casper - I knew boys like that - so it was no great feat of imagination. I was just writing about something I knew very well. I was just married at the time and my brother, who was about 18, kept a young kestrel in the shed at the bottom of the garden so I was able to assist him in the rearing of it.'*

Children today have no direct experience of the *Secondary Modern*, of that cataclysmic division at age 11. And the mining industry no longer dominates any town the way it does in the film. *'To this generation,'* says Hines, *'they probably wonder what the pits are... But the plight of Billy Casper doesn't change. There are still boys struggling, trying to find themselves that have something taken away from them.'*

Barry Hines's has never really wanted any more than to change the world, or as he calls it, the system. At age 30, when his second book *A Kestrel For A Knave* had been made into a successful film, breaking attendance records in Yorkshire, and his current play, *Billy's Last Stand,* opening at the Sheffield Playhouse, he had made a break, in his own life, from the grip of the system. *'At school I was just a runner and a footballer, completely non-academic,'* explains the author. *'I didn't* even know what school was about I'd never even read a novel.' Although this statement is true, certainly in Barry Hines's high standard of achievement, it is modest. After all, he was sufficiently academic to pass the 11-plus. Had he have failed, Hines's life may have been a lot closer to his famous protagonist – Billy Casper. *'I left school at 15 and went for a job as an apprentice mining surveyor at Rockingham pit. Why? It seemed like a decent sort of job. They said to wait until I had some 'O' levels, so I went back to school and got some. After I went back to the pit I realised after three or four months it wasn't for me. I was lucky enough to get back into to the school again in the Lower Sixth – I thought if I could get to Loughborough College I could at least go on playing football.'*

'At Loughborough, one bored Saturday afternoon, I asked the bloke I shared digs with if he had anything to read.' His flatmate was studying English as a subsidiary subject and lent Hines *Animal Farm*. *'I can't remember ever having read a novel till then. I suppose I was 19 or 20. We did a Shaw play for 'O' level but I can't even remember what it was.'* Ten years later and the author had written two novels, his first being the *Blinder*, which he regards as fun but basically *'kids stuff'*. At this time, working on his third novel, dedicating five nights a week to writing, this is after he comes home from teaching at Hoyland Kirkbalk Comprehensive. With very little time, and very little money – he used the cash from *Kes* to pay off his mortgage; the third novel he hoped would be his saviour – freedom of financial burden and a full time occupation as a writer.

But *Kes* had not finished soaring, and his three per cent of the box office enabled him to start the dream.

Like Billy Casper, Hines spent much of his childhood exploring the countryside, but unlike Billy, he was no academic failure. After passing the eleven-plus he went on to Ecclesfield Grammar school. Most of his friends had failed and had ended up in the local secondary modern – the model for the school in the film. Barry explains, *'The school was very tough and some of the boys used to go dressed in boiler suits and boots because they spent so much time rolling around the floor fighting. Their mothers said they may as well dress for the job, rather than ruin good clothes.'*

Many of the incidents his friends used to talk about after school found their way into the book and subsequently the film. Although Barry relished the humour of the day – he also realises with hindsight that those children who had failed the eleven-plus had effectively been told that they were unintelligent and many of them continued to believe it for the rest of their lives. *'In academic terms*

Billy Casper is a failure,' explains the author, *'he is in the bottom form of a secondary modern school. He has "a job to read and write" as he tells the Employment Officer. Yet once he becomes interested in falconry, he acquires a book on the subject, which is full of esoteric vocabulary and technical descriptions. He then goes on to successfully train a kestrel which requires both intelligence and sensitivity. If there had been GCSE's in Falconry, Billy Casper would have been awarded an A grade, which would have done wonders for his self-confidence and given him a more positive self-image.'*

The dialogue was very powerful and very real in the book. Paul Allen, journalist said, *'This was mainly due to Hines's down-to-earth fluency in a South Yorkshire voice which a spell in London and another with a BBC bursary in Elba (which helped a lot with the writing of the book) have done nothing to dissipate.'*

Barry and his mates, during the nesting season, had often taken a young magpie – trying to rear it, feeding it on household scraps. They provided rich entertainment with their mischievous ways, before flying back to the wild. Barry admits he would have never taken a kestrel from the nest in the same casual manner. It was not simply that they did not know how to raise a fledgling kestrel and it might die, it was more to do with a feeling of awe and instinctive respect for such a beautiful creature. Or, as Billy Casper passionately describes it when discussing Kes with the sympathetic Mr Farthing, *'Is it heck tame, it's trained that's all. It's fierce, an' it's wild, an' it's not bothered about anybody, not even me right. And that's why it's great.'*

Richard Hines was technical advisor on the film, *'My brother trained the kestrels and he did wonders on a tight schedule,'* says Hines, *'It's not like working with a trained dog. A kestrel has to be the right weight. They only fly if they're hungry so we would weigh them before a scene and if they were too heavy they had to wait to shoot the scene. It was imperative that Billy had to appear able to fly. the birds but he wasn't a natural. There was something magical about kestrels. They demanded an instant respect but David had none of that. He wouldn't have known a sparrow from an eagle. It took about a month of quite intensive training, but in the end he pulled it off.*

Barry Hines was on set every day and had viewed the rushes. *'I could tell it was going to be good. I had seen the TV plays that Ken and Tony had made and thought, "Yes, that's the real thing." If they couldn't make a good job of it, no one could. The thing that delighted me the most was that Tony, Ken and I were on the same wavelength. We made the film we wanted to without any interference from Hollywood.'*

People have often asked Barry Hines if the character Billy Casper was based on a real person. *'No he wasn't,'* confirms the author, *'But he's not unusual, the lonely misfit who doesn't belong to the gang. But even though Billy has a tough life and the odds are stacked against him, it was important not to make him weak, blameless character whom everybody picks on. This would have weakened and sentimentalised the story. Billy is a survivor, a tough little character. More Artful Dodger than Oliver Twist. When he is foiled by the bureaucracy at the public library, he immediately goes out and steals a falconry book from a bookshop. When McDowell tries to bully him in the playground, he gives as good as he gets in the ensuing fight. We gather during a conversation with Mr Farthing that he has already been in trouble with the law, and most dramatically, he keeps the money which his brother has left him to place on a bet.'*

A Kestrel for a Knave was published in 1968 (Michael Joseph) and was shortly followed by the film. Barry Hines worked very closely with the director Ken Loach and producer, Tony Garnett. *'What impressed me when I first met them was their determination to stick to the harsh reality of the novel,'* explains Hines, *'and not turn it into a sentimental - Walt Disney boy and his pet, type story. What was especially gratifying for me, was that some of the locations in the film were the same ones that I had written about in the novel, and it gave me an extra thrill to see them on the big screen.'*

How evenly was the divide I am not sure. We know Loach greatly collaborates with his writers. The novel's themes, dialogue and structure resemble those in the film, yet this does not imply that Hines took a majority of creative decisions in adapting the book – although all realised they had to eliminate the novel's flashbacks and introduce a dual temporality. Loach attributes his photographic style to Menges, but he chose to work with Menges; similarly, although the subject of *Kes* comes from Hines's imagination and experience, he, and Garnett, chose to film the novel. A large degree of praise has to go to Loach for his tight structure in handling *Kes*, the way he deals with the elements, regardless of script, and of course, in the casting and directing of actors.

It was not necessarily the birth of the *Three Wise Men* – Loach, Garnett and Hines – because they all existed; it was the creation of their friendship. The ingredients – like a classic cocktail – were paramount. Obviously Barry Hines's novel *A Kestrel for a Knave* was in existence before the three had all met professionally. Tony Garnett was responsible for bringing the author and the director together and from that seed *Kes* was born. '*Working with Barry Hines is a joy,*' said Loach, '*he and I – like Tony and I – were a similar age and from a similar background, and we see things in a similar way – the same kind of things make us smile.*' The film that came out of that first meeting was voted by the British Film Institute – the 7th best British film ever made.

There were a few changes in the adaptation of the book to the film, there usually are, however faithful the film-makers remain to the original novel. Often, scenes that work in a book do not on film and vice versa. '*I found it much more thrilling,*' says the author, '*watching Billy flying the hawk to the lure on the silver screen in Technicolor rather than in my head. Conversely, one of the key scenes in the novel, in which Mr Farthing asks the class to write "A Tall story" didn't work at all when it was being filmed and had to be abandoned.*'

In the book Billy writes a story for Mr Farthing and originally, although it ended up on the cutting room floor, they were going to shoot it as he wrote. '*It was tried with a hand-held camera shooting over Billy's shoulder, but it soon became apparent that it would have taken him too long to complete and an edited version would not have had the same emotional effect.*' Another major change was the ending. In the novel, following the fight at home with his brother, Jud, after he has killed the hawk, Billy runs away and breaks into a derelict cinema, which he used to visit with his father in happier times. He sits on a broken seat and projects onto the screen an imaginary scene of the hawk attacking a fleeing Jud upon the moors. '*This wouldn't have worked,*' explains Hines, '*because it was pure fantasy taking place in Billy's head, and the style would have been out of context with everything that had happened previously. In the film, the downbeat ending of Billy burying the hawk after his emotional confrontation with Jud was much more appropriate.*'

One of the great performances and one everyone associates with is the football match. It is a great mixture of comedy and tragedy. Comedy in viewing the events unfolding in the movie and tragedy surrounding the figure of authority in Glover's performance. '*Brian Glover who played the PE teacher was a friend of mine,*' explains Hines, '*We had taught together. He was an English teacher and professional wrestler. He used to get his pupils to read plays out loud and he was very good at acting out the various parts. I can remember him coming into the staff room after a lesson, saying, "They've just applauded me out of the classroom." When he heard about the film, he asked if there might be a part in it for me and I suggested the PE teacher who was in charge of the football match.*'

As filming progressed, Barry Hines saw the vision of his book unfolding before his eyes. *'It was cold and overcast the whole time, but everyone had a marvellous time,'* he said. *'With all the laughter going on during filming, I knew for certain that we'd be laughing at the finished thing. But the most exciting thing for me was seeing that Ken Loach was succeeding in capturing the spirit of my book.'*

Throughout the filming, Barry Hines's house at Hoyland Common was used as the production office. *'I didn't even have a telephone then, '*he recalled. *'The company put a phone in, on a little landing going up the stairs; they were on the phone all the time. What was good about it was that United Artists never checked up on this and I kept the phone for a year or two afterwards!'*

The movie *Kes* was a huge success and it helped to popularise the novel, although published as adult fiction, is widely read in schools and is still a set examination text. *'I often receive letters from children asking questions about the book,'* laughs Hines, adding, *'GCSE candidates I suspect seeking insider information. It's a surreal experience. It's like being back at school doing English literature 'O' level, only this time I'm answering the questions on my own text. I've sometimes considered sitting the examination under an assumed name to see how I would get on. Perhaps my interpretation of the book would differ from that of the examiner and I would fail. Who can tell?'*

Barry Hines has given many readings at literature festivals, schools and universities and many questions have been fired at him. These have ranged from incidental ponderings of a un-published author to highly technical questions about dramatic prose. One he remembers – the weirdest – was put to him from a school in Lancashire. Barry was sitting in the staff room waiting to talk to a happy bunch of fifth formers – it was their last lesson on Friday afternoon. A teacher sitting next to him, lowered the newspaper he was reading, as if struck by a sudden inspirational thought, and said, *'You know that novel you wrote,* A Kestrel for a Knave?' Barry nodded encouragingly. He continued, *'Did you write it on purpose or by accident?'* Barry was stunned – he could imagine someone penning a line or two of verse by accident – but a whole novel! Luckily there was a minor explosion in the science laboratory and the author was spared the embarrassment of coming up with an original line that matched the question.

Another question Hines was asked, mainly in the South of England, how did he know so much about the countryside when he came from Barnsley? *'It's an ignorant question,'* explains the author, *'but* understandable, because many people still have a vision of the north filled with - dark satanic mills, mines and factories, and not a blade of grass in sight. When I try to explain that the mining village in which I was born and brought up – just a few miles from Barnsley – was surrounded by woods and fields, I can tell they don't believe me. Read Sons and Lovers by D. H. Lawrence, I tell them.' In the village where Barry lived, miners used to walk to work across meadows, with skylarks singing overhead, before crowding into the cage at the pit top and plunging into the darkness. This vision was played out in the film as we see Jud (Freddie Fletcher) strolling to work – the poetic cacophony of nature meeting the dramatic juxtaposition of industry.

One of the great indulgencies with readers, I have done it myself, is to seek significance at every turn, especially where names of characters are concerned. The answer can often be quite mundane. 'Sometimes I spot a name I fancy in a newspaper or magazine and sometimes I make them up,' says the author. It's a skill that is both intuition and feeling – that the name fits the character in the authors mind. 'The original Billy Casper,' informs Barry, 'was a famous American golfer who I had read about in the sports pages.'

Quite often in popular novels people seek hidden meanings, trying to get into the mind of the author, pontificating, theorising and summarising actions, places and names. A Kestrel for a Knave was no exception, as Barry explains, 'I've received a lot of letters enquiring about the significance of the names of the two horses in the bet that Billy failed to place for Jud.' The author had to get the book down off the shelf to remind him of the names. Book in hand, he continues, 'Tell Him He's Dead and Crackpot, that's what they're called,' he shouts out triumphantly. 'Weird names I must admit, but nothing significant in them as far as I can remember. Writing a novel is hard enough without agonising over names of race horses.' So there it is, right from the horse's mouth – sorry, couldn't help that one.

A Kestrel for a Knave started life as a novel and has subsequently been adapted into a film, a stage play, a musical and serialised on radio. Barry adds, 'Kes on Ice, hasn't appeared yet, but don't bet against it.' When asked if he thinks there will be a remake of Kes Barry Hines shakes his head, adding, 'Despite the main issues still being relevant today, I feel the original film is such a classic that it would be impossible to even attempt to re-create it.'

The eve of the new millennium created a spin off from the book and film that might have surprised the author. The newspaper heading read *A Kestrel for a Name*... and it was just that. A Barnsley couple, Rachel and Mark Gough, named their daughter, Kes, after the movie. *'Mark is Barnsley through and through,'* laughed Rachel, 29; who was not born when the film came out, added, *'It was either Kes or Toby Tyke, and her grandma banned us from calling her after a giant bull-dog! I think it all started with Mark when he realised Kes was filmed at St Helen's School which he could see from his window in Monk Bretton. He reckons there's a shot — which we've not quite managed to spot — where you can see his dad mowing the lawn in the background and he's been hooked ever since. Mind you I admit I've got to be a bit mad too to call our first baby after a bird!'* This was not the first time the couple had taken up column inches in the local newspapers — when they got married both were wearing their Barnsley football strips, together with the best man and the bridesmaids.

Following the millennium Barry Hines was asked to write an Afterword for a reprinted addition of *A Kestrel for a Knave* (Penguin Books). It gave the author a chance to reappraise his finest work and consider how it would differ if it was penned today. *'The main difference, educationally, is that Billy Casper would be attending a comprehensive school rather than a secondary modern, which is an advance of sorts, even though the principles of comprehensive education have only been pursued in a half-hearted way. Unfortunately his job prospects would be no better; in fact they would be worse. In the late sixties, when the novel was published, Billy would have got a job of sorts, however menial. He wouldn't even get a job down the pit now, because in South Yorkshire where the book is set, most of the mines have closed down. He would probably go on a scheme of some description designed to keep him off the streets, but with few long-term prospects.'*

I wondered, with what Barry knows now, if he wished any changes to his most famous piece of work? *'In retrospect, I think I made Jud and Mrs Casper too unsympathetic,'* says the author. *'Perhaps I should have given them more space; shown Jud hard at work in the darkness, shovelling coal on a three-foot face. This would have illustrated the importance of his lost winnings when Billy fails to place the bet:"I could have had a week off work wi' that," he complains bitterly. A week of fresh air and open sky. And he didn't mean to kill the hawk initially: "It wa' its own stupid fault! I wa' only goin' to let it go, but it wouldn't get out o't'hut. An' every time I tried to shift it, it kept lashing out wi' its claws. Look at 'em they're scratched to ribbons!" I think I might have been tempted to wring its neck in the same circumstances.'*

'I could also have made Billy's mother more caring. In the scene

where she is getting ready to go out for the evening and Billy is reading his falconry book, she could have shown a little more affection, perhaps given him a kiss – I almost said peck,' laughs Hines, adding, *'But all the speculation   is pointless really, changes in characterization would have produced a different book.'*

The book has had a remarkable journey over the last 37 years – Hines calls it both gratifying and puzzling. *'Neither author or publisher are certain how a book will be received when it comes out. Sometimes, a quiet little book ignored by the critics, but recommended by word of mouth, gains a currency amongst readers, while a much publicized masterpiece flops. I bet they weren't popping the champagne corks at Michael Joseph when the manuscript of* A Kestrel for a Knave *arrived in the post. A slim book about a no-hoper and a hawk. But somehow the chemistry works, and over the years I have received many rewarding letters from readers, saying how much they enjoyed the novel or the film and in some cases how it has changed their lives.'*

Out of the many remarkable stories off enrichment that surround the novel, Hines thinks the best one to sum up the appreciation is thus, *'I read* A Kestrel For A Knave *when I was 12 or 13 and was haunted by it. I knew a few Billy Caspers – I was very nearly a Billy Casper myself. I found the love of music my escape. Kes mirrored some of the things that were going on around me. Billy's hawk was my music.'* The letter writer went on to say he had become a musician and enclosed his first CD entitled, *For a Knave.*

Penning the afterword to the new re-printed addition; with a 30-year lapse, can be both sobering and reflective. The author mused at the time, *'While writing this, I have often thought about my father, a coalminer who died before I started writing. He wasn't interested in literature, and neither was I as a teenager, when he used to come and watch me play football and run at athletic meetings. He read the racing pages of the Daily Herald and an occasional cowboy book, but that was about the strength of it. I started writing just after he died and I wish he could have lived to see how things had turned out. I would love to have seen his face when I handed him a copy of this new edition of* A Kestrel for a Knave. *I can see him now, sitting by the fire turning the pages and shaking his head. "Who'd have thought it?" he would have said. Not me, I would have replied. And we would have laughed at the improbability of it all.'*

10

The Cinematographer – Chris Menges

Sixties television produced a new breed of cameraman. Men who live dangerously, who risk their lives to get close to where the action is, yet are capable of great artistry. They are the last of the adventurers. At the top of the pile is Chris Menges, according to many at the time, to be the best cameraman in television.

I could have written a novel about my journey to meet the highly respected cinematographer and director, Chris Menges. His beautiful home is not far from Knighton, sitting on the Welsh border and facing a vista of rolling green patchwork hills. It took me less than an hour, I happen to live quite near, to reach the un-adopted tarmac driveway and 30 minutes to reach Chris's house. I covered nearly 2 miles, climbing all the while, of winding and trampled road, went through 3 proper farmyards with working dogs and un-tethered horses – and not the usual BMW's and satellite dishes. I opened and closed (very important) several gates, tried to tackle a 3:1 incline in second gear, went over 2 cattle grids and saw species of bird I had not seen before.

The rambling cottage was magnificent with its country garden of wild roses and summer flowers sprouting forth. Inside had lost none of its charm, with the same fixtures and fittings, including the original baker-light switches, which were present 50 years ago. I was shown into a cluttered office, with a back wall full of books and papers. From the desk you could see Wales stretching out in front of you. Just the sort of retreat you require when you are flying around the world making movies. One day you are lining up a shot in a busy town in Portugal - to frame Anthony Hopkins and Meg Ryan (*Papa* 2005 - pre-production) or in Miami Beach, Florida, directing Goldie Hawn (actually telling Ms Hawn what to do - wow) in *Crisscross* (1992) with hundreds of cast and crew milling around like an ants nest. This idyllic hideaway in Wales, where the only sounds that break the silence, is nature, is a perfect nest to fly back to. Away from busy, demanding lives of everyone in the movie business.

There was little around the cottage to offer any clues to Menges's profession, and then, tucked up a corner; not visible when you enter the office, were two dusty Oscars. I had only ever seen them on television – the Academy Awards, usually in the early hours of the morning, watching some actor or director etc. holding them aloft and mentioning the people who mattered to him or her. I nervously picked one of them up and held it in my hand expecting it to light up and send electric currents throughout my body, but alas – I had not won it and only the true bearer of such gifts can feel the power.

Chris Menges was born in 1940 in Kingston, Hertfordshire, England. His father – a musician, musical director, and composer who worked for the Old Vic Theatre in London for over twenty-five years – moved to England from Germany before World War 1. After his schooling, Menges began work with a documentary production company as a gofer. Eventually, Menges joined the ITV's hard-hitting television current affairs programme *World in Action* team in the early 1960s, under the wing of Dennis Mitchell, and became a journalist and cameraman for several important documentaries about South Africa. His first feature as an operator was on *Poor Cow* – Ken Loach's big screen debut. Towards the end of the sixties, Menges had graduated to cinematographer and worked on Loach's second feature, *Kes*.

At the start of the seventies Menges returned to the world of television documentaries. Menges himself was the subject of a documentary film produced by Allistar Moffat of Scottish television called *Shooting from the Heart*. He later worked on a series of television films including *The Gamekeeper* and *Black Jack,* both directed by Loach, and *Bloody Kids* (1979), directed by Stephen Frears. Putting aside *The Empire Strikes Back* (1980), Menges continued to specialise in small films dealing with contemporary British life. This included *Babylon* (1980), one of the first British features to tackle the sensitive subject of race relations. Others were *Looks and Smiles* (Ken Loach, 1981), *A Sense of Freedom* (John Mackenzie, 1981), *Walter* (Stephen Frears, 1982) and *Made in Britain* (Alan Clarke, 1983).

When Menges photographed *Angel* in 1982, a debut feature for Neil Jordan, this opened up opportunities for the big screen. He worked twice with Scottish director Bill Forsyth, on *Local Hero* (1983) and *Comfort and Joy* (1984). The former was produced by David Puttnam who subsequently hired Menges for *The Killing Fields* (1984) directed by Roland Joffé. The film was made on location in Thailand, and Menges adopted the humanistic, observational style, greatly influenced by the photography of Henry Cartier-Bresson. Menges drew on his experience of earlier documentaries, such as *The Opium Trail* and *Opium Warlords* – both shot in Burma. *The Killing Fields*, which was to give Menges his first Oscar, was lit to avoid any hint of travelogue glamour – which would have been totally out of place, and in the interior sequences Menges aimed for; an atmospheric claustrophobia.

Incredibly, the reunion with Joffé and Puttnam awarded him his second Oscar for the *Mission* (1986), with Robert De Niro. With this film the location was Argentina and Colombia with much of the action taking place in heavy humid jungle. Once again Menges was able to draw on his documentary experience, particularly *The Tribe that Hides from Man* made in the Amazon in 1968. By the mid 1980's with Oscar in each hand, he was probably the finest cinematographer of that decade.

Menges's directorial debut feature, *A World Apart* (1988), was a passionate account of apartheid in 1960s South Africa. His follow-up, *Crisscross*, was possibly a first foray into mainstream features and received mixed reviews. *Second Best* (1994), in which William Hurt portrayed an introverted Welsh postman who adopts a troubled young boy marked Menges's return to form. *The Lost Son* (1999), tackled many uncomfortable subjects including child abuse and prostitution, and while it is uneasy viewing it is nonetheless compelling.

A lot of column inches have been dedicated to Chris Menges's art. Similar to Ken Loach, Chris is another man of vision. And it is his images as well as the director's, we see when viewing *Kes*, the lighting, the feel, the mood, the beautiful shots on the windy green fields that surround the murky city. David Robinson, from The Financial Times, states, '*Menges's colour photography is very fine indeed, evoking without romanticising the dramatic contrasts of pastoral and industrial in the Yorkshire mining country. The wild beautiful dales colliding with the industrial filth.*'

Menges worked on Lindsay Anderson's classic 60's drama *If...* His experience with the Czech director of photographer on the film, Milroslav Ondricek, totally changed his perspective with regards photography. He bought this new insight to *Kes*. The scenes were all lit naturally, which afforded the actors greater freedom of movement, which, totally uninhibited, let them produce freer more naturalistic performances.

Menges felt that the results of his collaboration with Loach were the consequence of a shared vision that found an outlet with Barry Hines's story. Like Ondricek, Menges had a background in documentaries and he admired the Czech's fictional pictures with director Milos Forman, especially *Lasky Jedne Plavovlasky (A Blond in Love)*. 'His early films were superb,' said Menges, 'but the one I worked on, If..., was much less satisfactory. It's down to a meeting of minds and sympathy for the story. Ken and I were trying to find a very sympathetic, almost gentle way to capture the performances. He said I was the person who showed him the way, but really we were learning together by the experience. On Poor Cow, we lit the actors and then they did the performance, but with Kes Ken wanted something more simple and observational, to illuminate a room and let the performance develop within that room so that we weren't putting marks down and telling actors where to go. They could live in the reality as they found the situation and we could capture the performance.' The colour photography of red brick and green countryside by Menges carefully avoids the lyrical. The harshness is maintained, and Billy can melt into the streets, as he would in real life. His scruffy, unkempt appearance is mirrored by his surroundings. This is Casper's world – where he can play both victim and predator.

Loach and cameraman Chris Menges produced a vivid impression of a working class environment regulated by the job, Saturday nights at the pub and a flutter on the side, where talk is for information, vituperation or chatting up the girls and the hardest task of all is to break out of the mould. They are all on a treadmill and views of the pit loom and the siren sounds – almost beckoning and taunting Billy's future.

Both Menges and Loach have great respect for each other, not only professionally but also spiritually. Like a pack of wolves hunting, you feel both need each others talents to reach the height of success both men expect. Equally both have the ability to adapt. 'Ken is always evolving,' explains, Menges, 'learning the kind of film-making he wanted to make – it's very at the moment. I have just been working with Ken recently on Ticket (still in production 2005), which was wonderful for me to go back working with him. Observing Ken in Rome, a couple of weeks ago, where we filmed Ticket, he's refining, refining all the time about the style of the work he wants. Working with Ken it's always been a challenge to think laterally and not think in the way one is taught in mainstream cinema.'

With the passage of time, over thirty seven years, technology has advanced and changed – regards Loach and Menges the fundamental principles remained the same – be as inconspicuous as possible and catch the action as it develops.

'On Kes, the early equipment was so antiquated compared with now,' says, Menges, 'the film was much slower, the lenses were slower and the equipment bigger. We were unobtrusive hoping for accidents it might be dialogue, it might be action. Often in mainstream cinema the dialogue is very presented, things are beautifully composed and lit. Ken's trying to catch spontaneity and reality, it might be on the first take – it might not, and this is why I think Ken Loach stands out from all other directors.'

Loach promoted Menges from camera operator on *Poor Cow* to cinematographer on *Kes*, 'What actually happened, I did some extra shooting on Poor Cow when Brian Probyn (World in Action colleague) wasn't available and obviously it clicked with Ken I had something to bring to the table. So I got that opportunity on Kes, which for me was, at twenty-seven, was a very exciting moment, although I actually felt ill prepared to take on that challenge. It was just an incredible experience.'

It appeared that most of the experienced crew sensed that something special was happening. 'The day might end late and you might be totally exhausted – but you knew during the day you'd caught something. There were four or five key scenes in Kes that really were believable, really worked, and you were aware of that during the filming process.'

Chris Menges, as did the whole crew, took little notice of the adage, never work with children and animals. One would assume there would be a plethora of problems when you are filming kids, with little or no acting experience and half-trained kestrels flying about, but it all seemed to fit into place beautifully. 'David Bradley gave such a wonderful performance,' reflects, Menges, 'I mean all the boys did, but Bradley's was such a grand performance. Freddie's (Fletcher) was another performance, the anguish; I think he gave the film a really hard edge, which was so important so full marks to him. It was an excitement to be behind the camera, trying to catch those moments, so it was never stressful in that sense.'

One of the key scenes, nicely placed in the centre of the film, was the hilarious football match. 'That was complete chaos,' laughs, Menges, 'we shot the actual football match in a relatively short time – and it's priceless. It just came together – none of it was rehearsed beforehand. Ken doesn't like the rehearsal procedure. He used to say things to me before filming started like, "Somebody should come through that door, but they might come in this door – so watch out." He likes to catch spontaneity and you don't get that with repetition. Kes was a genuine film and I am very proud of the experience.'

'What Kes was so good at showing was the absolute boredom of *long hours either down the pit or some menial job. I think that sense of a working life with life running away from you and your just completely exhausted by the whole experience, it's so good in all of Ken's work but particularly in Kes.'*

When the cameras stopped rolling and the crew packed up and left Barnsley, there were no physical signs of their visit, just memories and, of course, the movie. Most of the young actors melted back into everyday life, and could reflect on their experiences with proud affection. They had all been in a film, most regarded a classic, but it was time to get on with life. This adjustment is difficult, but most seem to have managed it very well. Dai Bradley's exit from the limelight, even if he had wanted to, was going to be a lot more difficult. *'Ken had great misgivings about taking a lad out of a classroom and placing him up there on some pedestal – it changes everything. I saw him quite recently at the NFT* (National Film Theatre) *– I think that boy has been through an awful lot.'*

It seems incredible that when Metro Goldwyn Mayer, who had taken over the original copyright owners United Artists, were transferring the master copy of Kes onto DVD - they showed a total lack of imagination. *'Here I am,'* complains Menges, *'I photographed Kes, a really fundamental part of my life, when they, whoever they are; UA or MGM, decided to transfer to DVD – did anyone call me up and say, "Hey Chris, do you want to be a part of this?" I couldn't believe the quality of that transfer. If I'd have been there I could have gently worked on it, I could have made a much more exciting print – they don't care. You see it happening a lot. The distributor decides to release a movie onto DVD and they never contact the people who made the film – the director, the cinematographer - the eyes of the movie. My role would be to assist, be impartial, in a very generous way. Cinema is a photographic media. Everything you do in a film, as a cinematographer, is to serve the wishes and the needs of the writer and director.'* I vowed there and then to get in touch with the executives of MGM and push forward to get another re-transfer from video to DVD.

It was my publisher, whose original intention it was to include a copy of the DVD with every copy of the book – now we could all work together on a special addition of *Kes*. Chris Menges offered his full support immediately and when I spoke to Ken Loach he agreed to do the same. Ken, who would also record a commentary, offered me his team from Sixteen Films; Alistair Griggs and Camilla Bray, to try and track down the original soundtrack. Loach explained to me we would need the soundtrack, as some syncing had been done, especially in the early morning bedroom scenes, where dialect had unprofessionally been cut.

The transfer would take many hours of work – but Chris knew he could greatly improve the impact of the movie. These men are artists first, genuine film-makers who make films they believe in – and this was the proof of their commitment to their profession.

In the past, while trying to get rights to some *Kes* stills for this book, it had proved difficult to get an answer from MGM. I could have made a board game out of their telephone communication system. You would get a name, an email, then they would move on and you would have to start from the bottom again. As my friend always used to say – as one door opens another slams in your face. Now, though, I had a powerful film company behind me, Sixteen Films, and I hoped things would be a lot easier.

Later that week Tony Garnett offered me some more information, *'I don't think MGM own the rights to* Kes *anymore – it's Sony because they bought the MGM library. I mean you never really know who owns what. They call it all sorts of fancy names now, but it used to be called capitalism! They don't consult the filmmakers, they don't really care.'* Here, here. I just hoped that Sony's infra-structure and telephone network was as good as their walkman's – I've still got mine from years ago.

It actually all came together very nicely. Our contact with Sony led to me being invited to London to meet their departmental heads. Both Sarah Atkinson (Head of Catalogue Marketing) and Martin Hearn (Product Manager) shared in our acclaim for *Kes* and the idea of creating a Special Edition to include additional content to supplement the original work soon became a realistic possibility. I would like to thank Sony for their interest and look forward to the release of this new dvd.

When interviewed by David Chell for *Moviemakers at Work,* and asked what his most rewarding project was, Menges answered, *'It's difficult to know… I've mentioned* Kes *several times. It was the first film I shot, and I remember at the end of shooting that film the sadness of having to go, of having to leave, of having to stop. I think that's probably my most rewarding project.'* From a man who had faced danger and come miraculously through on a number of occasions and has worked on *Killing Fields* and *The Mission*, which he received Oscars for both, and his own success at directing – this was praise indeed.

The Score – John Cameron

John Cameron's musical score for *Kes* is not over-lush and does not fit a conventional pseudolyrical style. The powerful arrangement with its delicate touches blends beautifully with the films quiet affection and anger.

All the critics lined up to heap praise on 19 minutes of sheer inspirational genius. These musical experts included Pete Redmond (*Mojo*), Neil Davenport (*Metro*), Time Out London, Mia Clarke (*The Wire*), David Shepard (*Q Magazine*), Steve Nicholls (*DJ Magazine*), Maxim Magazine and Jason Fox *(New Musical Express)*.

John Cameron was educated at Corpus Christi College, Cambridge and graduated in Music and History. John's exceptionally broad experience as composer, arranger and music supervisor for film, TV and theatre has made him fluent in a wide variety of musical styles. He has worked with everyone from Laurence Olivier to Marty Feldman and Andrew Lloyd Webber to Donny Osmond. His trophy cupboard boasts, together with many others, Academy Award Nomination, New York Drama Desk Award and National Broadway Theatre Award.

Musical collaborations include *Poor Cow,* his first film with Ken Loach, using songs and themes written by Donovan and *Hawks* (1988) with Timothy Dalton and Anthony Edwards, which was co-written with Barry Gibb.

One of the first of John's forty-plus feature film and feature TV film scores was the music for Ken Loach's *Kes.*

John received an Oscar Nomination for his music in *A Touch of Class* (1973), starring Glenda Jackson and George Segal and directed by Mel Frank. The composer losing out on the night to Marvin Hamlisch for *The Way We Were,* sung by Barbra Streisand.

His last major music score was for the powerful war drama *To End All Wars* (2001) starring Robert Carlyle and Keifer Sutherland with a music soundtrack featuring The London Symphony Orchestra. Cameron also composed a track featured on *Ocean's Twelve* (2004) and David Holme's Soundtrack CD. John has recently completed composing, conducting and orchestrating the music for the Disney/ Touchstone 6-hour mini series *Little House on the Prairie* (2005).

In the theatre Cameron has been equally busy and successful, at one point taking up the prestigious position of Executive Musical Director, in 1991, of the Royal Variety Show. John has written the orchestral score for every version of *Les Miserables,* including the original Paris version (1979), the RSC productions (directed by Trevor Nunn and John Caird) in London (1985), Washington and New York (1986), which won him a New York Drama Desk Award. In May 2002 the National Broadway Theatre Award for best orchestral score was awarded to John again for *Les Miserables.*

When in 1991 it was decided to produce the definitive West End version of *Joseph and the Amazing Technicolor Dreamcoat,* John Cameron was brought in to bring a new slant to the orchestrations. He worked closely with Lord Lloyd Webber, to produce the wildly imaginative version of the production that was to star Jason Donovan, Phillip Schofield and Donny Osmond, amongst others.

John has also composed extensively for TV including the title music for *24 Hrs, ITV Snooker,* ITV dramas *Jack The Ripper* (1988) and *Dr Jekyll and Mr Hyde* (1990), both with Sir Michael Caine and provided the title music to BBC TV's *Crimewatch,* called *Rescue Helicopter.*

His band CCS, which he formed with Alexis Korner and Peter Thorup for Mickie Most's RAK label, had four top twenty and one top forty hits: *Whole Lotta Love, Walking, Tap Turns on the Water* and *Brother* (last two written by John and Alexis Korner), and *Band Played The Boogie* (With lyrics by Cameron**).**

He went on to arrange all the Hot Chocolate hits from *Emma* to *Heaven Is In The Back Seat Of My Cadillac,* including *You Sexy Thing, Every One's A Winner, You Win Again, Put You Together Again* etc. John's work with Heatwave included arranging the hits *Boogie Nights, Always and Forever, Grooveline* and *Gangstars of the Groove,* as well as the first two and the fourth albums.

In 1980 he collaborated with David Essex on the movie score, single and album, *Silver Dream Racer.* He also conducted the Royal Philharmonic Orchestra on the concept album of Essex's *Mutiny!* He was principal arranger for the Jose Carreras albums *Passion* and *Pure Passion* and arranged, conducted and produced Carreras' new CD *Around the World.*

When I caught up with the composer in middle April he was dashing backwards and forwards getting ready for the big opening of *Alfie* (written with Eden Phillips) with Darren Day. John guided me in from Berkhamsted Station and I had a pleasant few minutes drive to his beautiful cottage – a world away from the busy M40.

I opened the five barred gate, patted John's golden Labrador and stepped into the house. At first there was little evidence of the composers forty odd years in music. Then items start to emerge. It may be an impressionist jazz painting or sheet music or a magazine reviewing Cameron's latest offering. The wonderful vista outside; the freedom, would ease any acidic remark from some stuffy critic.

The latest news on John's never-ending career, he is working in L.A. with the Gypsy Kings on a musical version of *Zorro*. He even offered to come back for the launch of this book, which I thought a wonderful gesture.

My first question to John was how he was offered the chance, at twenty-four, to write the score for *Kes*. *'I was working with Don (Donovan), the time of Sunshine Superman, Epistle to Dippy and Jennifer Juniper etc. and he was asked to score* Poor Cow *and he asked me to arrange the music. So we all went into the studio and it was quite fashionable in the sixties for folk musicians to record the film score, basically everyone got round, looked at the screen and improvised it. Eddy Joseph, the executive producer, turned round to Don and said, "Who is actually going to write the score for this – we start dubbing next Wednesday?" and Don turned round and pointed at me.'* Never having scored a movie before, the composer; outwardly, totally unfazed by the prospect, rang up a friend of his father's, Elizabeth Lutyens who proceeded to give John a ten minute lesson. *'We looked at the picture, the next day, on the Thursday, we got the timings on Friday, Saturday I was playing rugby and I wrote the whole score on Sunday. We had it copied on the Monday, recorded it on the Tuesday and then dubbed it on the Wednesday, as promised. It could only happen in the sixties,'* laughs John.

It is always fascinating when a child or young adult realises his or her vocation in life and follows a path that is almost pre-destined. John Cameron joined the church choir and started playing the piano at age six. *'The cross-over time was when I was about twelve and being in a music shop with my mother. I was a snotty nosed little grammar school boy.'* John adopts a clipped BBC grade announcer's voice, *'Have you Beethoven C minor overture thirteen? And my mother said quite normally, "have you got I saw Mommy Kissing Santa Clause?" I sought of gave her a look of dislike. And then I heard Singing the Blues on the radio and I thought – I like that. Rock and Roll had started to come in. I could play that. Two years later I was playing twice a week in the Dukes Head in Croydon – I'd crossed over. I kept all the straight studies and ended up reading music at Cambridge, but the Jazz, rock and roll and everything else never went away.'*

John's father, Norman was taught violin by Beatrice Lutyens. He was heavily influenced by Eddy Lang and Stéphane Grappelli, Django Reinhardt and Joe Venutti, and he loved rock and roll. *'My mother (Doris) used to play the piano like Fats Waller,'* remembers John, *'so it was like; just go out and play, just do it. So I came out of Cambridge with this sort of attitude.'* The musicians the young composer met after leaving his place of learning further compounded his own philosophy — the boundaries were in your own mind.

Impressed at how Cameron worked Loach offered him the chance to score *Kes*. With no knowledge of the book, access to the shooting locations or prior viewing of the rushes, Cameron was wheeled into a Soho studio and presented with the final cut. *'We discussed how to express certain things in the movie and I came up with the idea of using a penny whistle and the alto flute,'* remembers John. *'I'd been working a lot with a guy called Harold McNair, wonderful player. I explained to Harold I wanted him and I wanted an alto flute — but he then told me he didn't have an alto flute and had never played one.'* In classic sixties style he told John he would buy one that day and just needed a weeks practice. *'We're all in the studio seven days later and he's playing stuff that has almost become seminal alto flute playing.'*

Different directors work in different ways. Sometimes a composer can be bought into a movie project quite early; well before the movie people have started filming. Moods and objectives can be discussed, and these eventualities may affect the way the film is shot. The more common procedure is at the final cut or certainly when the film is basically shot — the composer is given a virgin screening. *'The thing about* Kes, *it was perfect without any music on it. I think the challenge was to write some music as if it came out naturally — it wasn't telling the audience what to think, what to feel,'* explains John. *'This is why I used penny whistles, solo instruments and base clarinet — things that would not feel out of place in the context of the movie.'*

The line-up of experienced musicians Cameron chose for recording the *Kes* score was impressive. He had played with them — all versatile, flexible musicians who had the skill and instinct to play different genres. Pete Redmond from Mojo stated, *'the studio line-up is a roll call of British jazz musicians - Ronnie and Danny Moss on clarinets, David Snell on harp and the incredible Tony Carr on drums. The largest dollop of respect, however, must go to Jamaican-born flute-master Harold McNair, whose wistful, swooping tones underpin the whole score.'*

A film may take years to get from script to screen, but when the producer gets the green light (or is it red in the movie business?), things happen very quickly and everybody wants jobs completed yesterday. 'I actually had around two and a half weeks to put the score for Kes together,' says John, 'which is total luxury. After that the basic process is you look at the movie, you talk to the director and establish a style; a language and the type of music you want to put into it. What size of orchestra – is it going to be a big lavish affair or all solo instruments or whatever? Then, almost the most important thing is the spotting session. You basically sit with the movie and say "right, the music will start there," and the director says, "No, I want it to start there." And you say, OK, but I'd like to start after that big sound effect. So you're really deciding where the music has its best entry and out. An editor will then give you the timings – the better the timings the better you are able to write the music. It's great working in the States because they not only describe the scene but they will give you measurements to a hundredth of a second and that way you can do your maths without keep looking up at the screen to compose. Next you build a kind of skeleton that does all the changes that are demanded – any time you want to hit sync point you can make that – and then you cloth it in music.'

Viewing the relatively finished product, without music, in some instances may be a detached, cold experience, but not so for John Cameron, 'I was just taken up with this kid and this amazing story. It was a performance I had not seen the like in film. It had a theatrical feel to it, a grittiness you get in a really great stage performance. Reality, really.' Many people, some connected with Kes, have discussed the issue of using the broad Yorkshire, in particular Barnsley, accents. 'I still can't understand the first 30 seconds of the movie and then my ear gets attuned. Obviously the American distributors must have thought they all came from another planet,' laughs John.

I wondered how it was possible for an artist to switch off when watching his or her own work. John explains, 'I can watch Kes now and enjoy it. If I watch something three months after I have done it I see all the cellotape. I'm thinking – oh I could have come in a bit earlier there.'

'We have about four generations of children in our family and as they come to us they all want to watch Kes. I watched it recently on television with our youngest Amy and I had this terrible realisation that I've probably never done anything better.'

In fact Cameron gets more internet web hits from the work he composed in the mid sixties that at any other decade. It was recently that David Holmes discovered a number, Explosive Corrosive Joseph, Cameron wrote in 1967, loved it and included it in the movie and soundtrack Oceans Twelve (2004). 'There is a certain time when things cease to be old fashioned and become timeless, like Explosive...'

All productions carry a fear of failure hanging over them – that may out-weigh the optimistic view of a classic, runaway hit; a smash. At least when the movie is finished the composer, in this case, can walk away and begin the next project. 'The great thing about the theatre is it is dangerous every night,' laughs John.

There is probably no other occupation in the world that has you keep proving yourself and starting again, almost daily. Reputations are either heaped in praise or murdered in cold blood by some critic. 'My son lives in Australia now and he's an economist – he's got a proper job and wears a suit. He phones me up and says "I don't know how you do it - every six months you put yourself up against the wall in front of a firing squad and hope that no-one will hit you.'

'The one thing I can say in this business; I don't think I've ever done a project where I haven't met somebody I'm glad I met.'

Although *Kes* soared high and eventually yielded the praise it deserved, Cameron's score to accompany the film could not be purchased. Although in the sixties soundtracks to movies were rarely released.

Out the blue the composer received a telephone call from John Benton-Hughes owner of *indie* record label Trunk. Cameron takes up the story, 'Johnny is a freak buyer of late 60's and early 70s library music written by certain types of composers, a bit like myself. I'm not sure but I think he was looking for an album of mine called Swamp Fever (KPM); it had Harold (Harold McNair), Danny Thompson and Tony Carr – it had become a kind of cult thing and it was changing hands at some stupid price – I haven't even got a copy myself!'

'The conversation went on and Johnny said "You know my favourite soundtrack is Kes. Has it ever come out?" When John explained that it had never been released the record producer asked if he had a copy. This was not all that simple as the *Kes* soundtrack had been recorded in the studio straight onto film. 'We never recoded to tape, what I eventually gave Trunk was a safety master, we recorded straight to optical – mono. Orchestra playing away – bang, straight onto film! It was cheaper – a straight mix. We didn't even go with a three-track dub on it. In those days if it was an expensive dub you would have a three track with strings on one, woodwinds on another and percussion on the third.' Eventually Cameron found a copy, someone had made during the recording, in a plastic box in the garden shed. 'It was a little quarter inch reel-to-reel with no leader on which is why the start goes a bit wearier...' John adds, 'there was just this crinkly bit on the end.' Trunk took the copy away and immediately transferred it to Digital Audio Tape (DAT).

So some thirty-five years later the fans of *Kes* could buy the soundtrack on CD and vinyl. Many did purchase the soundtrack and still do in music shops, e-bay and Amazon, even though the music runs for only eighteen minutes and forty-nine seconds. 'The whole thing about Kes was that the music was very spare like the movie,' John added. 'Ken did not want to waste a second of music that wasn't needed. Ken was incredible to work with.'

Benton-Hughes commented on its release in 2001, 'I know it's only 20 minutes long, but I think this is the best piece of British pastoral folk music ever recorded. There's no other soundtrack to touch it and, yes, Kes still has a strange emotional effect on people.'

'Kes was my first film score as a composer,' explains Cameron, 'and after thirty years of Symphony Orchestras and Rock 'n' Roll bands, an Academy nomination, a Drama Desk award, Opening nights, Razzamataz, Les Miserables et al., there's something that draws me inexorably back to Kes. Perhaps it's the plaintive simplicity of Harold McNair's solo flute, perhaps it's because the film itself is such beautiful work, I know I get as much satisfaction from this score as from anything else I've ever written.'

Jarvis Cocker loved the score and on the release of the LP and CD in 2001, set the mood perfectly and commented, 'The sound of a long-lost child-hood... The smell of a damp school cloakroom, from an age when comics were still printed on newsprint... But this is more than just another product of the nostalgia industry – put on this music and immediately you'll be soaring through the air, free of your earthly shackles: for this is the sound of a human soul in flight. A beautiful daydream antidote to an all too real South Yorkshire nightmare. "Tha' won't get me down t'pit.' 'Pig, Pig, Sow, Sow.' 'Tha' dun't like being called a bastard does tha'?" This is the real thing. This is beauty so fragile it hurts. This is music with the Jesses well and truly off.'

When we were organising one of the book launches, which was to be held at Edward Sheerien School, we all thought it a great idea for some of the pupils to perform part of the score from Kes. I contacted John to ask if he had a copy of the original sheet music. 'I think it's yellowing in the shed somewhere,' comments John. 'If you get the school to contact me, I will find out what instruments they have and then I will arrange some music specially for them.' It doesn't get any better than that.

One of the most versatile composers in Britain today, it became apparent that this man John Cameron was a book all by himself. He was certainly too busy to write one. In a perfect way John's music is his biography. Some people deal in words, some people collect words and catalogue them to place in a journal and some produce notes and musical arrangements – it's hopefully all art and John Cameron's contribution to the world of music is unsurpassed.

12

The Life of Brian – Brian Glover

A Teacher, a Wrestler, a Writer a Movie and Shakespearean actor
- Brian Glover was just your average Yorkshireman! (www.ayup.co.uk)

Directly attributed to Brian's appearance in *Kes*, Brian was interviewed by the famous impresario of theatre land, Binky Beaumont. A West End production, of Terence Rattigan's *A Bequest to the Nation*, playing Captain Hardy, followed and Brian Glover was a jobbing actor.

As he stepped off the stage at the end of the production Brian entered television and met his second wife Tara, a script editor for the BBC, it was 1972. Thus began a warm, close relationship that would last up until Brian's death in 1997. So in less than half a decade he had been an English teacher, professional wrestler, big movie actor, West End stage actor, including musicals (although he could not sing) and met his sole-mate. The train journey never slowed for Glover, he never looked back and he never ran out of steam. The Yorkshireman was taken out of Yorkshire, as Brian Glover moved to London, but his Yorkshireness remained intact. It was a deciding factor in his movie and stage career. He also received little or no bad press. *'The press can turn a lot on celebrities, especially now, they build them up and just turn on them,'* explains Tara Glover, *'but they never did with Brian. I can't think of a single negative thing.'*

It took two and a half hours from my home in Shropshire to the Fulham Road in London and half that time again to find a parking space. After just a few minutes in Tara's company I realised my time travelling and parking time had not been wasted. In fact we chatted for so long I had to move my car and place it in another parking zone. I had already been told by people in the business, including Freddie Fletcher, what a wonderful charming woman Tara was, and I was not disappointed. The apartment where we conversed was spacious and skilfully decorated with pieces that had obviously impressed the Glover's and not bought to impress. The vista from all four corners was magnificent and took in the Chelsea jet-set land of the sixties – even the dome of St. Paul's was visible. In the opposite building the plaque explained that Joyce Grenfell had lived there in the seventies.

Following many advertising voice-overs, his real talents were recognised at the National Theatre stages, in Panto, TV and on the big screen in all manner of roles, he was one of our most beloved stars. And it did not stop there. He was a writer too, of over 20 plays and short films. His lively appearances on BBC's *Question Time* lit up the screen. Brian also wrote a weekly newspaper column, which he started around 1990, for the Yorkshire Evening Post – right up until his untimely death in 1997. *'The job of writing these articles was a bit of a tyranny,'* states, Tara. *'He was doing all these other things and writing plays, and this was like having a permanent deadline. Every week it was, "What shall I write about?" And then he would get it written, phone the copy in, and then for two days it would be great – but then it would be coming around again!'*

His film CV is one of the richest you will ever see. From parts in *Dr Who* and a clutch of Shakespeare (memorably as Bottom in *A Midsummer Nights Dream* - 1981) he was in a number of Hollywood high rollers including *Alien3* (1992), *The Great Train Robbery* (1979), *Company of Wolves* (1984), and *Leon The Pig Farmer* (1993). Prolific work at the National Theatre included work on *Saint Joan* and *Don Quixote*.

The public loved him for his gleeful comedy work. A favourite for many is the episode of *Whatever Happened to the Likely Lads* (No Hiding Place – Brian Flint), when Bob and Terry were trying to get through a Saturday evening without finding out an England football result in advance of a TV highlights show. Brian's grinning mug seemed to find them wherever they hid. Then he was Heslop, the sleepy lad from Sidcup in three episodes of Ronnie Barker's *Porridge*, his broad Yorkshire hidden inside a Cockney routine. He was also Arthur Daily's best mate Yorkie in *Minder* and had big roles in *The Sweeney*, *Dixon of Dock Green* and *Return of The Saint*.

At his best though he was the voice you knew instantly from advertising slogans. His was the voice that told us that *'Milk's Gotta Lotta Bottle'*, that a loaf of bread was made *'Wi Nowt Tekken Owt'*, and that *'Tetley Make Tea Bags Make Tea.'* So ingrained in public consciousness is his sloganeering that when he appeared in a West End revival of the Canterbury Tales the fly posters advertised it as *'Chaucer Wi Nowt Taken Out'*. His long career, dotted with respected classic works on stage and screen, kept Brian Glover's name truly high profile and well respected.

Colin Welland – the only real household name in *Kes* found himself eclipsed by a stocky, balding Lundwooder called Brian Glover. Off screen a close friendship developed between the two actors which lasted until Glover's death. Out of all the remarkable performances it is probably Glover's role as the bullying, vain games master Mr Sugden that is most remembered. Similar to playing down the sentiment, the humour teeters on the edge of caricature but deftly keeps within the parameters of humorous reality.

'The humour in it was the teacher dealing with the boys,' explains Loach, 'and taking the mickey out of them, but not realising they are taking the mickey out of him as well. Brian cottoned on to that exactly. He was like an overgrown schoolboy, but never went too far because he was a teacher.'

There was a definite chemistry between Glover's character and Bradley's. It may have been a similar relationship between a terrorist and his hostage, but it worked very well on screen. Bradley comments, 'Brian was a character - something enormous. He was a pop-up character - great fun. The sequence where he hits me with the ball just before the showers, he would actually come with one of those really heavy leather balls and just throw it at me in the face. Just to see how I'd react. We worked together after Kes in a play at the Cottesloe Theatre at the National Theatre where he played God and I played Adam, which was a perfect set up because he could easily be God. He's a wonderful man.'

Regards the actual football match, Bradley remembers, 'They chose the worst days of the summer for that scene. They had a local fire engine come round and flood the field with hundreds of gallons of water. Although it was August, it was bloody cold and freezing.'

All through the vital Manchester United versus Tottenham Hotspur fifth round cup tie on Match of the Day, Sugden played both loan striker and bad tempered referee. After having first pick of the squad, Padgett; the best player, Sugden dispenses with the gentlemanly tossing of the coin – grabbing the ball he announces, 'We'll play with the wind, down hill.'

Glover was in his late thirties when the film was made and his time was split between teaching and wrestling. His ring name was Leon Arras The Man From Paris, although he had toyed with Eric The Blond Bomber. 'He was wrestling in Wilmslow and there was supposed to be a Frenchman on the same bill named Leon Arras The Man From Paris,' remembers Tara. 'Well this Leon Arras didn't turn up and when Brian entered the ring he was introduced as... Leon Arras The Man from Paris – which somehow stuck. He kept the name for years afterwards. Some time later Brian was in a bar in Liege; France and this huge wrestler walks up to Brian and says, "Mio Leon Arras The Man From Paris." And Brian *stands up and says, "Mio Leon Arras The Man From Barnsley... and why didn't you turn up at Wilmslow?"'*

He had started his working career on the Barnsley Chronicle in the advertising department, before taking up teaching. He taught at Racecommon Road and Longcar Central schools. *'He was my teacher at Longcar,'* comments Michael Joyce (McDowell's friend), *'The character he played, Mr Sugden, wasn't really that much like Brian – he was far more articulate - although he could be very fierce if you upset him. He has clipped me around the ear a few times.'*

Barry Hines, says of his PE teacher Sugden, *'He is an amalgam of PE teachers I have known. People say he is exaggerated, but I've known PE teachers who do cheat. You don't have to exaggerate. You destroy your case if you do.'*

Ken Loach, a great believer in visual impact, had long cherished the moment on screen when Mr Sugden, the bullying games master, would appear. He wanted to make it memorable and his eye for detail and his quest for perfection did not diminish when filming the football match.

A bright red tracksuit top covered Brian Glover's Manchester United football strip, with delusions of grandeur pertaining to be Bobby Charlton. Red, Loach knew, was an extremely punitive colour and nothing was going to detract from it. Throughout filming Loach had instilled in his wardrobe mistress an aversion to anything else red. Even to the point of sending her to a local second hand stall in Barnsley market. *'The wardrobe woman, after looking around at the different garments, commented on how clean they were,'* says Trevor Hesketh, *'The stall women said, "Yes, they should be – they're all clothes that have been left behind in launderettes – I buy them in a ton at a time". When the wardrobe girl says, "That's what I want – a ton – but nothing red!"'*

With his bright red tracksuit top off, underneath was a vivid red Manchester football shirt. Loach even had a special crew going around painting out any red items – such as doors, fire alarms, fire buckets, woodwork etc. The team used a special grey paint that simply washed off. At one point the coal wagon turned up, to deposit coke for the fight scene between McDowell and Casper. Loach's eyes lit up – *'I want to use that lorry,'* he stated. The problem was it was mostly red. A plan was devised and the school caretaker, who the production team had employed as odd job man, led the un-suspecting coalman away, while the team moved in and painted it grey.

The football strips created another problem for the continuity girl, Penny Eyles – I wrote this before Penny put me in my place in a later chapter. Another days filming was required and the muddy strips of both boys needed to be kept for continuity – but dried. Trevor Hesketh takes up the story, *'So the girl troups off to the local launderette with around twenty strips to put in the dryers. But the attendant says the price of two shillings includes powder, washing machine and dryer. The girl explains she does not want to wash items only dry them. Following a long discussion – the attendant was adamant not to lose money – they had to purchase powder, wash them and then they could use the dryers. A member of the production team was called and the problem was solved – we paid two shillings per strip – but only used the dryers!'*

Chris Menges called the soccer shoot complete chaos. In fact the only continuity problems all stem from the match. Things were not helped when on the second days filming Brian Glover turned up for work with his knee bandaged, he was livid, as a professional wrestler he hardly ever sustained injury. Loach decided against writing the injury into the script and shot the whole scene again, Brian now wearing his bandaged knee – adding two days to the film schedule. Again the fire engines had to turn up and douse the whole pitch to recapture its winter muddy state.

Many have commentated on Brian Glover's realism and his ability of getting into the skin of PE teacher Mr Sugden, an experience where the join is totally invisible, great casting and great acting. Loach makes stars; builds reputations but does not exploit them. Unfortunately success means you will probably never work, in a leading part, with the director again (the exception being Robert Carlyle – *Riff-Raff* and *Carla's Song* & Ricky Tomlinson – *Riff-Raff* and *Raining Stones*).

Bernard Atha, who played the Youth Employment Officer, and Glover, shared a similar unnerving experience with regards certain governing bodies. Atha had already received criticism from the very body he was portraying – the Youth Employment Services. Brian Glover in the guise of his alter-ego Mr Sugden could have offended quite a few people across the board - Teachers, referees, humanitarians, pacifists, the Manchester United Football Supports Club and Bobby Charlton.

Condemnation came in the shape of the Carnegie Foundation. Leeds Metropolitan University, who enjoyed a reputation for excellence in sports education and training, that dates back as far as 1933, when the Carnegie Foundation was set-up, creating a College of Physical Education in Leeds and the very first male PE Teacher

Training establishment in the county. They placed as much emphasis on *education* as they did on the *physical.*

Atha takes up the story, '*The criticism I received was nothing compared to the abuse Brian received for wearing the Carnegie badge in Kes. Carnegie was the most famous PE college in those days, out ranking Loughborough. It was a very macho, upper class, in terms of education, organisation, very independent. They bred a mix of very high quality athletes and physical training administrators. So when they saw Brian strutting about in the shape of Mr Sugden, with the Carnegie badge emblazoned on his red tracksuit top, they were furious. "That would never happen with a Carnegie man. It's dammed outrageous." Were some of the comments from the college.'*

Although their motif, the ancient Greek figure of discobolus throwing the discus, can be plainly viewed on Sugden's right breast of his Fred Perry top, it's hard to take him seriously. And it is possible that the PE teacher had *acquired* the emblem without ever going through the gates of the famous college.

'*To most people it was just a badge, meaningless; to Carnegie it was a great slur. You must remember at the time one of the Carnegie five's was playing for England, a man called Slater was an international football star, they had the British Champion pole-vaulter, our two most famous rugby players had come through the college – they had a high profile, prestigious reputation to up-hold and Brian, in their eyes, did nothing to support this.'*

What the Carnegie College of Physical Education must have thought about Woody Allen's comments when he said, '*People who can't do – teach. People who can't teach – teach PE!*' They must have wanted to hang him from the Twicker's cross bar using Bobby Charlton's football laces.

I am pleased to say time has healed the strong views of yesteryear. When I contacted Carnegie College and School of Physical Education I spoke to David Henderson – the top man. To my surprise we chatted for fifteen minutes about *Kes* – he is a big fan of the movie. In fact that weekend he was going to a wedding in Leeds where the groom was an extra in *Kes*, '*He was seen standing on a street corner as Billy Casper is running to the newsagents, because Jud had taken his bike.*' David states, '*I think he was paid two shillings and sixpence.*' Although Mr Henderson was too young to remember the controversy as it unfolded - the story has been passed on from tutor to student. I spoke to one of the trainers; he remembered the incident very well. '*It was a strange time – and the film was so good at highlighting this character and people believed it. The true legacy is that we often show that sequence to students how NOT to train youngsters.'*

Most of the cast in *Kes* partook in various publicity talks and Brian Glover did his bit, in between wrestling and of course teaching. *'I took Barry Hines and Brian Glover to York University for a discussion on Kes,'* remembers Bernard Atha. *'When we got to the university we had to go past the kitchens. And suddenly all these women started shouting at Brian and booing. I couldn't think what was happening; we'd only just got there. Brian turned to me and out the corner of his mouth said, "I was wrestling in York last week and it was my turn to be the baddie!"'*

The description of how Brian got his first role is typical of the man. Barry Hines was a fellow teacher in Longcar Central School. Glover had asked his former colleague if there might be a part in *Kes*. Hines then made the suggestion of Brian (then aged 34) for the role of bullying games teacher Mr Sugden. *'Ken Loach was improvising a fight with loads of kids, and he asked me to stop it like a teacher would,'* said Glover. *'Well I'd stopped a good few playground fights, and I had the confidence of being in the ring all those years, so I just grabbed these two kids and banged their heads together!'* Amazingly, although the performance was very successful Glover continued to teach for another two years.

His portrayal of PE bully Mr Sugden on a school football pitch will live forever. *'I'm Bobby Charlton today, boys!'* he announces pulling off his pristine tracksuit to reveal his Manchester United shirt, then goes on to be a combined striker, referee and TV Commentator - flattening fifteen year olds in his wake. Barry Hines states, *'Although I was a PE teacher, the PE teacher in the film is far more extreme than I was in real life.'* Legend has it that the character was based on a Kirk Balk Comprehensive schoolteacher whose former student, Nick Eaden, was a Barnsley's right-back.

The memorable football scene is one of the funniest in British film history. For people who hated games at school – the competitiveness, the showers, the cold – seem to derive special pleasure and comfort from the hilarious scene. It starts when the balding games master, Sugden, works out his personal fantasies of sporting glories on the boys. The beefy, cheeky athletics master, Sugden dominates every sequence; with the peaky Billy, swallowed up in Mr Sugden's borrowed shorts, is a hopelessly inept gaolie who spends most of his time shinning up the goal posts and turning somersaults. Even here, one feels the misery of being the fat boy or the under-sized un-talented boy who is always last to be chosen when sides are picked, then hearing the groans of team mates at his forced election.

The great British director Stephen Frears said of the role, *'People always talk about where they were when Kennedy died, well I can remember where I was when Brian Glover appeared (Mr Sugden) in* Kes. *I can't remember a better entrance in a British film — now I'll make a preposterous claim, well that's like Orson Welles in* The Third Man. *It's on that sort of level. Just one moment and a whole world is exposed.'*

I feel it a great honour, with the help of Brian's widow, Tara, to have permission to write his biography. He was a wonderful man who I had grown up watching on television and on film. To put his varied and experienced life into words is both exciting and challenging.

Brian once recalled; *'I enjoyed doing it (Kes) and I had nothing to lose. It's an excellent film and I am thankful to it.'*

13

The Lad – Billy Casper & Dai (David) Bradley

Billy Casper – The Character

Dai Bradley, or as he was known then; David, was a child star born to play Billy Casper. It is true that every school up and down the country all had at least one Casper – sometimes there would be a class full. Ken Loach admitted when looking for the lead role he only visited three Barnsley Secondary schools for that very reason; he knew, somewhere amongst the faces of the kids he auditioned there was his Billy Casper smiling back at him.

Even Loach could not have hoped for a better candidate to play the anti-hero. I believe he could have trawled RADA and most of the distinguished drama houses up and down the country and not found a better Casper.

He is no sensitive plant wilting on the ash-heap; he's a sturdy little weed totally native to the soil and straightens itself up after everyone's feet have passed over it. He has no literary aspirations or notions about rising above his class. He is everyone's target. Big brother, Jud, clips him around the ear as he carries out mundane tasks. Mum orders him around, like some young naughty pup, as she gets ready for the bingo or a night out at the pub. Teachers raise there voices in anger on the first beat; not waiting for an insolent grunt or feigned deafness. The head at the school has caned Billy more times than he has been disappointed with modern youth. They all participate in Billy's misery.

Casper's a tough, scraggy, weasel-faced, undersized adolescent; he can give as good as he gets. His thin mouth appears to eat itself when nervous. When he walks into any classroom his eyelids droop, a mixture of tiredness; after delivering early morning newspapers, boredom and arrogance. The latter bought on by the establishment's unconvincing efforts to drill him full of information that has no relevance to his life. Billy knows it and he recognises the apathy in the teachers' eyes. Most wanting a post in a better school; a grammar school, working with the children who have passed the eleven-plus, children with a future. The pay and the prospects the same, but to some misguided teachers – it is a leg up. An escape from the *failures* sitting in front of them – possibly mirroring their own failure as teachers.

Casper's kestrel hawk is no lovable pet but a magnificent creature of the wild, which like its handler can be trained but never tamed. The hawk soars high, as the boy could soar, if society had not already stunted and clipped his development. It is through the bird that the boy finds consolation for the things of which life has cheated him. Through this supreme experience of talking in class about the bird, Billy finds for the first and only time a genuine sense of communication with his classmates. This scene in which he is persuaded by a relatively kindly schoolteacher, Mr Farthing (Colin Welland), all others are portrayed as obtuse disciplinarians, to tell the class about his kestrel is great theatre. One sees him coming alive. A few scenes later when confronted by the Youth Employment Officer (Bernard Atha) being tempted with offers of becoming a plumber or an electrician; the shutters go up and his utter indifference paralyses one's own nerve ends. When the officer cheerfully suggests he might like mining, his vehement refusal reveals whole generations of resentment. There is nothing for Billy to do, when faced by idiots, but to stare out of a window and answer at random – disengaged from reality.

Although the ending is tragic and extremely moving, the film is in no sense pessimistic. Through an intimate and very localised story, it throws out a fundamental and universal challenge. How much longer are we going allow human potential to be ignored or so cruelly crushed?

For Billy Casper, trapped between an insensitive home life, an unimaginative school and a disinterested future, there is no freedom. His relationship with the bird becomes, for a short while, a fulfilment and liberation. While the bird is flying free – we feel the same hope for the young lad.

Dai (David) Bradley - The Natural Actor

British director, Alan Parker, praised Bradley's performance, saying, 'Did this kid even know anything about kestrels before Ken came along and said this is now your passion? When you watch this film, you'd think this kid has been interested in birds for his entire life.'

After a quick succession of TV, theatre and film character rolls, following his performance in *Kes*, the telephone mysteriously stopped ringing, his agent got hungry, and Dai looked towards other job opportunities for income. Some took him away from the world of acting, some, more recently, placed him on the fringes – he was recently working as a dresser for a West End play; he could still smell the grease paint but the roar of the crowd was not for him. Was there really *life after Kes* for Bradley?

Dai Bradley was born in 1955, the son of a seamstress, Nora Bradley and North Gawber Colliery miner Horace Pop Bradley, in the South Yorkshire mining town of Barnsley. *Kes* was his first professional acting role, at the age of fourteen. '*I started out at school in Christmas pantos,*' reminisces Dai, '*which were terrifically successful – in fact more successful than the local town professional panto – and suddenly we heard a rumour that Ken Loach, Tony Garnett and Barry Hines were thinking about making a movie, and then they came and auditioned about forty kids from our school, and luckily they chose me.*'

There was obviously great excitement as the movie people swept through the town in the middle of summer 1968. Director and producer scouted the town and surrounding areas for cast members and suitable locations. '*I came from a typical working class background,*' says Dai adding, '*my prospects were pretty mediocre, so to have the opportunity of being involved in making a feature film in Barnsley was unbelievable.*'

Bradley points out, quite incredibly, '*Barry Hines actually used to teach at the school I went to.*' Although Hines never actually taught the youngster, Bradley had seen the teacher walking up and down the school corridor and during assembly. He had little knowledge of the tremendous impact the teacher turned author would have on his life.

There were obviously similarities between character and actor. Like Billy, Dai lived on a working class estate, had failed his eleven-plus and had an interest in nature, although he did not come from a broken home. '*There were others who were good,*' explains Loach, '*but David was extraordinary and very, very talented.*'

Bradley still believes *Kes* paints an accurate picture of the South Yorkshire of his childhood. '*It wasn't my life,*' comments Bradley . '*Billy didn't have much in common with me and he didn't get on well at school. I enjoyed school. I had a very good relationship with many of my teachers and I enjoyed football. Billy knew about the training of birds. I knew nothing about birds whatsoever and I've discovered it doesn't just relate to my* communities. I've had African-Caribbean people come up to me and, with eyes watering, have said Kes was one of the most wonderful films they had ever seen so it's a cross-cultural film which has surprised me and in some respects I'm really kind of thrilled by that.'

There was another coincidence that initially caused problems. Like Casper, Bradley had a morning paper round, which meant his day started at six-thirty a.m. 'It wasn't affecting my acting,' recalled Bradley, 'but Ken and Tony Garnett noticed I was looking tired and asked me what I did in the morning. When I told them I delivered newspapers, they offered to pay my wages not to do it. We were often shooting six days a week and, a few weeks into filming, in September, I told Tony I wouldn't be available on Saturday afternoons any more because I sold football programmes for my local team, which allowed me free admission to Barnsley's matches. So I also got a couple of quid not selling programmes.'

Ken Loach drew a remarkable performance from Dai Bradley, selected from many local boys who auditioned for the role. His near-anorexic features were tough rather than soft. They said of Marlon Brando; 'He had the body of a gladiator and the face of a poet.' It could be said of Bradley; he had the body of a poet and the face of a gladiator. Peter Crookston described Bradley, for the Sunday Times, 'He's built like an underfed whippet, all sinew and sharp, lubricated knots of bone.' Realistically nature had already hinted at support roles.

Performance is not a strong enough word for the impression of living and being which all the actors, in a mixed cast of amateurs, semi-professional artists and a professional, achieve. Loach's gift for making fiction resemble life is not a matter of simple naturalism. Each of Hines's observations, wry or amusing, touching or bitter, adds point to Loach's theme. Where does the acting finish and the direction begin? I believe two expert forces came together. The powerful director, cutting his teeth on televisual drama; breaking into movie making and a young raw 14-year-old with bags of talent and plenty of enthusiasm. A star with the X factor – he only wanted a chance to shine and Loach gave him the stage and the young lad never let him down.

There were originally two hundred hopefuls up for the part of Billy Casper. The shortlist was actually whittled down to about thirty young boys where they converged on the Queen's Hotel in Barnsley. They were given two scenarios to act out – the playground fight with McDowell and his visit to the library to find a book on falconry. 'For the first one, we were given a script, but there were no lines for the library sequence,' recalled Bradley. 'Where as the previous three kids had gone *straight up to the librarian and asked for a book, I elected to do something different. I walked around the walls of the room, as if looking at different shelves. Eventually, the librarian said; "Excuse me, can I help you?" I replied; It's all right I'm just looking for a book. We then started to get very gently into a conversation.'*

It is quite extraordinary, even at this early stage, that the young inexperienced Bradley should sense the opportunity to go against the flow. He possessed an innate force, an almost inbred desire to perform and wring out every ounce of energy for any given scene. He was a maverick artist in a sea of mediocrity. He held the power of divine artistry, but what made it extra special – at fourteen it was just another toy to play with.

For weeks Garnett and Loach agonised over their decision to offer the role to Bradley – they new it would make a big difference to his life. Bradley had already told the pair that he would probably be forced to go down the pit – and acting was the only way out for him. Unlike Billy Casper, Bradley was a good student, as his form teacher, Trevor Hesketh, points out. Although he had little idea of what he wanted to do after he left school and in the end, when Bradley took his final exams – the results were very disappointing. Dai comments now, '...*Because of the whole snowballing effect of Kes, I didn't stay on to take any examinations. I went to a Secondary Modern school but I felt the opportunity provided by Kes was there and I should grasp it instead of waiting eight or nine months.'*

However, he knew that he did not want to follow in his father's footsteps. *'I spent an hour in a mine as a boy and I knew I couldn't handle that kind of life. It was a gruelling existence. When I look back at my dad, I realise that each day he spent eight hours working and eight hours sleeping. That means he spent two thirds of his life in darkness.'*

When Bradley finally received the letter from Loach inviting him to take the role, Bradley recalled in wonderment, *'It was written in purple ink. I'd never seen purple ink before!'*

The teenager was given just fifteen pages of script and had to promise not to read the book to find out how the story ended. It was the beginning of Loach's practice of handing out pages of script as filming progressed – with some lines blanked out.

Bradley had great respect for Loach and their weeks working together greatly impressed the young actor, *'Ken is a genius, there's no doubt about it. He's a very gentle man even in his most infuriating moments, he never raises his voice. He's able to pass on his feelings to the* people he's not particularly pleased with, so you desperately want to do the best for him. He enables you to improvise, so long as he knows where it's going.'

Bradley was not a typical child actor. John Threlkeld, from the Morning Telegraph, commenting after the release of *Kes* in Barnsley, says, '*David is free of the sickly innocence of Freddie Bartholomew or the nauseating brashness of Walt Disney's freckled troupe.*' Speaking at the time of the Barnsley premier, March 1970, Bradley said, '*I do not think the film has changed my personality at all. I hope I do not become big-headed and my friends of two years ago are still my friends today.*'

Celebrating the success of *Kes*, the young soccer fan Bradley was invited to Manchester United's training ground. When Bradley met his idols from the soccer world; Sir Matt Busby, Bobby Charlton, Dennis Law and Pat Crerand, the latter had some advice about friendship, '*Remember your pals when you get a few quid.*'

Colin Welland said one of his most vivid memories was the scene where Billy delivers the talk in the classroom and says it felt like a part of his actual life. For Dai Bradley, it was a part of his life – indeed, a life changing experience. He recalled the filming, during his school holidays, as '*like being at Blackpool Pleasure Beach every day*', explaining, '*It was one roller coaster ride to the next.*' A car picked him up at seven-thirty to take him to each day's location, filming would finish at four in the afternoon, then he learned the rudiments of falconry, before returning home for a meal and to learn his lines for the following day. When Bradley was not in a scene he actually worked on *Kes* in a number of assistant roles, '*I remember the times I wasn't actually shooting, I was the number three assistant to the camera crew, so I would carry cases around and I used to be number two assistant to sound. I'd hold the boom when they were doing shots that were not on film. It was just an enormous and wonderful experience for all of us.*' David Robinson, said of Bradley's performance, '*He is as extraordinary as Billy Casper; so utterly absorbed and unself-conscious that he does not seem to act at all. He is a skinny little thing with a pinched face, with unexpected muscle twitches. He never once smiles, or – except perhaps with his kestrel – lets drop his defences of suspicion.*'

I am sure his performance on set was helped by the wonderful team Ken Loach had built around him. Bradley said of filming, '*It was like one long holiday. The atmosphere with the crew was like family. Most of the kids were mates from school.*'

A lot of newspaper and magazine text in late 1970, following the general release of *Kes*, pontificated the gap between Casper and Bradley. Some summarised a great future for the actor claiming he would be, unlike the futureless Billy, a millionaire by the age of twenty. The reality was very different which proves that talent and determination may not always be enough, they may be ingredients for success but, unfairly, not the recipe. It is true, when Bradley reached manhood, his meagre frame did not fill out – and he carried his boyish appearance through the legal drinking age and into his twenties, and little has changed since. Even in 1999 when he was on the books of Inspiration Management he was described as 5' 7"slim build and athletic – which was very close to his equity description nearly 30 years before. This made leading man parts unrealistic. With such a strong performance under his narrow belt; character parts should have been in abundance. But I think it worked against the young actor who started with little experience and big ambitions, I think he was so convincing people thought Bradley and Casper were of the same mind and he was as much Billy as he was Dai. There was nothing wrong with his dedication to his craft. His Equity card (F65461) boasted accents and dialects as Native Yorkshire, Scouse, Brummie, Lancs, Welsh, Scots, American and Cockney and the skills included able swimmer, horseman, fencer, athlete and light tenor; albeit untrained.

Of course criticism came from other established sources. *Kes* co-star Colin Welland's commented in a Sunday newspaper several years ago that Bradley had ruined his career as, *'he'd become all posh.'* The actor says his accent faded due to a regime of speech lessons in Leeds to strengthen his voice, and classical roles. During visits home his friends would chide him of his lost origin of speech. *'They would get really annoyed,'* he says. *'They thought I was taking the mickey so they told me off.'*

At age sixteen Dai Bradley certainly felt that his strong Yorkshire accent would be a hindrance and elocution lessons at a voice-training centre in Leeds, were sort. He was basically striving, in six weeks, to master Standard English. *'My accent can hold me back. I do not want to be stereotyped, and I would like to do Welsh and Scottish parts, and even Geordie,'* said Bradley at the time. It was at this period the modest son of a miner, decided not to go to acting school. *'I will spoil my style. If 20 students go through the same course at acting school, I am sure it can knock the individuality out of their acting. They are all taught the same things.'* There was no doubt Bradley was a thoroughbred race horse, the lack of training may have hindered his progress, but at what cost no one will every realise.

Sudden fame often has drawbacks. For Dai Bradley, it meant losing his name. When the teenage star of *Kes* applied for equity membership, he was now sixteen and eligible, shortly after his big break, he discovered another David Bradley was already on its books. He had contemplated dropping the 'e' from Bradley or David W. Bradley — the 'W' standing for Ward his mother's family name. He even flirted with Ward Bradley. Not really keen on any of the names he had come up with; Bradley telephoned his namesake, an aspiring theatre actor (Sheffield Playhouse) a few years older, with a proposition. *'Listen,'* he argued, *'why don't you change your name? I played Billy Casper, that little kid in* Kes. *David Bradley is my name and people will always remember me. If you don't change your name, they'll think you did the part.'* The other David Bradley's response was unequivocal, *'Bugger off, you pillock.'* 'He was right, of course,' laughs Bradley, who changed his Christian name to Dai. *'He's carved out a very nice career for himself. He's probably more in work than I am.'* Unfortunately that statement turned out to be true, and Dai Bradley's fragmented acting career was dogged by stagnant periods. Towards the end of 2004 Bradley's name sake had appeared in all the *Harry Potter* movies (2001/2/4/5) playing Argus Filtch, has credits in fifteen movies, twenty TV programmes and a dozen TV appearances.

Ironically, the man that equity recognises as David Bradley starred alongside Freddie Fletcher (Jud Casper in *Kes*) in *Another Sunday and Sweet F.A.* (1972). In this football drama, as if haunting the star of *Kes*, he actually also played the goalkeeper.

Dai Bradley carried on regardless and excelled in his stage work — reaching a new level of professionalism with his acting talents on display in *Equus*. It was an enormous blow when he did not get to reprise his stage success in a film version of *Equus* (that fell to Peter Firth) and although he had supporting roles in a handful of movies, his screen career had virtually come to a halt by the start of the eighties.

Fate almost sent Bradley's career spiralling upwards into TV history. Around 1982 Franc Roddam, the creator and director of *Auf Wiedersehen Pet,* was assembling the cast with writers Ian La Frenais and Dick Clement. All agreed that Dai Bradley was ideal for the part of Neville Hope (eventually played by Kevin Whatley). Some writing had already been scripted with Bradley playing the innocent Neville. In fact the ensemble went to see Bradley's latest acting role (and would be for some time) in *The World Cup; A Captain's Tale* (1982). It was at this viewing they picked up newcomer Tim Healy who was to become the unforgettable rock, Dennis Patterson. Why the actor eventually lost out is unclear, but it would have been very interesting to see and Bradley would have had his dream to play a Geordie – on a series that has scanned 21 years.

Loach selected Dai Bradley from Form 3S at St. Helen's Secondary Modern, to take the leading role in his film. Certainly, Dai is convinced that without Ken Loach and Tony Garnett he would never have left home. When he finally did fly the nest (deliberate pun) he knew he was on his own. In 1973 he commented on breaking free and leaving Yorkshire to follow the dream of becoming a jobbing actor, 'They do have a certain responsibility; Ken and Tony, of course, but they owe me nothing. If I'd saved somebody from drowning I wouldn't remind him of it every time I saw him. I'd expect him to say, "Have a beer and forget it." I wouldn't want whiskies all the time; nobody can play God. I might make it as an actor sometime, I might not. We'll just have to wait and see. One thing: there won't be any blame. I'd just say thanks to Ken and Tony for five, ten or twenty-five great years.'

The groundbreaking success of Kes changed Bradley's ambitions. The quiet schoolboy, who had rarely left south Yorkshire, found himself alongside Loach being quizzed by critics at film festivals. Loach's naturalistic style was widely praised, as were his actors real performances. In 1969 Bradley won BAFTA's most promising newcomer award. He was to be bestowed with other awards in the future – Winner of the Golden Bear, also for Kes. For King and Country he was honoured by the South African Film Board and for Absolution he was awarded a Commendation at the Oxford Film Festival. 'Filmwise, Absolution is something I enjoyed doing with Richard Burton and Billy Connolly,' explained Bradley recently, 'That was great fun, but the role of the actor, unless you're in the top 7% or 8%, is a kind of roller-coaster and my career has been a roller-coaster in a lot of ways, but then I don't see life purely as being solely about acting. That's what I do for a living. That's what I enjoy doing obviously but life is about experiences and taking challenges as opposed to be fretting about where the next job is coming from.'

Bradley experienced another Kes-like moment of grace following a charity performance of a play in Beverley Hills. 'I walked into a charity reception at the Beverley Wiltshire Hotel,' remembers the actor, 'and a thousand people were all standing up applauding. I thought, oh-oh, someone's coming. I thought Burt Lancaster or Tony Curtis had walked in behind me so I made way for this big star I thought had followed me into the room. I felt incredibly embarrassed.' The ovation was, of course, for Bradley.

When the film crew arrived in Barnsley at the beginning of the 1968 summer break, a career in acting seemed about as likely for Dai Bradley as a transfer to grammar school. It was not that he did not have the talent or inclination, he had both – he had fast earned for himself a reputation as the star comic turn in St. Helen's yearly pantomime. This was another strange similarity with his screen altar ego Billy Casper. He was regarded a bit of a loner – certainly, as other pupils were concerned. Of course there were very different circumstances that lead to Casper's aloofness – he was basically trying to distance himself from McDowell and the troubles it created, 'in coffee bar's and that,' as Billy tearfully points out to Mr Farthing. Dai Bradley received enthusiastic reviews from mainly teachers and parents. One extra, who whished to remain nameless, stated 'He was a bit like Billy, a bit of a loner, not trouble, but a teachers pet – due to the acting and that. The teachers like that.' He certainly had a remarkable talent, but whether he realised it at fourteen during the school pantomimes, I am not sure. The reviews at the time, obviously before Kes, during these shows were quite glowing. In Sinbad the Sailor, February 3rd 1968, a journalist wrote in the Barnsley Chronicle, 'Perhaps making the biggest hit with the audience was the black-faced Ali Aly, played spiritedly by young David Bradley. His mere appearance on stage had the audience in fits of laughter. His diction was good and his over-all performance excellent.' In The Piper of Troone, the same journalist wrote, 'He was remarkably good as Charlie Dimple. He had no nerves and is more polished than many of the adults who have performed for years in amateur dramatics. I predict a great future for him in drama if he stays with it. Wonderful, David.'

Everybody assumed it would be the same old story of unfulfilled potential. Leave school; find a job, next public performance the altar. Dai's headmaster, Mr Clarence Hirst, said, 'David, I felt, would have fitted well into a bank or into lower law – a solicitor's clerk, something of that sort.'

This is quite a leap from the sort of job you would expect Casper to follow – or be pushed into. Not that anybody is suggesting Bradley and Casper should have any shared character traits or instincts – there is no inexplicable link. Dai or should I say David, is a real person, and Casper is an imaginary character; the penned thoughts of author Barry Hines. The two are married together by the producer and director and some slight correlation may exist. I think it is ignorant to assume the two are some how fused together – similar to Sir Michael Caine and his character, Alfie (1966). Some un-informed journalists could not separate the two.

Certainly after the film was made Bradley went off in a

completely different tangent. I am sure David and Dai separated at some point, and some of the old David was left behind at St. Helens. After all he had been photographed by David Bailey and had had his hair trimmed by Keith at Smile – before filming he had heard of neither.

Dai Bradley spoke of his first taste of being an actor and his flirtation with stardom '*I remember the first time I saw myself on the screen; it was rather like loosing my virginity my heart was going like fifty to the dozen. I was fifteen and a half, and suddenly the whole publicity bandwagon started to roll, and I found myself in the position of a door being opened to become an actor. I was entirely grateful to Ken Loach for giving me that opportunity.*'

The acting profession could be sneered at and not totally acceptable to all concerned, as the headmaster of St. Helens underlined in 1973. '*Since David went into this acting line,*' comments Mr Hirst, '*the most important thing he's done is to change attitudes. Acting – even cooking – around here used to be seen as soft, sissy, not a man's work. He's removed quite a lot of that feeling. We have a boy with us now we are trying to get into drama school. And another little girl has joined the Black and White Minstrels.*'

It was around the time of the interview with The Sunday Times that Bradley, still living in Barnsley, hit his bad patch. He was resting for about three months. Although he was bored and depressed he point-blank refused to sign on, especially in his home town. He said of this lean time, '*I was too embarrassed to take the dole, I suppose, I'd feel I was letting them down. You see, as far as my parents and my friends in Barnsley are concerned, I live in a fairyland world and to them it's just something fantastic. I come in and I say, oh, I worked with Sir Laurence Olivier last week and they can't believe it. On the other hand, they're coming to realise that famous personalities are just ordinary people, which is the way it should be. For instance, I feel I can talk to Sir Laurence man to man, rather than star to ... to whatever I am.*'

At around this time Bradley found a crafty way to learn his lines. He used to take the whole script home with him and on his tape recorder, tape all the parts except his own – leaving spaces to reply. He then simply plays back the tape responding at appropriate intervals.

Although the telephone stayed dormant for quite long periods of time, Dai Bradley acted in a number of films and television series throughout the seventies and early eighties. In 1970 he was one of the *Flaxton Boys* in Yorkshire Television's boy's own adventure series filmed at Ripley Castle near Harrogate; in 1972, public feelings put aside, he had a small role in *Kes* co-star Colin Welland's *Play For Today: Kisses at Fifty.* In 1973 he played the part of Barty in a children's film, *Malachi's Cove,* adapted from the story by Anthony Trollope, with Donald Pleasence and Arthur English, and filmed at Tintagel in Cornwall.

Dai moved to London in the early seventies and at the National Theatre, had his first great theatrical success as Alan Strang in Shaffer's play, *Equus,* about the dilemmas raised by psychoanalytical theory and the place of passion in a world of suffocating normality, which toured the world - including a stint on Broadway for two-and-half years. Directed by John Dexter, and starring Anthony Perkins, this production won the Tony Award for Best Play on Broadway in 1975.

In 1977 he appeared in *The Fire That Consumes,* a controversial French play about the emotional tensions between boys and their teachers at a Catholic school, directed by Bernard Miles, with Nigel Hawthorne as l'Abbé. Based upon the boyhood experience of the author Henry de Montherlant (1896-1972), who was expelled from his school by a not irreproachable Abbé for his sentimental friendship with a younger boy, this translation by Vivian Cox, staged at the Mermaid Theatre, was the first English production of the play, which had come to England in its original form in 1971. The Sunday Times review of 23rd October, 1977 said of Bradley's performance, '*As the child so tragically fought over, finds exactly the right note of wanton innocence.*'

1979 saw him as a young German soldier, Kropp, in a remake for television of Remarque's anti-war classic *Im Westen Nichts Neues (All Quiet on the Western Front)* starring, among others, Donald Pleasance and Ernest Borgnine. Playing the soldier again, he appeared in *Zulu Dawn* (1979) with Burt Lancaster, the prequel to the classic 1964 film *Zulu* starring Sir Michael Caine.

The pysychological thriller *Absolution,* written by Anthony Shaffer (*Sleuth, Wickerman, Death On the Nile, etc.,*) and starring Richard Burton, although made in 1978, was not released until 1981 in the UK, and 1988 in America. In this Hitchcock-esque story set in a Catholic boarding school, with references to Shakespeare's *Julius Caesar* and Gilbert & Sullivan's *Patience,* Dai was one of the two boys who, for separate reasons, attempt to reveal the serious flaws of their priest-teacher Burton by exploiting the seal of the confession. The fate of his character, the crippled Arthur who has a pedantic knowledge of ancient military tactics and a genius for mimicry, was in some ways a variation on the themes in *Kes* and *The Fire That Consumes*.

New Year 1980 saw Dai's return to Africa for the gruelling experience of filming Elspeth Huxley's autobiographical novel *The Flame Trees of Thika* in Kenya. Three generations of child stars - Hayley Mills, Dai Bradley and eleven-year-old Holly Aird - combined for this classic period drama of the end of Empire set on a colonial coffee plantation in 1913. Elspeth Huxley flew in to give her blessing to the production, adding a welcome boost to the weary cast and crew and an extra note of authenticity to the story.

In 1982 he returned to the world of Northern comedy-drama with *The World Cup - A Captain's Tale*, starring Dennis Waterman and Nigel Hawthorne, which tells the story of England's surprise win at the inaugural World Cup of Football in 1910. Filmed in Northumbria, *The World Cup* was directed by Tom Clegg, of *The Sweeney* and *Minder* fame.

From the mid-eighties, apart from his directional debut, he also starred, in Johannesburg play which he hoped to see transferred to the West End, he pursued interests away from the stage and screen. He even indulged in the spiritual teachings of the late Indian guru, Krishnamurti. Dai says of his experience, '*When I first heard him speak I wept buckets of tears.*'

During this period, away from the stage and camera lights, Bradley had concentrated on writing, including a children's novel. He also spent much of that decade renovating an old chapel outside Bath. After Bradley and his agent parted amicably at the start of the decade, he put acting on the backburner and embarked on string of ill-fated projects. A board game idea failed, as did his television drama series set around the world backgammon championship, *Shake, Rattle and Roll*. Then he wrote a film about medical ethics, which was abandoned when the same scenario was played out in reality with the Diane Blood fertility case.

Many things have happened to Dai Bradley in the years that followed *Kes* – a mixed bag of highs and lows. He commented on his time as Billy Casper – those seven mad weeks – '*Today, I can look back on it with great fondness and wonderful memories.*' It seems that *Kes* is still a part of Dai's life and he can reflect positively on his childhood stardom, '*Although I haven't seen the film for some years,*' Dai continues, '*it still holds a special part in my life – as it does in the lives of the others who were in it.*' Thirty five years on Bradley is still recognised in the street. '*Yes, quite a lot actually,*' he says, '*I was doing a promotional shoot* only a couple of days ago in the local park near where I live, and there was a little lady who recognized me and said: "you were the little boy in Kes weren't you?" I was so pleased that she enjoyed the movie.'

On a philosophical note, Bradley recently commented on his famous role, 'I don't make a great fuss about Kes, I don't surf the Kes bandwagon. Before doing the film, I'd only acted in school pantomime. It was an extraordinary time in my life. I look upon the film with joy rather than pride.'

Meanwhile, Dai Bradley, whose performance validated Loach and Garnett's reasons for turning Barry Hines's story into a film, proved that there was life for a Barnsley schoolboy beyond the local pit, but his fate made him a popular candidate for - Where are they now? features over the following decades.

Following the re-release of Kes, on DVD, in August 1999, to mark the thirtieth anniversary of Loach and Garnett's first feature together, Bradley visited Pontefract to talk about the film and his role as Billy Casper, and discovered why the film has such timeless appeal. 'I'm amazed it's still on the National Curriculum,' he says. 'But these youngsters seem to identify 100 per cent with Billy Casper. It seems to be a movie that's well thought of in all communities, appealing to a whole range of people.' Ironically, the actor on the re-birth of Kes was unemployed. And this from an actor who has received a BAFTA for best newcomer, best actor nominations from Los Angeles Drama Critics' circle for roles in Equus and from the Johannesburg Theatre Council for The Wound.

Like Carol White in Cathy Come Home, Bradley became synonymous with his screen role in Kes. But as the actor acknowledged, 'It all started through Ken Loach, and Kes was the catalyst... One of the things I happily accept is that, if people only remember me for Billy Casper, then that's fine. It was a wonderful experience and obviously it had a great effect on so many people.'

Commenting on his whole incredible experience of the acting profession, Bradley says, 'However you interpret failure and success, I personally don't see it as purely to do with vocation. It's to do with how you affect other people's lives - not just family, but friends and strangers. And that comes through work and your attitude to work, and your experiences. And like most experiences, being in Kes was not about life or death; it was an adventure, a spiritual and emotional adventure. It's up to the individual to decide whether it's worth travelling that route, or whether another journey is worth their while. If you have a passion to follow that dream, then follow it. It may not last you a lifetime, but there'll be other dreams, and at least you'll have had the adventure. I would imagine that all of the people who have worked with Ken - those who didn't make it in the acting profession and those who did - pretty much all of them would say they'd do it all again.'

There is renewed hope that Dai Bradley may return fulltime to acting following a television movie in 2001 called *Station Jim* starring George Cole. And even more recently *Asylum* (2003) where he plays Father Michael. This last outing was chosen as the closing night gala film for the 2005 Bradford Film Festival. Bradley's old form teacher, in real life and of course in *Kes*, Trevor Hesketh was invited along to the premier. 'He was absolutely wonderful, was David (Bradley), and played a great part. Hazel and I met him after the showing – everyone was very complimentary and excited. They are trying to get the funding to go national – and if they do I think it will be a great success.'

Dai has been working on an autobiography but says he has no plans to publish it for a few years. When I was originally discussing *Life After Kes* with Bradley – he was always very conscious of me stealing his thunder. The conflict of interest, as he put it, has curbed his total commitment to my project. I have even offered my many months of research so he can talk to his former friends and colleagues.

My personal view is that my work in no way impinges on his biographical life. I always felt confident that *Kes*, with its great ensemble in front and behind the camera, its powerful political message – was bigger than any individual. Dai has a remarkable story, one that I originally wanted to write before I embarked on this extraordinary journey through *Kes* country.

14

The Brother – Our Jud

In a way Jud Casper, Billy's brother, or half brother as is intimated throughout, is a bigger threat than his mother, teachers, pupils and the establishment. At Easter he will leave the teachers behind, and you feel, most of his friends. The establishment – any authority, employer, librarian etc., Billy comes in contact with; he either ignores or deftly sidesteps. Casper's mother, with all her lack of caring, insensitiveness and single-minded pleasure – has affection for her son. With the circumstances the way they are, regarding Billy and Jud, they have to share the one bedroom, are going to be strange bedfellows for some time. Billy will keep letting Jud down and vice versa – although there is a begrudging proudness for his fighting skills – '*Our, Jud's 't' cock of t'estate*,' as Billy describes him to McDowell.

They are together at the opening scene – with no respect for each other and they are left hating each other at the end of the film and you feel it is going to go on for many years. Jud is bigger and stronger than his little brother and time is not going to change that. Even when physical strength diminishes in Jud, his mental persecution will carry him through his declining years.

It was a great thrill for me to meet up with Freddie Fletcher who played Jud Casper in *Kes*. Apart from the fact that he never gives interviews, only when it is about a specific project he is currently working on – a movie or television series, and only then begrudgingly. This is not born out of any fear for the press or the spotlight. Similar to Jud Casper, I do not think Freddie Fletcher fears anything or anyone. With Jud it was his cocky, brash, fighting ways that gave him his air of supremacy. With Freddie it is down to the fact that he knows who he is. He has no reason to put on any false mask. He is happy who he is and what he stands for. This has protected him from the elevated and over-stated falseness of the fame game. It is a world full of people who believe their own hype and others who have dropped by the wayside, crushed without the drug of fame to feed their egos.

The press can be merciless vultures preying on the rotten carcass of past demeanours and difficult times. Freddie had trod vary carefully around them. *'If I have done something on film or for television and I have to talk to the press I will – to satisfy the promoters,'* comments Fletcher, bitterly. *'But I will never talk about my friends and family. I've had bad experiences in the past and I just stopped giving interviews.'*

When I first called Freddie Fletcher, it was Barry Hines who pointed me towards Grimthorpe, and asked if I was addressing Mr Fletcher, his retort was, *'Who wants to know?'* Quite rightly so, he wanted to know about the project and what the finished product was going to be about. When I satisfied him about my integrity we arranged to meet up in the near future.

Of all the actors, crew, extras etc., I was especially looking forward to meeting Freddie Fletcher. His character, Jud Casper, was like a shark swimming around an island with brother Billy marooned in the middle. Jud was a frightening, explosive character, a hard drinker, a womaniser, a fighter, a bully, and a hard working miner. With his lean muscular physique, blond hair and six-foot height – he was a million miles away from his younger brother.

The scenes in the confined terrace house were very dominating and dramatic – it was very claustrophobic with Jud, Mrs Casper and Billy, sharing the small space. The house originally to be used for the downstairs interior scenes, belonged to an old miner. *'When Ken was filming the scenes in Billy's house he quickly realised there was not enough room,'* comments Trevor Hesketh. *'Ken asked me if I could track down a pre-fabricated unit, so they could build it with one wall missing. Luckily I had seen someone taking down some pre-fab units close to where I live and we purchased one of those.'* In fact the bedroom scenes where Billy and Jud share a bed were filmed in an old ladies house. Because some of the shots were filmed late evening or early morning, and it was the woman's bedroom – she actually slept downstairs and never bothered the actors and crew.

Freddie Fletcher was born in Grimthorpe, famous for it's colliery brass band, which was immortalised by Mark Herman's *Brassed Off* (1996). Freddie was offered a part in the movie, but turned it down. *'A lot of the locations were in and around Grimethorpe, pubs and clubs etc. I really didn't want to work in my home town.'*

Freddie attended Raley school in Barnsley. It was Grimethorpe Youth Club Centre, with his best friend John Grayson; who was to play his best friend in the film, where Freddie was selected and offered the role of Jud. Remarkably he had no previous experience of acting and reserved no notion of becoming an actor. Freddie was just eighteen years old and earning his money as a painter and decorator. 'It was Mr Hitchin, I think who put my name forward, me and John (John Grayson), I believe he was a friend of Barry Hines. I'd never read the book, but they said John Hitchin's friend was making a film and they were looking out for different characters. The audition, as far as I know, was not necessarily to play Jud, it could have been anyone. I had to go round the school; I think Ken Loach and possibly Tony Garnett were there.'

The audition, like all Loach's auditions, was completely unscripted. They gave Freddie Fletcher and John Grayson a scenario. 'What they said to us was, as much as I can remember, was that my character had put John's sister in the family way and he had come round my house to see if I was going to marry her or whatever and we just made it up from there. So John pretended to knock at the door, I let him in – we started arguing and then started scraping; and all hell let loose.'

Although Freddie had never met Dai Bradley before Kes, he did know Lynne Perrie (Mrs Casper) – he used to listen to her sing in and around the clubs of Barnsley. The scenes that featured Lynne and Freddie appeared to have a natural chemistry that leaped out at you. 'We had no definite script as such; I mean there was a script. Ken just gave us certain scenarios or arguments to act out, at the end if any of us thought of anything – to keep it going and see what happens. I used to enjoy the cross banter in the house with Lynne. I had no feeling if what we were doing was any good, I hadn't a clue. When I look at Dai's performance – it was unbelievable. Ken Loach was lovely to work with and you wanted to do the best for him.'

Fletcher appeared in Marie Giese's When Saturday Comes (1996) starring Sean Bean. Unlike the usual merry-go-round of a casting director contacting the agent, who then informs his client with the possibility of having a screen test - Freddie was saved from such formality. 'Beanie (Sean Bean) actually called me up – totally out of the blue. They'd been filming at a local brewery in Sheffield. One of the workers there turned round to Sean, in the middle of filming, and said: "I know an actor; his name's Freddie Fletcher." Beanie knew the name from Kes and asked the guy if he had my number. I obviously didn't know him then. So the phone rang and this voice says: "Hi, Freddie, this is Sean Bean here." I said fair enough so ok who is it? He says: "No, really this is Sean Bean. We're filming in Sheffield can you meet me for lunch?" And because of my film character in Kes they called me Judd in When Saturday Comes. In fact all of Beanies film buddies where all going: "Ah it's our Jud and quoting from the film." Due to the fact that filming was already underway, the part was not large, but we see flashes of the older Jud Casper, as barman Judd, as he quells an unruly crowd, drinking in his pub.

Since the film was shot in 1968, the 37 years have not taken away Jud's mask. Although his hair is cropped short, you can still see Jud's piercing eyes as well as the physical strength that is usually attributed to someone in the armed forces. *'I do get recognised; it depends where I go really. I hadn't seen* Kes *for many years, but I saw it around Christmas time, my wife had never seen it all the way through. I mean you forget what you looked like then. My lad who's eight said it looks nothing like me – but it sounded just like me! But they all said he looked like my Dean, the middle one, who's coming up to seventeen.'*

The premier to a film can often be the first time an actor has seen himself on screen. This is particularly true with all Loach's films, as he does not let the actors watch the rushes. *'I remember being mortified when I first saw myself on screen and then you hear your voice. You really don't realise what you sound like.'*

Having a two year gap from filming Kes and its eventual general release – it was very difficult for the actors to secure work. *'When we had completed the film, nothing happened much. I had an agent in Leeds and he used to get me auditions. Then after the major release this guy who was directing the* Queenie's Castle *series had just seen Kes and he contacted my agent. He chose me* (to play Raymond Shepherd), *together with Barry Rutter and Brian Marshal, and we made up the cast and joined Diana Dors and Lynne Perrie.'*

The TV series Queenie's Castle was first broadcast on bonfire night in 1970 and ran for two years. There were 18 episodes each lasting 30 minutes. *'When I first got the part for Queenie's, we – me, Barry Rutter and Brian Marshall actually went down to Diana's (Dors) house in Sunningdale. Alan Lake (Dors's Husband) was supposed to play the brother-in-law but unfortunately he had had a scuffle with a pub landlord and ended up stabbing him – and Lake got 18 months in jail. Eventually Tony Caunter, great actor, stepped into Alan's role. I met Alan a few times, he was a lovely bloke – he used to pretend he was gypsy; he got gypsy blood in him. He actually came from a council semi in Stoke,'* laughs Freddie. *'I stayed at Diana's house quite a bit, Alan was away at that time, and she used to take us three boys, and in those days I didn't know London very well, all over the place. She was a lovely, lovely woman.'*

Freddie appeared in films including Terror on the Britanic (1974) with Richard Harris, Anthony Hopkins and Omar Sharif and Some Kind Of Life (1995) with Jane Horricks. Together with other TV series like Fox (1980), Fletcher also worked on Alan Bleasdale's G.B.H. (1991). And he has done the odd TV movie including Clouds of Glory:

William and Dorothy (1978) starring Felicity Kendal, written by Melvyn Bragg and directed by Ken Russell. *'The phone went one day and a guy says this is Ken Russell – well I said Bollocks! And put the phone down. Luckily he telephoned me back and offered me the part – I spent five or six weeks on location in The Lake District.'* Freddie even turned down a part in *The Full Monty* (1997), due to a family member's illness.

When not working, although Freddie's career has been steady, he certainly could not be classed as resting as some actors like to say. He has been a farmer, painter and decorator and a short spell down the mines. *'I turned my hand to anything, basically to make a crust,'* says Fletcher. Freddie was also a fearsome rugby player.

It is always interesting to find out what path led to a career in acting and Freddie blames it totally on Ken Loach. *'I mean I used to do drama at school, I used to love it at school. I wouldn't have thought I would have ever acted in films if it hadn't been for Kes.'*

It was quite a boring question now to ask if there was any rehearsal because there was not any. It struck me that the nerves must have been very taught if you are subjecting non-actors to perform with all the professional crew standing around waiting for the magic to start. *'I was never nervous, not even in that first take. That's one thing I have never ever ever ever suffered from; nerves in my life,'* states Freddie categorically. *'I always knew I was trying to do my best so failure was not a problem to me. Whether I did something right or wrong wasn't an issue. The whole atmosphere on set was like that - I don't think anyone was really nervous or on edge. Dai certainly didn't appear nervous and that from a fourteen year old boy was unbelievable.'*

I think everyone I spoke to showed concern for Dai Bradley, and his bumpy ride with fame. Working close with the young lad from Barnsley many friendships had been forged. *'I think he'd gone from a secure home and he started really from the very top,'* explains Freddie. *'And he had a long way to fall – he had to try and keep up there. I think all this and going to The National Theatre and being away from home – I think he must have been very lonely. I think the worst thing Dai did was lose his accent. I always wanted him to make a million – actually I might get the ten bob he owes me from 1968,'* laughs Fletcher.

This most certainly appears to be true as he cut away his roots and, not intentionally maybe, distanced himself from friends back home – who found the new Dai with his posh accent, difficult to cope with. This may even have been their own insecurities as well as his own, but his friends stayed where they were and he melted back into television, movie and theatre land.

'I went to many castings and some I didn't get,' states Freddie, 'because I had a Yorkshire accent and some I did get because of my accent. There are Yorkshiremen all over the world. There are Scotsman and Londoners – if you can do the job, fine. If not I'll go to another audition. I really have not got a problem with it.'

One of the stories that cropped up during interviews was the edited out fight scene in The Cudsworth Arms, between Freddie Fletcher and another extra. 'He said the same thing to me, Ken Loach as he said to the guy who had to pick a fight with me,' Freddie explains. 'So he said to both of us, separately, without the other knowing: "when one muscles in to get a drink, start an argument and throw a punch at him, he'll be ready for it, and then take it from there – we'll stop before it goes too far." So I think fine, no problem. The thing was I didn't know Ken had told him to throw a punch as well – and I was on my own ground – this bloke wasn't. All the blokes in the pub all knew me. So when he thumps me, I wasn't expecting it so we ended up having a bit of a scrap and luckily no-one else joined in. I can remember the tussle on the floor and two of the Olson twins, they were both karate black belts, ready to start.'

I recently watched an old episode of Peak Practice (yes it was UK Gold) where Freddie was the main protagonist – he actually played an epileptic fireman. It was wonderful to see him act – dominating scenes, delicately side stepping the obvious actor rout and showing strength blended with subtle fragility. The one thing that struck me was that Freddie was a damn good actor. He could hold his own, and if had wanted to, although he put his young family first, he could have been up there with the best of them. What makes Freddie special is that this does not affect him – it is not a lost opportunity in his eyes but another path that has given him different riches. He puts his family foremost and everything else comes a poor second. 'Looking after and supporting your kids is real life,' states Freddie seriously, 'and acting is just another job that puts food in their bellies and shoes on their feet.'

The memory of our Jud, cock of t'estate, as Billy described him will last forever and so will my meetings with Freddie Fletcher. It was a great performance and his powerfulness and menacing presence on screen has not diminished over time and meeting Freddie as even enhanced the image. There is little correlation between actor and character, yes, if you thump Freddie Fletcher he will probably thump you back and if you buy him a pint he will buy you one back. He is a true gentleman of Yorkshire. All his children are an asset to him, an extension of his values and beliefs. Freddie is content with himself and the people and friends around him. He will never forget his birth town, because that is what shaped him and made him what he is.

15

The Mother - Lynne Perrie

Originally I had planned to meet up with both Lynne Perrie and her much-in-demand brother, Duggie Brown. We made several plans, but Duggie just never seemed to stop working, playing golf or a combination of the two. In the end I had to wave the white flag and conduct separate interviews. I had heard a lot about Lynne; in fact a lot that I had heard had come from her own words in her expose of *Coronation Street*, called simply *Secrets of the Street*. I have never watched a complete episode of *Coronation Street*, I just do not watch soaps, I actually find it quite distracting, like listening to someone's conversation in a pub – which I suppose is the overall appeal. Perhaps, secretly, if I start to watch them, I fear I may get hooked on all the soaps and greedily devour every transmission. And of course that is about three hours a day taken up for the rest of my life.

Lynne played a wonderful part in *Kes*, even though she had never acted before. Similar to a lot of performances in the movie, I feel she recorded her personal best. Perrie could act, the world could see that, and that single performance set her up for life.

For 23 years Lynne Perrie has stalked *Coronation Street* as the fearsome Ivy Tilsley/Brennan. Before her big break in *Kes* she was singing on the brutal Northern club circuit. She had club experience in Britain, Germany and South Africa, and had appeared on the same bill as the Beatles and the Rolling Stones.

Lynne Perrie came into the world as baby Jean Dudley on April 7th 1931. The venue was opposite Parkgate steelworks in Marsbro, Rotherham, with the forge hammer going continuously day and night. It was her grandma's house, a temporary residence, while Lynne's parents waited for a council house. 13 years later another *Kes* star was born into the house in the shape of Barry Dudley; Lynne's brother, later changed to Duggie Brown. He was to follow in his sisters footsteps, before appearing in *Kes*; as the milkman, and tread the boards of the Northern club circuit.

It was one Saturday night, with her best friend Doreen, which changed her life forever. Lynne Perrie had always sung, not to an audience, but at home, in the bath – the usual. Now it was a talent competition at the Maramba Club in Rotherham. Doreen did not except no for an answer and physically pushed her on stage. Following the nervous performance; she did not win, a drummer, Ken Copley, approached Perrie, he was looking for a singer to front his brother's band. Lynne auditioned and got the job. At the first rehearsal she learned they were all buskers and none of them could read music – which made musical arrangements slightly more difficult.

'But luckily they were a great Jazz band,' explains Perrie, 'and used to play in whatever key I was singing.' She received five shillings every Saturday night she played with the band. Which was a lot of money to Lynne – she was just fourteen years old. This was the start of a lifetime in showbusiness.

At her peek, during her singing career, it included a six-week tour with the Beatles. Lynne said at the time, 'I've played every room in the country.'

After getting married and having a child, Stephen, Lynne, after a three year break, resumed her singing career. Her husband's uncle was concert secretary at the nearby Progressive Club, and needed a turn for the Sunday night. Although it was a disaster, Lynne returned the following week, with a little more confidence, and bought the house down. The Rotherham Trade Centre followed and so did a further 27 bookings; on the night! Bathed in success and now earning £4.50 a performance Jean Dudley changed her name to Lynne Perrie inspired by the Yorkshire Olympic Silver medallist Gordon Pirie. Jean Dudley and Lynne Perrie would never look back.

'If it hadn't been for the clubs,' offers Perrie, 'I'd have never got my break in the movies, which of course led to my television career.' Perrie was singing in the Ba' Ba' Club, in Barnsley, when Ken Loach and Tony Garnett popped in for a quick pint. She had no idea who these movie men were, as they watched transfixed, and had no idea the impact they would have on her life.

Loach and Garnett invited the singer to join them at their table and complimented her on the act. They explained that they had been auditioning all day for the part of the mother of a Barnsley lad in a movie, called Kes, they were making. They explained that the character, Mrs Casper, husband had run off and she went down the pub every night and would leave money so her young son could get fish and chips.

'That's exactly what I do with our Stephen,' chirped Perrie, 'I go out working and leave two shillings on the mantelpiece for his dad or the babysitter to get him a bottle of pop and some chips. And tell them not to let any other kids in who'll go jumping over the furniture.'

Loach and Garnett looked at each other, knowing that they had found their Mrs Casper - Billy's mother. When they offered the job to Perrie, she was a little surprised.

'I'm not an actress, I'm a singer.' They explained that they had auditioned forty-seven actresses that day and she was more natural than any of them. The singer explained she was not free as she was booked to do a fortnight singing in Wales. Desperate to secure Perrie for the role – Loach promised to let her finish filming at 4pm and provide her with a driver. The deal was struck.

Ken Loach organised a vehicle, a Vauxhall Viva and a local driver, Eddie West, to run errands and take Perrie to and from Wales. The idea was to give the car to the driver after filming as payment for driving services. There must have been some problem, because the driver was let go and a replacement was found – all in the space of a couple weeks.

'I used to leave the set on location in Barnsley and head for Wales,' says Perrie, 'I didn't like the studio car and ended up letting the driver take my Mark 10 Jag so I could get to sleep on the back seat. It cost me £80 in petrol for the fortnight and I only got £40 for doing the film. There were no repeats or anything. The movie was a great hit around the world. I would have been a millionaire by now if I'd had the repeat fees from that film.'

Like so many performances in Kes, with art imitating nature - Perrie became Mrs Casper, she had previously lived and breathed the role. Although the part was not huge it was pivotal and knitted the scenes of Billy's depressing home life. There were wonderful kitchen sink exchanges with Perrie and Freddie Fletcher playing Billy's brother, Jud. At times the gulf between them was almost hatred, both blaming the others existence on each other. The only thing they had in common was their impatience towards the young Billy.

The only caring side, and it was a mere glimpse, was when Mrs Casper is out drinking at the club and she appears to show genuine concern about her elder son. Perrie pulled this off magnificently, with serious interaction between the other actors and extras. It is a testament to her first acting role as you ponder where Mrs Casper begins and Perrie ends.

The world premier of Kes was not the great occasion Perrie had envisioned, the ticket stated formal dress, and was an invitation from the directors of United Artists Corporation Ltd and Associated British Cinemas Ltd. 'It was my first ever film role and I was so excited – until I found out it was being held at the local flea pit cinema in Barnsley!'

It was the ABC Cinema in Peel Street. There was no limousine — she could have actually walked from her house.

Regards the film, Perrie has a philosophical view, 'Kes *undoubtedly made me because I never had to do another audition after that, I got roles in a string of TV plays including* Crown Court, Slattery's Mounted Foot, Queenie's Castle, Follyfoot, The Intruder *and* Leeds United *and of course,* Coronation Street.'

16

The Actor – Colin Welland

Colin Welland was born Colin Williams, in Leigh, Lancashire on the 4th July 1934. He is married to Patricia Sweeney, since 1962, and has four children; Genevieve, Catherine, Caroline and Christy. His life could have been relatively normal, as he grew up to be a teacher in his hometown, before embarking on a career as an actor. Ironically, for his first major feature, *Kes*, he was to return to his former occupation.

Colin attended Newton-le-Willows Grammar School; Bretton Hall College; Goldsmith's College, London, before taking up teaching and receiving a Diploma in Art and Drama. Four years later Colin joined the Manchester Repertory. He played the impresario Big Andy in the West End musical *Man of Magic*. In these early days Welland became a broadcaster, but it did not last, as he was fired for broadcasting the news without a tie. *'I actually remember Colin reading the news,'* says cartoonist Bill Tidy laughing, *'nobody could understand a word he said.'*

Welland first became a familiar face on British television when he landed the role of Constable David Graham, one of the original characters based at Newtown police station in the long-running police serial *Z Cars* in the 1960s. The series broke new ground, introducing a fresh realism to such cops-and-robbers shows and the regular stars all became household names. Welland stayed with the show for some time, as PC Bert Lynch's second partner on the beat, before eventually leaving for new pastures. He reappeared, together with other stars from the early years of the show, when the last episode was filmed in 1978.

'I came into the British film industry through television in the 1960s,' says, Welland. *'It was a wonderful education: I started on half-hour plays, moved to 50-minute plays, and ended up writing 90-minute plays, by which point I was fully equipped to write a movie.'*

Colin Welland is widely respected both as an actor and as a writer for television, the cinema, and the stage. Rotund and unfailingly good-humoured, he has given invaluable support in a range of plays and serials.

Thus established in television as a performer, Welland went on to appear in various plays and movies, often also contributing to the scripts (he was voted Best TV Playwright in Britain in 1970, 1973 and 1974). True to his Lancashire roots, his plays often had an earthy Northern humour and dealt with themes accessible to the working-class man in the street. He also enjoyed huge success as a writer for the cinema, notably with his screenplays for *Yanks* (1979), starring Richard Gere and for *Chariots of Fire* (1981), an Oscar-winning smash that was heralded (somewhat prematurely) as signalling a new golden era in British movie making. Welland himself picked up an Academy Award for Best Screenplay. As he delivered his acceptance speech, he told the ceremony guests, *'The British are coming.'*

Modestly, Colin commented on his most famous Oscar winning piece of work, *'Films are a high-risk investment, there can be fantastic rewards, both artistically and financially, but like the oil industry, you need to sink 12 wells in the hope that one will bubble up. Nobody knows what's going to make money.* Chariots of Fire *made money because it came out at just the right time: there had been the 1980 Moscow Olympics and people wanted something heroic again. At any other time, it might not have worked.'*

Among subsequent films that have garnered their share of praise have been *A Dry White Season* (1989), starring Donald Sutherland and Marlon Brando - a drama dwelling on the cruelties imposed by the policy of apartheid in South Africa (co-written with Euzhan Palcy), and *The War of the Buttons* (1994), another delve into the often dark and violent world of children. Also much admired was his appearances in such films as Willy Russell's *Dancin' through the Dark* (1990), which was set in familiar north-western territory, in the bars and clubs of Liverpool. Colin also penned *Twice in a Lifetime* in 1985 which starred, among others, Gene Hackman and had Sir Paul McCartney composing the score.

Perhaps the most memorable image from Welland's lengthy career as a television actor came in 1979, when he was one of a first-class cast that was chosen to appear in Dennis Potter's award-winning play *Blue Remembered Hills,* which recalled the long-lost days of his own childhood. In company with Helen Mirren, Michael Elphick, Colin Jeavons and John Bird, among others, all of whom were adults playing the roles of young children, Welland cavorted gleefully around woods and fields, his bulk grotesquely crammed into a pair of boy's shorts. Potter's brilliantly realised play, exposing the native cruelty beneath the outwardly innocent world of children, was hailed as a masterpiece and Welland himself, not for the first time in his distinguished career, was singled out for special praise.

Without doubt one of his most famous rolls was the kindly Mr Farthing. And one wonders how that mirrored his own career in teaching. I think Loach alighted more on the teaching experience he possessed rather than his acting skills. *'I was the only professional actor with a major role and initially I felt inhibited by my formal experience,'* says Welland, *'But I'd been a teacher for four years so I took to the role like a duck to water. The classroom scenes were filmed in an actual school so I spent a week beforehand teaching there to get to know the boys. Ken wanted people to be as natural as possible.'* A testament to his former occupation as a teacher was rewarded when many of the pupils insisted on finishing the assignment he had set them prior to filming. *'It helped considerably that I was surrounded by real kids and real people. It was a terrific experience. I look at the film now and remember it as if it was a part of actual events in my life.'*

In one of the classroom scenes, Welland's character asks Billy to regale to his class an account of how he trained the kestrel. *'The whole class was enthralled by Billy's story and their reactions were completely real,'* said Welland. *'It was completely unrehearsed. We were genuinely moved and that's what comes across. That's what makes the scene so vivid.'*

Welland and Loach, the director had filmed him in three episodes of *Z Cars,* as PC Graham, were friends and the pair lived near each other in the village of Barnes. *'Ken isn't the sort of bloke to cast you because you're a friend,'* said Welland. *'He cast me because I was what the character was. I had been a teacher in a secondary modern in Leigh, in Lancashire, exactly the same sort of school as the one in Kes. He would probably have cast me if I had not been an actor. I was so delighted to work with him again.'*

The marvellous performance given by Colin Welland was a cinematic treat and he well deserved his BAFTA for Best Supporting Actor. Loach knew and respected Welland and the feeling was mutual. The actor adored the way in which the director would try and elicit a performance. *'Ken was always trying to surprise the actors,'* says Colin. *'In the school assembly scene Ken had organised a real member of staff to pick a particular boy who had been coughing and drag him out of the room. At the last minute, Loach told the actor playing the headmaster to pick a completely different teacher who obviously chose the wrong child. So in the finished film, the unlucky boy was really protesting his innocence as he's dragged out into the hallway. There was a tremendous freshness about that scene.'*

Colin Welland has made his mark on British and American cinema and leaves a legacy of quality and passion. From walking the well heeled floors of *Z Cars*, through his many TV and movie roles, his screen writing career - the everlasting image I will have, was that he was the only friend Billy ever had. The playwright Wlilly Russell, an ex-teacher from Toxteth, said of his perfomance, *'He was wonderful in Kes. He was absolutely spot on.'*

If only one teacher understood the significance of such a powerful message, and changed their outlook, maybe there would be less Billy Caspers hitting the street. If the change will not come from above, as in the government, then it must come from within. I would like to think that Colin Welland, the former teacher, played himself in *Kes*. Maybe the movie industry's gain was the teaching professions loss?

The Location – The Barnsley Jewel

17

John Warrack, of the Telegraph wrote, *'Coming from Sheffield, near Barnsley, I am glad that this film was made there. To use such a location for a legend makes up for a lot. It was beautiful... I needed this film to tell me how much.'*

The first historical reference to Barnsley is in the Domesday Book of 1086, where it was referred to as *Berneslai*. The name has its roots in the Saxon word Berne, a barn or storehouse and Ley, meaning a field. Nearly a thousand years later it was to be the central location for a Hollywood funded movie.

While the film was being made the country had had been going through a type of revolution - summed up in a two-word phrase; The Sixties, which conjures-up a kaleidoscope of images - there's the pop music with Beatlemania and rag-trade London extravaganza called the Swinging Sixties baring the mini dress, and dope smoking hippies picking flowers and making love not war. Peace was in the air and you could hear the vibrations echoing around the planet, as the whole youth world tried to join the party. It was now 1968, as half the British inhabitancy was trying to recover from an eight year binge of sex, drugs and rock 'n' roll, while the other half had gone horse complaining about the noise. Ken Loach and his young film crew turned up at Barnsley to make a movie that was as far removed from the sixties scene as a passport photo booth was from photographer David Bailey!

Although Barry Hines went some way to place his central character, Billy Casper, in South Yorkshire – he was really only the builder. Ken Loach was the architect – he picked the site. Barnsley, with its world-renowned Royal 3lb chop, hostelries, linen industries, glass-making and of course coal-mining and the famous market; at one time the largest open-air market in the North of England – it was all going to be placed on the celluloid map. For a short while the world would be able to peek inside the life and times of the Barnsley people.

Before the film-folk descended on the town in the late sixties, Barnsley was a thriving industrial conurbation. Although the profitable Barnsley seam had dried up by the end of the 1940's, 24 other seams throughout Yorkshire gave Barnsley its most important industry. Less than twenty years later, hard on the heels of the 1984-85 Miners' Strike, the 16 pits left and 15,000 mineworkers were almost totally eradicated. By 1992 only two pits survived, Grimethorpe and Houghton Main, by the end of that year they too had been nominated for closure. The lights had gone out in Barnsley.

Ironically, 120 miles away in Wednesbury, I too became a victim of the Miners Strike. At around 1983 I was a coalman delivering coal to the Midlands. As coal became scarcer, my customers began to get cold feet, literally, and drifted towards manufactured ways of heating their homes.

I was very sad to let the business go. It was a care-free job, out in the fresh air. I worked with Albert Holland and Tom Hickinbottom, known as *Ode Tum*. I am momentarily transported back, sitting in the dilapidated weighbridge, cooking bacon on polished slack shovels. The fire was built up expertly by Jacko, who I had inherited when I bought the coal round. His former employer did not have the heart to let Jacko go and neither did I. So come cold winter morn or hot summer afternoon the banked-up fire blazed away in the corner of the room. We all sat and laughed, as we swapped bawdy tales and fascinating stories.

I can remember vividly, one frosty winter morning, with ice under foot, threatening to send us flying; together with a hundred weight of coal, sitting in the kitchen of Mrs Apphopkins. She was a lovely old lady, and had invited Albert and me into her modest house. As I was sipping tea and holding my plated mince pie, a large overweight Labrador sat drooling a few inches from my food. '*Is he hungry?*' I asked, with the dog not blinking, staring transfixed. '*Oh no,*' smiled the old lady, '*it's not that. You see you've got his plate!*'

During the sixties, Barnsley was a mining town first and foremost – keeping busy around a quarter of the town's population. But there were off-shoots from this such as glass making and engineering - all male dominated industries. A traditional Barnsley industry was linen weaving and so many women and girls were encouraged into garment making factories locally and in Huddersfield – unfortunately the industry fell, giving way to the lighter and cheaper articles manufactured in Ireland and Scotland. Lyons opened a huge bakery at Carlton (near St. Helen's School), which employed many girls, mothers and indeed men. Apart from a few Polish refugees comparatively few immigrants have moved into the area. Brewing was also important and the pickle factory in summer.

When I first arrived in Barnsley, apart from my recollections from the film, this was the first time I had seen the town in the flesh. I was struck, at first, by the beautiful countryside. I do not know what I was expecting - it was a naïve vision to assume the trees and grass would have been blackened by industry. The neat rows of miners' cottages dominated some streets and others gave way to new modern starter homes. I could tell changes were taking place in Barnsley – I wondered how much of the old was being destroyed and how many of the old were being left behind?

The town centre, in the sixties, consisted of 5 large open air markets – which were extremely popular, surrounded by shops and pubs. *'There were shops like Woolworth's, Marks & Spencer's and Littlewoods,'* says, Trevor Hesketh, a former teacher who appeared in *Kes*. *'One department store near the Town Hall was Butter Fields and Massies (now an Australian theme park). However the chief retailer was Barnsley British Co-operative Society which in its many shops and emporiums sold everything from can openers to food and lavish clothing.'* Virtually every family had a co-op number and a dividend was paid annually in June or July when it was used towards holidays in say, Blackpool or Scarborough.

Under Government boundary changes for a few years, Barnsley became capital of the new South Yorkshire County administration office blocks and a new Council Chamber were erected on two of the market sites - the outdoor market being moved to what is now a car park near the town centre. *'The building of a new indoors/semi indoor and market building with surrounding shops heralded the new era as a County town,'* comments Trevor.

All this changed again under further Government Boundary changes when the south Yorkshire Council was abolished and Barnsley, Rotherham and Doncaster became Metropolitan Boroughs. *'The West Riding County Council disappeared and the population of Barnsley grew to 250,000,'* explains Trevor, adding, *'by taking in surrounding townships (and moorland), which had been under the W.R.C.C. authority.'*

Entertainment was very important to the inhabitants of Barnsley. *'In the town centre, there was the Theatre Royal with variety shows, pantomimes and drama,'* reminisces Hesketh. *'There were three large cinemas - the Odeon, the Ritz and the Alhambra, now a shopping mall, plus the Pavilion and the Princess, the Globe and two flea-pit's the Britannic and the Electric. Only the Odeon remains today.'*

There were Working Men's Clubs and other drinking clubs all over. Families were encouraged to go to many of them; as most had Children's rooms.

It had been suggested to me by a few interested parties that *Kes* had a lot to answer for. Some believed it showed a vision of life in the late sixties and the rest of the world had not realised everyone in Barnsley had moved on. Playwright and screenwriter Willy Russell knew Barnsley well – then and now. *'I was around Barnsley for a long time,'* he explained, *'and the problems that Barnsley had (laughing), were nothing to do with Kes. Let's face it, it was due to a city, like Liverpool in a sense, there was no reason for it anymore. It was put there to meet the needs of an industrial age and then everything changed with the closure of the pits.'*

It was while I was discussing *Kes* with Willy Russell, that he mentioned a folk singer called Dave Burland. *'He's brilliant on Barnsley,'* enthused Willy, adding, *'his observations are really spot-on, he's a fantastic singer as well.'*

Willy was right. I chatted to Dave and time passed very quickly, as it often does when you and a stranger just click. *'Everybody talks about the Working Men's clubs in the North,'* says Burland, *'but Barnsley had a great scene in the sixties for folk music. It just suddenly evolved. It was mainly pubs that used to house the singers and it just grew from there. In the sixties, in Barnsley, you could play 26 nights a month.'* And Dave usually did. Dave Burland is one of the most respected performers on the British folk scene. He has also presented many programmes for Radio 2.

For Dave Burland, after leaving Holegate Grammar school, in Barnsley, the road to success was not straight forward, and he stopped off on the way to be a bank clerk. His former boss commented at the time, *'I'd quite like Burland if he didn't stop singing Danny Boy all the time.'* Dave said of his years crooning in those hallowed banker's halls, *'I was the world's worst bank clerk, yes I secured that title fairly convincingly, and then I became a policeman from 1960 to 1968.'*

To be a policeman anywhere during sixties Britain was quite an achievement. The culture, certainly around London, one of free love – most activities was against the establishment and their bastions; the police. The whole ethos of the sixties movement was one of booze, dope, freedom and easy living. Was Barnsley any different to any other town outside of London? *'My time as a policeman, I did feel separate, or me and my colleagues – you see it was a borough force. I think the whole strength of my force was 138 – to police the town itself. It was very parochial; it did mean you got to know everybody who was knocking about the town. It was tough – it was a tough town. It wasn't so much rough as rough and ready.'*

While London was swinging, Barnsley carried on and showed little interest with the new free society. Industry was booming and the lads and lasses hit the town, every night, to paint it red. It was busy and that meant work for the bobbies on the beat.' *I found the policing in and around Barnsley very interesting, I enjoyed it and it was informative and fairly instructive,'* explains, Dave. *'The relationship with the police and the public was much much better in those days. There was no revolt because you were on the beat. And I think that has been a huge mistake. I mean nobody really likes the police, but there wasn't the vehemence there appears to be today.'*

Burland handed in his uniform and the sixties were almost over. And so to was the insular nature of policing in Barnsley. *'I left and it all changed,'* explained Dave, *'they amalgamated with West Yorkshire and South Yorkshire. It just became one big force to cover the county.'*

For the next 31 years Burland performed all over the world, mainly in a solo capacity but with occasional forays into team handed music making. He was on the road, earning a living as a musician. Although his performing took him away from Barnsley, he remained a resident of his beloved town. *'When I walked the beat in the late sixties – and I look around today, I don't think Barnsley has changed all that much,'* comments, Dave. *'It has changed regards buildings and outlook, but the people are still the same. The loss of the mining industry was a crushing blow for the town. I think people are eventually getting over that – they're certainly coming out the other end. I do love my town, I mean I can see its short comings.'*

Like many Barnsley folk Dave is concerned about the recent ideas and extravagant talk over the plans for the town. *'The council are trying to dramatically change Barnsley. When the mining industry fell, they thought they had to show people that the town was not just decaying or dieing – which I don't think it is. There's a lot of entrepreneurial skills coming into the town now.'*

Life went on. On the films stifled release, in 1969, everything was normal in the town, as Trevor Hesketh explains, *'The annual Club trip was the highlight of the social year. Many entertainers did their training on the club circuit; several of the cast of* Kes *were club entertainers. Pubs were popular, although no food was served in those days, except for meat pies and sandwiches.'*

I missed out on the sixties, as I was born at the beginning, but purveying my favourite DVD's I see that nearly all my films were made during that period. *Billy Liar, The Loneliness of the Long Distance Runner, A Taste of Honey, Girl With Green Eyes, Saturday Night Sunday Morning, The Family Way, Two Way Stretch, Whistle Down the Wind* and yes, *Kes* of course; and the list goes on. In fact they were nearly all predominantly black and white. I even got to the stage where I would only watch films that had no colour. To my shame I even watched certain movies that were shot in beautiful Technicolor and I used to manually turn off the colour on my TV. This was not as the director envisioned his tour de force. I can safely say I am now cured of such purist forms of sentimentality. Although Ken Loach always wanted his masterpiece, *Kes*, filmed in black and white, United Artists flatly refused to do so. I am very happy, although washed out and de-saturated, with the colour of *Kes*.

The main location for *Kes* was St Helen's school, which opened in September 1963. Trevor Hesketh was appointed Head of English Department in January 1964. *'The previous occupant only stayed one term as he had already got a job waiting for him abroad!'* laughs Trevor.

In the post-war years Barnsley Council concentrated on building Housing Estates to accommodate families from the central area of town. These estates sprawled on the outer edges of the borough. Trevor states, *'One such estate was Athersley. Such a huge area required several primary schools and two secondary schools, vis Edward Sheerien School in Athersley North and St Helen's Schools in Athersley South and a special school for Disabled children in the same road as St Helen's.'*

St Helen's was a Community School with strict boundaries including Athersley south, Smithies and Carlton (a small village) plus the area known as *Klondyke*. *'Similarly Edward Sheerien school had its own boundaries and therefore the two schools were quite separate and a degree of rivalry existed between the two,'* explains the former teacher.

Selecting the best pupils, like sorting out a cutlery draw, the silver spoons and the most shiny knives and folks were picked out first. *'Barnsley had a generous policy of creaming its more able pupils, based on the eleven plus exam,'* says Trevor. *'The brightest went to Barnsley Grammar School for Boys or to the Barnsley Girls High School, both schools took in W.R.C.C. pupils as well. The next layer of cream was divided equally between Mark St Central School and Longcar Central School; both mixed sexes - whose academic achievements were very good.'*

Further down the barrel, getting towards what the educational system was rapidly labelling dregs, were the so-called failures. *'The remainder went to Secondary Modern Schools,'* explains Trevor, *'some of which were mixed sexes, but at the age of 13, there was a further streaming when suitable brighter pupils, sometimes called Late Developers, went to a new school in a Rectory called the Technical School - not to be confused with the Mining and Technical College which had been built in the 1930's.'* So there it was, a few no-hopers rattling about in a cesspit put together by the government. The system had failed them and they only had a dangerous job down the pit or some unskilled boring job with long hours and short wages.

So, what did one do with the apparent rejects that remained at the secondary modern schools? At St Helen's at least the facilities were extensive. *'Mixed sexes were the norm, formal teaching in classes of 30 and 40, sitting in rows at individual or dual desks was the usual,'* comments Trevor. *'The School was spacious, and had many features including an indoor swimming pool, which was shared with local schools, Youth Club, an extensive area for Practical Subjects, a good Gymnasium, School Hall with stage, Science Labs and many large airy classrooms.'*
St Helens housed an attractive library with beautiful oak shelves, but sadly hardly any books, and a dining room with kitchens. The only thing lacking was sufficient office accommodation.

At this stage the school leaving age was 15 and some pupils opted in later years to stay on an extra year to take public exams such as C.S.E. *'In English we entered some students to take G.C.S.E, in which coursework counted as much as exams.'*

Subjects taught in school were English, Maths, Religious Education (compulsory by law), Geography, History, Sciences (Physics, Chemistry, Biology), Music, Art, Needlework (girls), House craft (girls), Woodwork (boys), Metalwork, Technical Drawing (boys) and P.E & Games (separate sexes). *'There were peripatetic teachers for instrumental music, remember this was a brass band area,'* informs Trevor. *'Shorthand & typing was taught at Barnsley Technical College for - suitable girls.'*

It appears the day to day workings of St Helen's was a blue-print for the films central structure. *'There was a daily school assembly – prayers, bible reading, hymn, short address and notices not unlike the assembly in* Kes,' laughs, Trevor.

There was a school uniform but it was not compulsory. Many parents could not afford it. It was chiefly worn by the girls – a brown skirt with a yellow blouse – boys were the usual grey trousers with white shirt, girls of course did not wear trousers.

School discipline was good, in general. Punishment was either by lines, detention or extra work. *'Punishment was used as the ultimate sanction,'* says Trevor, seriously. *'It was only administerd by the headmaster or his female deputy. This was then recorded in the punishment book,* which would be shown to Governors or inspectors etc. Chief offences were smoking, petty theft and arguments.'

The school in the film did dwell on the more unruly pupils. After all this was drama, being played out with real people in a real school. Although the join in most cases was almost invisible, this was after all a movie. 'Attendance for St Helen's was on the whole good,' smiles Trevor. 'There was a certain amount of truancy, whereby, say, an older girl had to stay at home to look after a sick child, because the parents were both out working. Teenage pregnancies were almost unheard of - only two in my 20 years at the school. Drugs! – never heard of them!'

'The School attendance officers were very helpful and understanding and a local police liaison officer was a marvellous man – knowing the families of the area.'

The youth club was popular with pupils in the evenings and the school was used for adult education. There was a dearth of books until money became available in later years to gradually stock up with library books and textbooks.

Trevor Hesketh was very much in the mould of Hines's kindly Mr Fathing, who is the only teacher to be-friend Billy Casper. 'In order to combat the sense of failure among many of the pupils,' explained Trevor, 'one had to discover their particular interests.'

'Sport was of great importance. The headmaster, Clarence Hirst, was secretary of the English Schools FA and had long been associated with Barnsley Boys, a highly successful school's soccer team. The school had an annual trip to Wembley to see England Boys play. School excursions were very popular, as were trips aboard.'

The famous pantomimes had long since carried a professionalism that was only witnessed at legitimate theatres throughout the country. The idea of the annual school pantomime started as a school project, which involved virtually every department of the school. The cast always included members of staff and pupils of all ages. Trevor Hesketh was a major part of the performances, treading the boards along side many of the future *Kes* stars, including David Bradley – the young talented lad, born to play Billy Casper. 'Scripts were usually hired although at least one was written by a member of staff,' says Hesketh. 'Most rehearsals were at lunchtime or after school, but a few non-participating members of staff complained when final rehearsals had to be in lesson time. Pupils studied the law relating to licences, seating and aisles. Parents became involved and every pantomime was a huge success, playing to packed houses.'

Looking back all those years, reflecting on all the ups and downs of school life, the former teacher can feel contented at the whole experience. *'Altogether, St. Helen's was a caring, very happy school,'* confirms Trevor. *'In my opinion, it was a big mistake for the authority to close down Edward Sheerien School and to rename St. Helens as Edward Sheerien, when they combined.'*

St Helen's most famous pupil Dai Bradley had his own fears about his home town. Dai thinks Barnsley has changed tremendously in the intervening years. *'I saw on the BBC's* Look North *programme a few days ago that communities are still struggling to get over the demise of the coal mining industry,'* commented Bradley recently, *'The centre of Barnsley has changed since I was a boy. We had a wonderful open-air market but that's now partly indoors, and I hear if this new architectural plan of linking Liverpool with Hull goes ahead the architect wants to convert Barnsley into a Tuscan town. That could be quite interesting. I wish it would do more to cling on to its past, to clean up the old buildings because the modern ones have no character. I'm hoping the Council will retain the history of my home town but I'm not sure that it will.'*

I found this chapter hardest to write, like painting a familiar scene with my eyes closed. I was not from Barnsley, and had moved around a lot in my career to become a writer, and somewhere I lost my roots – an official identity. In a way I envied the people of Barnsley, who had gone through so much, and had given so much, but through all their hardship nearly all had remained faithful to their birth place. I did feel I had the instincts of the salmon, but I had reached two weirs and I was not sure of which one to choose. The challenge was on, and researching the book, I learnt much about people and more importantly, I learned a good deal about myself.

So the scene was set. A slice of Barnsley in the sixties – a version that was told to me. I am sure I could have spoke to others and written a different story – we all have views that differ from our fellow Man. It was essential, in my mind, to converse with people who loved Barnsley for what it was.

My wonderful journey was well under way, it had taken me into the homes of my heroes. The real people of Barnsley had been willing to adopt me for a time while I was writing my book. They gave me the benefit of the doubt, and I hope I have not let them down.

I have given the last words to this book to the leader of Barnsley Council, Steve Houghton, so he could offer his vision of the developing Borough. I thought it only right to give some words to the Barnsley people, well person – but he is passionate about his home town. He is a rounded individual with honesty, integrity, talent and most importantly – humour. Dave Burland expressed his fears for the new town most succinctly. '*I think it's bloody ludicrous. I don't officially go round trumpeting the fact – but it just seems totally bizarre to me. They talk about the wow factor and lasers in the sky?*' laughing, Dave adds thoughtfully, '*my, I've been wrong on things before.*'

18

A Wet Summer in Barnsley 1968

The scene is the colliery town of Barnsley – shades of D. H. Lawrence, the mood from the start is powerful – all the images submerging the mind in Billy's scruffy, oppressed, insignificant little life.

That summer in South Yorkshire was remembered by all those who took part with incredible affection, despite the fact that it was one of the wettest in living memory.

With the adaptation of *A Kestrel for a Knave*, Loach began a pre-production process that he would follow in all subsequent work. *'Barry showed us the places we had imagined in the book, including the school he had taught at,'* reminisces Loach.

These historic places include Old Hall Farm; which was re-named Monastery Farm where Billy took the chic from the nest, St Helen's County Secondary School (now Edward Sheerien School), Carlton Road, Athersley South where Billy went to school. This was also Dai Bradley's school. Loach found a retired miner's house on Hoyland Common estate and this was used as Billy's family house, although a pre-fabricated structure was used for most of the downstairs interior shots. It was Fitzwilliam Street where the butchers van scene was shot. The Rockingham and Skiers Spring collieries at nearby Birdwell were used for relevant pit scenes. A field near Hines's Hoyland Common home was used when Billy flies the bird. This was also the place where Richard Hines's used to fly his kestrel in the early days – the basis for the book. It was also the site Bradley would train to fly the kestrels after he had finished the day's filming.

The Cudworth Hotel is where Billy's mother and brother enjoy a night out. The hotel is now called The Dards and is run by David Glover – who played Tibbutt in the film; the other captain opposed to Mr Sugden. The Library in the film was Barnsley Civic Library, which Billy tries to join (Zoë Sunderland who played the librarian worked there). Clayton's Betting Shop in Lundwood was filmed where Billy failed to place a bet for his brother. And it was Savage's fish-and-chip shop in Hoyland Common, where he spends the betting money. It is Barnsley market where he walks the kestrel on his wrist. The James Miles Bookshop, in Leeds, is where we saw Billy steal the book on falconry.

Although all the school scenes were shot at St Helen's, Loach scoured three schools in the Barnsley area, including St Helen's, to find his Billy Casper and cast other child and teacher roles. The others were Raley and Longcar School – the latter where Hines (he also taught at St Helen's) and Brian Glover taught.

One farmer, a tenant of a field between Hoyland Common and Wentworth Station, was driving past his land when he noticed a crowd of about 8 people in his field – which he used for grazing although there was no livestock in it at that time. *'I was going passed and I saw this party of people in my field. As I opened the gate and walked over a bloke come across to meet me. I said "what the hell are you lot doing – this is my land?" He said they were making a film called* Kes. *At that he reached into his pocket and fished out five pounds. I studied it for a second and said, "carry on" and left shutting the gate behind me.'*

19

The Ensemble – The Soldiers

Most of the main cast, support cast and extras all played out their lives on screen. Pupil friendships, professional vocations and family circumstances, in the whole, perfectly balanced and blended realism with drama. Although a lot of this heightened reality was due to production foresight, inspired casting and bold direction, none of the fresh actors let the crew down. The film was forever going to be a snapshot of their lives. Some even reviewed the experience as if it actually happened, others could stand back, at a later date, and see what they were and also realise what they had become. For some it was a life changing experience.

On my forty-third birthday, recently, I decided to take my partner and family to Carding Mill Valley, Church Stretton, nestling in the valley between the Long Mynd and Wenlock Edge. I had last been there exactly 35 years ago, to the very day. It was 1970 and obscurely the time *Kes* was having difficulty securing a national release.

Oliver, Goldie and our young daughter, Summer, were building an inadequate dam along one of the many minute tributaries that spider down from the mountains. It was the very place the old white mini bus, my granddad chauffeuring, had pulled up all those years ago. Around ten of my friends from Haden Hill School had got out – and we all joined in - playing pinball hockey, worrying sheep and harping on about the picnic.

From a slight incline I stood silently imagining the scenario develop – the mini-bus chuntering up and stopping close to the stream. My silence was noted by Gabby and she commented on it. I told her I would have given anything to go back three and a half decades and see myself playing in the fresh water with all my friends. Being the birthday boy, happy to be the centre of attention, fooling around with my pals – a mixture of young minds I get on with and the cool trendy ones, or tough ones, I want to get along with. If I was granted that wish, to go back in time, for a second I promised I would not approach my younger vision. And then again if I did breakaway – what on earth would I say to my younger self – any pearls of wisdom would be wasted on an immature mind – I eventually settled for – *you're going to all right, until your forty-three anyway.* It would have made no sense and have probably sent me spinning towards a life-time of therapy. An hour later, video camera in hand, zooming in on Summer's dam building, I suddenly realised she would have the opportunity to review her life 35 years on. Of course she could not communicate anything, but I thought that was probably a good thing.

Although a slightly twisted version of events, the people involved in *Kes* could also review their lives, in preflashed de-saturated Technicolor. Fame can be an unusual drug, which can expand egos and deflate reality. The people of Barnsley took a bow and retreated into the wings to carry on as normal, well before the adulation and applause died down. For that strength of character I salute everyone who enjoyed the experience for what it was and congratulate the ones who drew and grew from the experience.

Bob (Robert) Naylor - *McDowell (the bully)*

It was a great performance; the overbearing bully, the aggressive scowls, the threatening postures, almost like watching a lion stalk a group of underfed lambs, all played effortlessly by Bob Naylor. A sort of Yorkshire Flashman from *Tom Brown's School Days*. Everyone, at some time, had felt that certain type of fear, the cold sweat running down their necks, the rapid heartbeat, as the bully, every school has at least one, entered an unsupervised classroom or playground.

Bob, together with his friend Michael Joyce was from Longcar School. The boys were from the fifth form; some of the near-by schools did not have one. This made Naylor a late fifteen, as opposed to the other cast kids who were fourteen, appear larger than life. The older boys, who were officially aloud to work full time, were on higher wages of £5 a day instead of £3 – amazingly Bob was just paid as an extra. This age difference also helped the story along – as Naylor playing McDowell was bigger than most of the other pupils – with the lean menace and frame of a rabid whippet.

'*They actually wanted the school bully from our school to play McDowell, but he wouldn't do it, I don't remember why,*' laughs Bob, adding,' *it was Barry Hines and Brian Glover who asked me to go up to the Queen's and audition for the part. It was the fight scene, I think I had to improvise – we just had to ad-lib the initial confrontation.*'

For someone who had never trod the boards, whether school pantomimes or amateur dramatics, one would assume that a hectic movie set would be quite nerve-racking and daunting. *'I never really felt nervous as such,'* explains Naylor, *'it was after all a school environment – a territory I was very familiar with. It made it easier for you to believe that these things were happening and you were really just attending school. It's like the young lad (Martin Harley) who gets the cane in the headmaster's study – when he was getting a good telling off, getting the stick – he totally believed it! When he started crying, started to get going, Ken just said keep rolling.'*

It seemed incredible that someone who had a substantial support role, McDowell shared many scenes with Casper, Naylor should not only be classed and extra, but also paid accordingly. *'We were just young and daft back then,'* comments Bob, dryly, adding, *'I'd never done any acting before or since. I wished I'd taken it up at the time. I mean Brian Glover got into it, but I think he secured an agent quite early on or was approached. Kes was a great springboard. I was that young, I didn't realise the opportunities – but I really enjoyed it. It was fantastic. And I think there was a niche for actors with Yorkshire accents.'*

Dai Bradley aside, a few took the plunge into the world of acting, most notably Freddie Fletcher, Brian Glover and of course Lynne Perrie. The two, I believe, who should have given drama a go was David Glover (Tibbutt) and Bob Naylor. *'I often wondered what would have happened if I had pursued it – I should have really taken some advise about it – I could have been the next Bruce Willis!'* laughs Bob.

McDowell, with his obvious contrast to the weedy frame and pinched face of Casper, seemed to encapsulate the fear of the playground bully. He prowled his space arrogantly making every corner of his domain feel his presence. The hangers on obeying his wish, fearful of his reputation. His physique was natural, a prowess and muscle definition that was genetically produced, rather than some artificial health centre with bevelled mirrors, exotic plants and under floor heating. McDowell was fit – which was due, one feels, to running around playing football and fighting, rather than jogging and drinking fresh goats milk.

It must have been very difficult at times to decipher between real life and the make-believe existence of a movie set. *'Brian Glover used to be my games teacher, and although everyone goes on about the football match – he was exactly like that when he took PE with us,'* laughs Naylor. *'In the film Sugden picks Padgett first to be on his team because he's the best player. But in real life, at Longcar, Mike Padgett was the best player and Brian would always pick him first.'*

Brian Glover not only played great characters in his busy career as an actor, but was himself a great character. These vignettes of Glover's life show what a wonderful sense of humour he had. We know from others how inspirational he was – but he was also a winner that wanted to win. *'I remember, before Kes, he bought these special Adidas ice-white trainer's – they had just come out,'* comments Bob. *'Brian was saying, before the match, hey boys look at these, aren't they fantastic? We'd all got scrag-out plimsolls on. As we were playing everyone was trying to tackle Brian and scuff his new shoes – it was all in good part. And you could never bowl him out at Cricket either, he would be batting and also be the umpire. If you were lucky enough to hit the wickets he used to shout no-ball! So it didn't count.'*

After shooting had been completed, some members were taken to a sound studio in London to re-dub their voices on the soundtrack. It was assumed no one outside Yorkshire would understand the Barnsley accent.

Ken Loach and Tony Garnett adopted the cast of youngsters and almost became their surrogate parents, *'I remember about half a dozen of us watching the Cup Final on the TV in Tony's flat,'* says Naylor, *'He'd gone to Wembley to watch the game so we raided the drinks cupboard.'*

Bob, who is married with three daughters; an eighteen-year-old and twin sixteen-year olds, lives at Mapplewell. Although Bob left school in the middle of his A-levels, the daughters are making up for lost time. *'The twins, Stephanie and Lindsey are doing great, both of them got 10 G.C.S.E's apiece and the eldest, Nichola, has just got 4 A-levels – grade A's in biology, physics and Chemistry and B in Maths , she's studying Physics and Astrophysics at Sheffield University, so I've been really blessed,'* says Bob proudly, adding, *'and they all love Kes.'*

Bob Naylor spent more than three years travelling to pubs all over Yorkshire testing beer pumps for the brewers Whitbread. After studying analytical biology at college in Sheffield, he worked at the brewery's laboratories.

Over 20 years ago, Bob went to work at Manor Bakeries at Carlton, where he met his wife Jackie. He is shift manager there. *'They make my life hell at work whenever Kes is shown on the telly,'* explains Bob. *'The first time it was on, a packed canteen gave me a standing ovation when I walked in. I got so sick of having the mickey taken out of me that I told people I get £200 in royalties every time it is on TV – just to wind them up further and get my own back. I let that go for about eight year before I told them it wasn't true.'*

David Glover – *Tibbutt*

I personally think, as previously mentioned, there were plenty of personal bests during *Kes*; but without doubt Tibbutt was another wonderfully naturalistic performance – without the cosseting of the main stars. It was almost to the point of non-acting, as if we see the person and the character synchronised. To a point I can see this happening on stage, where a performer can get in to his or her part and build a performance, with only a couple of breaks, over a three-hour period. But a film set is totally different, within a few feet of the actors (although Ken's team is further back than most), in the early stages at least, there is a bunch of strangers - professional crew, who are usually familiar colleagues. The constant stop - start, keep reminding the performer he is in a totally alien situation. The stress of all your peers wanting a wrap. Through all of these unnerving distractions, David Glover delivers one of the great unselfish character parts of the sixties. A rich time for raw, naturalistic, unleashed talent – it could have easily been Tom Courtney. The fact that within a year, before the film was even released nationally, David chose a completely different career rout. A testament to his strong will and resourceful nature.

Even by his own admission, David Glover was a mouthy fourteen-year-old who was good at football, and was a natural for the role of Tibbutt - the loudmouth classmate of Billy Casper.

He was living in Smithies and was a pupil at St Helen's Secondary Modern where many of the school scenes were filmed. He auditioned for the role of Tibbutt at the Queens Hotel.

'Barry Hines and Ken Loach visited a number of Barnsley schools looking for youngsters to take part in the film,' remembers Glover. *'I was asked to go to the head's office, auditioned and got the part.'*

The scenes in and around the school were shot during the six-week summer holiday in 1968. Because the majority of the cast had no experience of the techniques of acting – they were encouraged to go with the flow and the crew would work around them and catch the action. David recalls, *'Lines spoken by youngsters in the class room were written on the blackboard.'*

The famous football scene in which Tibbutt was captain of Spurs against Mr Sugden's (Brian Glover; no relation) Manchester United – actually took a few days to shoot.

One of the greatest exchanges takes place when Sugden shoulders Tibbutt violently to the ground during an illegal tackle. Tibbutt picks himself up and, before he can stop himself, shouts: *'The fat twat, he want's bleedin' milkin.'* Sugden sends Tibbutt off, admonishing:

'We'll play this game like gentleman.' On his walk of shame to get an early bath, Tibbutt says to himself, 'big fat bastard.' In a final show of defiance he rams up a two finger salute. This became a catch phrase for other pupils who had seen the film. No-one can be sure how much detention that moment spurned; but I would think quite a lot.

Vaughan Allen, from The Big Issue, painted a particular *Kes* memory spawned from this display of rebelliousness, *'One of the happiest of my school memories is the day the Head was driven from the playground by united ranks of kids. Half way through a typically listless homily, someone raised two fingers in the traditional British V-sign. Then another, and another, until the whole class stood before him fingers up-raised. Of course, we were made to suffer. But no one doubted that for a few moments we had broken free of the rules. We had won a small battle in the never-ending war of school life.'* *Kes* had been shown to the class the day before. *'The iconic image of Tibbutt, sent off in the famous football match impressed us all.'*

In 1969, less than a year after the film was made; and yet to secure a circuit release date, David Glover ventured somewhere Billy Casper would never have trod, he became a miner at Dodworth Colliery. He left the pit in 1986 and is now a licensee of The Cudworth pub, renamed The Dards – ironically where some of the scenes from *Kes* were shot. This saw Billy's mom and his brother, Jud; boozing; enjoying their night out.

Zoë Sunderland – *Librarian*

True to form, when Ken Loach wanted to shoot the library scene in his film he turned up at Barnsley Civic Library and asked three librarians to test for the role. He also booked the library for the scene – although the authorities insisted it was to remain open throughout the shoot. The girls who were selected for the audition were asked to deal with an obtuse member of the library and act natural – as if they were dealing with someone off the street. One of the crew took the customer's part and Zoë Sunderland and two other girls were selected.

Strangely enough, unlike the other two girls – both had worked there some time, Sunderland had only been working there for a couple of months – fresh back from working in Canada for the Bell Telephone Company – she was just 22 years-old.

'I can't really remember much about the audition,' says Zoë, *'I know I had to pretend to deal with an awkward customer.'* Sunderland must have

impressed the team as they offered her the part there and then.

'It was at least a couple of weeks before they returned to film the scene – I'd just come back from Ireland. It was incredible to see all the equipment, lights and everything and all the crew. I remember thinking how long are they going to take – I had no script but I knew it was quite a short scene – but outside was this cobbled back yard and when I went out the back there was a huge tuck wagon. I couldn't believe all this was happening just to film David Bradley and me – who I had not met until that day. I was a little nervous but not as much as I thought – I was just really excited.'

In Barry Hines's novel, *A Kestrel for a Knave*, the extended library scene is quite simple and may have been over stretched if the actual printed words had been used in the film. Loach decided, with the help of Garnett and Hines, to give the two actors a rough guide and leave them to improvise. It is an important scene as it shows Casper in an unnatural environment, but it proves the lengths he realises he has to go to, to obtain the skill to train the kestrel. Also, when he is faced with bureaucracy and red tape and cannot get his book, he solves the problem by going out and stealing the volume.

'I'm not sure what they told Bradley, but they gave me a rough idea what to say – things to mention. The library was open at the time – and we were using a corner of it. An old woman came up to the counter and stood listening to our dialogue, with Bradley trying desperately to become a member. It was incredible, she didn't realise they were filming us – with lights, cameraman, technicians, crew, mics and everything pointed at us. Bradley just carried on and so did I. Eventually the woman butted in and started having a go at David – really laying into him for being so rude and sticking up for me.' At one time this was the scene Loach was going to use. He knew that you could not improve on reality – filming someone who had no idea they were being filmed. Unfortunately, the scenario did not quite fit and it hit the cutting room floor.

Bradley and Sunderland were in good company. It is very rare on a hot set for a *stranger* to wonder into shot. The very nature of the business usually guards against any un-credited bodies or erroneous noises to affect the wrap. As time passes, as more sets are created, more money at stake to totally take over a location, it will become less frequent.

There was another such rare incident when Blake Edwards was filming in Austria. It was one of the famous Pink Panthers and Graham Stark was playing one of his many memorable snivelling, grovelling parts – as a concierge of a hotel, a very established hotel, that refused the Panther team exclusivity. Like Barnsley Civic Library the hotel would only allow the director a limited use of certain areas. Then, just before filming started, Blake Edwards had a master stroke. He thought it might be a great gag to have Stark made up like Adolph Hitler – the concierge uniform he was wearing was already very close to a German storm trooper. Unfortunately, and Stark knew it, with the talented make-up artist fixing the hair and adding the infamous moustache – he looked more like Hitler than Chaplin ever did. There was no comedy in it – it was in fact macabre - and the first words out of the make-up artists mouth was, *'bloody hell, Graham.'* Even Blake, as Stark made his way from the sweeping staircase had to admit that an icily frisson ran up and down his spine. Although the veteran director realised he could not squeeze any humour out of what was turning rapidly into a sick joke.

Stark had been made up, Sellers was on set, they had booked the reception for a couple of hours filming and Blake decided to roll and see what happens. Of course it was impossible – with a man like Sellers staring into Hitler's eyes, his best friend Stark, and trying to deliver queued lines without corpsing, was impossible.

Eventually time had beaten the director, with nothing in the can, and the hotel reverted back to normal service. With Sellers standing at the side of the counter observing all and the chilling figure of Stark dressed and looking exactly like Hitler an old lady (why are they always old ladies?) shuffled up to the reception and asked Stark for her room key. After finding the key and handing it to her the woman stared into the face of what she thought was the concierge. She did not speak and took the key in deep thought without realising what was terribly wrong. She walked off towards the lift and then turned back, as if hoping everything was back to normal – it wasn't – Stark stared back. Shaking her head she disappeared into the lift. Both Stark and Sellers looked at each other and joined the cast and crew in helpless laughter.

The library scene was in the can and the crew packed up their gear and departed. *'I got paid £15, and then they all went.'* remarks Zoë, adding, *'The next thing I had from them was an invitation to the world premier.'* The opening of Barnsley's own film as was written on the official invitation, was on Sunday March 29th 1970 (7.30pm) at the ABC Cinema, Peel Street, Barnsley. Each ticket admitted two and the dress was formal.

'I didn't actually go to the premier,' giggles Zoë, *'I was just so embarrassed. I thought I'd made an absolute idiot of myself and decided not to go. Afterwards people were coming up to me and recognising me*

from the film – and I'd never seen it! A few years later I did watch the film, it was on television, but I had to leave the room, as I was about to come on. Finally, last year, nearly thirty-five years later, I watched my bit. I felt very uncomfortable – I thought I kept looking at the camera.'

It is great banter between the two actors – all very natural. The comedy builds throughout the scene – with Bradley as the comic and Sunderland the stooge. It is one of the scenes, after the football match, which most people remember and quote.

Roy Turner – Good footballer

On the first day of filming Colin Welland's former occupation as a teacher was required rather than his acting skills. Three boys from Raley school were sitting in a row – George Speed, Roy Turner and Stephen Crossland. *'We were all very excited about Colin Welland being in the film,'* recalls Turner. *'We were all Z Car fans and we waited patiently for him to enter. As he walked into the room, I can't remember who started off, but we all chorused the theme music to the show. Colin spun round and leant over us menacingly and said, "I've finished with all that now. Do it again and you'll be out of here." We only meant it as a joke and thought he would laugh – we were cheeky young kids.'*

One of the most natural players on the football field playing for Spurs, in the important fifth round cup-tie at Old Trafford, was Roy Turner. It was Roy, the thin lad wearing the orange football top and the distinctive number three on his shorts, *'I was very proud of those shorts,'* remembers, Turner, *'we had been watching Celtic play and they had these numbers on their shorts – I had not seen it before. We were playing an important school match and we all had our numbers sown on. Unfortunately I had a pair ruined during the shoot. We had been cadging cigarettes off all the crew. We particularly hit Chris Menges, the cameraman, very hard. He smoked these great foreign smokes – French I think. We pestered him that much that the day before the football scene he bought a bag full of cigarettes and gave them to us. It was really cold when we were playing and there was a lot of standing around waiting. I had put a packet of cigarettes and matches in my back pocket of my shorts. Speed I think it was, ran over and did this incredible sliding tackle that was not in the script. Of course I fell on my backside with a thud and the matches ignited. There was a bang and my shorts were on fire emitting puffs of yellow smoke. The camera wasn't running, but all who saw it said it would have been great in the finished film.'*

There was one scene that the director insisted on getting right. He was having problems as the scene relied on a couple of actors hitting their marks in a complicated bit of business. The script required a player to dribble the ball from the centre half, in between three players and then shoot. The ball hits the right hand side of the woodwork as Casper inexpertly dives to his left. The shot then ricochets back and another player strikes the ball towards the goal, Casper recovers and dives athletically but fails to save it. Manchester United 0 Spurs 1.

The main difficulty was getting the first player to hit the cross bar, from about 10 feet. Loach had tried a few players before giving Turner a trial. *'On my very first attempt I did it.'* comments Turner, proudly. *'Bradley dived left then right and the other lad followed up with a goal. The director then wanted another one just to make sure. It took another 33 takes before I did it again and everybody hit their marks.'* The actual shot used was an amalgamation of two takes filmed. It is worth noting that the lad who actually scored was wearing an Aston Villa top - Tony Garnett, the producer, has been a life long supporter of the club.

Our intrepid hero was not finished there as the action cuts again to Turner, his gliding, graceful movements expertly steering the ball past eight sliding tackling bodies. The round pink face of the games master; Sugden, blowing heavy in the background, as he watches Turner shoot the ball through a diving Casper's legs. Jim Ryder informs the deflated Sugden that Spurs are in the sixth round of the cup. Sugden replies, *'Sixth round – I'll give you six of the best!'* Glorious stuff.

John Grayson – *Jud's best friend*

Grimethorpe Youth Club Centre was where John Grayson; assistant youth leader and Freddie Fletcher used to go. Mr Hitchin who used to run it was a personal friend of Barry Hines. Tony Garnett, together with Hines's turned up one evening, in mid session, to see if they could find anyone for their film. The two men Grayson and Fletcher – who were best friends, were asked to read for their particular parts – they must have natural Yorkshire accents. As it turned out, with art imitating nature, they were to play best friends on screen. *'I was only in a couple of scenes, at the Cudsworth Arms, enjoying the night out with Jud and also at the pit. He was just coming to work and I was just leaving. My first line was "'Ah-up, Jud, ow you goin?"' which was ironic really because I had to go all the way to London to re-dub it. It turned out that the overseas market couldn't understand that and I* replaced it with '"Ah-up Jud, 'ow you doin?'.

'It was an amazing time in London – at Elstree Studios, where we did the re-dub, we watched them making a film at the studios with Ringo Starr (The Magic Christian 1970). We then went back to the Millstone Hotel, Kensington High Street. I remember the name because I have an ashtray from the hotel bar!' That night, the ensemble had actually finished re-dubbing in one afternoon, everyone stopped at the Hotel. 'The next day we stopped at Tony Garnett's house. It was cup final day and Tony had gone to watch the match – which was actually a few streets away at Wembley. We watched the game on a huge colour television, at that time the biggest I had ever seen. I opened the window and I was watching the telly but listening to the roar of the crowd from the actual match.' The match was between Leicester and Manchester City. The date was Saturday 26th April 1969. The final whistle went and it was Manchester City 1 and Leicester City 0. John remembers the trip back home on the train. 'Going back north late on Saturday afternoon – the train was packed. I wasn't really a football fan, but to see all these Manchester City supporters celebrating their F.A. Cup win - it was amazing. They had loads of drink and food and we all joined in. If Leicester City had won it might have been a different story.'

Michael Joyce – McDowell's friend

Michael Joyce was sitting behind Casper and next to his screen best friend, McDowell when the other boys returned from getting the cane. 'It took some time to shoot the classroom scene,' remembers, Joyce, 'we were in there for about 12 hours at a time. We lost a few hours due to torrential rain – it shorted some arc lights outside they were using to create a summer feel.' It was actually late summer, but the rain and cold turned many sets to middle winter. 'We had one day where the sun was really shinning, we were filming inside the classroom and the director said we could all go home as they were going to shoot Bradley's scene in the woods. I got my money for the day and I was back in Barnsley town centre by 9.30am. I was paid five quid a day, I was 16. Me and Naylor were both mates from Longcar School, in their fifth form – so we were older than the other kids. They only got three pound a day because they were 14 and 15.'

Loach was happy to have art imitating nature when the real school bully from Longcar was ear-marked for the part of McDowell. When he turned down the part, Rob Naylor stepped forward. His friend, Joyce, was quick to set the record straight. 'He (Bob Naylor) could fight, but he never picked fights. He wasn't a bully in real life – nor do I think he was the toughest lad in the school, but he could look after himself. He wasn't cock of the estate, but he was 3rd or 4th so he could fight.'

One scene Joyce was glad the particular piece of film died in the editing suite. 'It was bitterly cold when we did the football scene with Mr Sugden, which was strange because Brian Glover was my teacher in real life. We had to keep starting and stopping and the cold would get you. One shot where someone had to tackle another, tall thin lad, but not get the ball off them and then shoot and hit the cross bar – it took about 30 takes. Anyway, I got caught short and when I turned round the camera was on me. Luckily it was a ruined take due to the striker missing his spot, otherwise the obligatory shot of the back of my head would have been in the final cut.'

Again, amongst this intimate cast of teachers and pupils – the author Hines used to teach Joyce. 'I was quite good at English and Barry Hines had invited me along to the audition at the Queen's. Actually I wrote an essay and mentioned the bit about coughing in assembly, which was used in the film. But Barry probably had read thousands of essays and was bound to use the odd thing.'

The family atmosphere not only existed between the cast and crew, but often the family would swell due to a friend or wife of a crew member. Chris Menges, the cinematographer, had bought his girlfriend along. 'I remember one day Chris Menges was setting up a shot and there was a girl with him and a kid, obviously his. I asked Barry Hines, who was sitting next to me, if that was his wife? Barry said it wasn't - they weren't married and I must have made some comment or looked surprised – it was 1968. Barry turned to me and said, "illegitimacy doesn't mean anything to intelligent people." You've got kids I said, are you married? "Yes," he replied. You must be bloody thick then! He would probably laugh about it now, but back then he wasn't very pleased.'

For some members of the cast, especially the young lads in the film, all thought a career in the movies would be a great way to spend there adult life. Michael Joyce was no exception. 'We all had ambitions that when we became eighteen we would all be film extras. In the years following the whole thing collapsed. The money I had earned from the film didn't last long either – I blew it on a scooter. But looking back it was a great experience.'

Over the years Joyce has had many different jobs, but for the last seven he has been working in a Heroin Specialised Detoxify Clinic. 'Day one we sedate the patient,' explains Joyce, 'and day two they're up and around, but still sedated, and we have to keep them entertained. Because it's so specialised these people are from all over Britain. Anyway, we've got loads of films to put on, but I had a copy of Kes leant to me by my wife's father and I put it on. They were all clapping and cheering – and I couldn't understand why. But the age of a lot of them, around fortyish, they'd all done it at school in English, read Hines's book and they all identified with Billy Casper.'

Julie Shakespeare – *Narrated story in class*

Kes was not big on female roles and I was very fortunate to secure Julie's services for my book. Julie gave one of those natural Loach performances where you assume she did not realise the camera was on her – but she did. It was a beautiful portrayal of excepted class shyness and there was no hint of awe struck nervousness of working on a busy film set.

I was particularly lucky to get Julie's testimony. Again, blood-hound-Hesketh came up trumps – which was quite columbo-esque as the former actress had spent the last twenty years in Greece. It was even more ironic that Julie had only returned to the UK to put her daughter, Eleni, through secondary school. After all the criticism Kes had fired at the government's educational system – Julie had flown thousands of miles to return to the very structure Ken and his team had lambasted nearly forty years earlier.

'My daughter, Eleni, started her Barnsley life at age eleven,' states Julie, 'having lived and been brought up in a foreign country. Her dad is Greek, but the mixed marriage children are bought up to speak English. She is quite well spoken. Well as you can imagine for the first six months she had to fight every inch of the way – but she has done it now and has even started picking up some of the accent.'

Barnsley will always have a place in Julie's heart. 'I always used to come back every year when I was living in Corfu, for just a few days, so I never really got back into the swim of things – the day to day life stuff – but this time I've returned to Barnsley I have vowed I will never leave again,' explains Julie. 'It's just so lovely being back, I had forgot how wonderful these people were. When you travel it's a great, great experience, you learn so much and meet so many people, but since my return the people here are exactly the same and treat me as if I have never left. I remember coming back in my early years, my twenties, and almost despising the area and the people – inverted snobbery really, but now I've grown up, become mature, I realise what it is all about and what I have missed.'

Julie Shakespeare was on set throughout the summer shoot. 'They just asked us to come in everyday,' says Julie, 'we - the extras, they didn't tell us what was happening or what we were going to do. We all hung about for the six weeks holiday – but there was no boredom – it was just so exciting. I was fourteen with all these movie people milling around and all this equipment, it was just amazing.'

Eventually Shakespeare had the call to go on set, it was the classroom scene – where Bradley delivered his famous kestrel training speech. As far as Julie was concerned she would just melt into the background as just another anonymous classmate, little did she know that the camera would be pointed at her, capturing her every word and movement.

'The director came in,' explains Julie, 'as we were seated in class, and said we were going to be talking about fact and fiction. Colin Welland was going to take over the class – and we should all act as we would in a real lesson. He then went on to explain that Colin would pick on someone to tell a true story. I had deliberately sat right at the back, me and my friend Jillian – out of the way. Because under no circumstances was I going to speak.'

Again the director ran over the scene and pleaded once more to act naturally and put the crew and cameras out of their mind. Once the crew had got into position Colin Welland entered up stage right. At that point Colin became Mr Farthing taking an English class. As he built up the lesson about fact and fiction, the screen class started to relax and a familiar mixture of concentration and dissociation authentically filled the room. 'I was listening away,' says, Julie, 'and for a short while it was just like a normal class and all of a sudden I heard Colin call my name out! I thought o my God, and then, of course, as you see in the film, asked me to tell a factual story – and I just did it. In fact I think they only filmed it and cut it about three or four times, I know it was wrapped really quickly.'

Although Casper's speech, which followed Julie's, had a formulated agenda, the young actress had no such structure. 'While we were in class, the director asked us to think of a story – a bit cheeky, a bit unusual,' laughs, Julie. 'At that time there used to be all-night parties, which I was not aloud to go of course. But I knew of this one party where the police had been called because of the noise – so I thought if he picks on me I will mention that, and that's what I did.'

There are two things that stick out in Julie's mind – the catering and the crew. 'The food was fantastic – anything you wanted and at any time,' remembers Julie. 'I have to say the crew were all magical. They were just so respectful and friendly. One of the crew had a sports car; a sports car in Barnsley at that time was unheard of. We used to take it in turns as he drove everybody around the estate. We could not believe that all these movie people just treated us so well. They were all super.'

The premier showing of *Kes* in Doncaster was fondly remembered by Julie. *'It was all so special. Although I turned up to the prestigious showing, we all had to make our own way there, on the back of my mate's scooter. And of course watching the film, for all of us kids, was incredible. I mean we really had no idea what the film was about because for most of us we had just been in odd scenes – so when it all came together, to see the finished product, I don't think any of us really fully understood what we had been involved in – even in a small way.'*

For Julie Shakespeare the film has matured like a good wine. *'I mean I especially love the film today because I'm older,'* comments Shakespeare seriously, *'I understand what it is trying to say. I saw nothing wrong in the depiction of life back then, because it described my life – it was me. David never came from a home like that; he came from a very good home. They might not have been very rich – but they were a loving stable family, so was mine. But there were families around Barnsley at the time, who were exactly like that.'*

'I love my Barnsley and although I have spent as much time away from the area as in it – I always come home.'

Shortly after the national release of *Kes*, while it was well on its way to being described a classic, Julie moved away from the area. *'Barnsley to Buckinghamshire,'* she laughs. *'I went there to work in a family business, a country pub, for about twelve years. I was in those days, very broad Yorkshire and they all knew I was in that film. They used to come into the pub especially to see me – it was really embarrassing. It was actually very hard for me and I had big problems – they were all so posh. But of course I came to realise, they didn't have a problem with me, I had a problem with them.'*

Many have remarked about the passion in Bradley's narrative, during the classroom scene. It unfolds so delicately, as you see the enthusiasm build in the troublesome Billy. Eyes sparkling with concentration – it was a rare glimpse and possibly the biggest single message that the governmental educational system had got it all so terribly wrong. *'I didn't know, none of us did, what David (Bradley) was going to talk about. But when he did, it was just so amazing and interesting. It was a wonderful performance. Although David differed from Casper in many ways, that was David's appearance, and he always looked a little forlorn.'*

The now famous pantomimes where some of the *Kes* stars would emerge, is favourably remembered by Julie, *'My real passion* was music; singing and dancing, and because of that I used to be in all the pantomimes. David was the real star who carried the whole production – he was magnificent. For about four years they used to run for a week and were sold out every time – and that was David. The metal work teacher; Mr Dyson, especially, complemented and encouraged David's performance – they were a bit of a double act. Mrs Corner, she was my best friend at school; so encouraging, she also organised the pantos. It was totally awe inspiring – it was my happiest times at the school, I shall never forget those days.'

Mike (Michael) Padgett – McDowell's friend

Probably the best footballer of the bunch was Mike Padgett, who came, together with pals Bob Naylor and Michael Joyce, from Longcar school. 'Barry Hines was our games teacher,' says Padgett, 'and occasional English teacher at Longcar Central School. Sometime in early summer in 1968 Barry asked me and three other lads from our school, Glynn Bowser, Rob Naylor and Mick Joyce to get involved in the filming of Kes at St Helens School. I was sixteen and due to leave school in August that year.'

The four boys trouped along to the Queen's Hotel for an audition. Ken Loach selected the scene where the innocent lad gets caught with a pocket full of cigarettes. 'We mixed in with some lads from St Helens,' explains Mike. 'Rob (Naylor) was picked to play McDowell and we were asked to play in some of the football, classroom and playground scenes. We were outsiders in a sense and knew hardly any of the other school kids but we fitted in quickly during the six weeks or so of filming.'

It was Barry Hines, a great footballer himself, who recognised Padgett's soccer talents and suggested he should take centre stage for the football scenes.

Mr Sugden, cuddling the ball, fidgeting to keep warm, picks Padgett, before Spurs team captain Tibbutt, has a chance to choose. Even when there is the chance of scoring a penalty, Sugden's enlarged ego prevents him from doing the right thing. 'I definitely should have taken the penalty ('Let Padgett take it, sir,' the team members shout),' laughs Mike, adding 'I don't think many of us had read A Kestrel For A Knave and we never saw any film script so most of us had no idea what was coming next. Me and another lad were taken to one side by Ken and Barry and asked who we thought was the best - Dennis Law or Bobby Charlton. We argued our case and then were put in front of Mr Sugden to defend our positions with the camera rolling. I'm the one who suggests to Mr Sugden that Denis Law is better than Bobby Charlton. Not a good idea!'

'I can't remember how many days we spent on the football field,' comments Padgett, 'and in the dressing room shooting those scenes. It didn't seem very long. Brian Glover took over every scene with what looked to us like making things up as he went along. Ken Loach was laughing his head off like one of us.'

The whole crew appeared to go out of their way to bond with the young kid actors. Taking them to the sweet shop, trips in sports cars, handing out cigarettes and providing the entertainment. 'Ken's favourite saying was "That was great. Now just one more time," towards the end of the filming a camera technician brought in a Men Only magazine and showed us a photograph of a bedroom scene with the bloke unzipping his pants in front of a woman. In biro the technician had written "That was great. Now just one more time." Ken went red and laughed along.'

Mike Padgett was neatly secured in the bullying McDowell's gang. In the playground scene before the fight the gang are smoking and trying to look tough. 'Colin Welland had already worried us when we first met him,' explains Mike. 'We were in the assembly hall ready for filming when he walked in. We all started whistling the Z cars theme tune (not the first time someone had done this) and he spun round as though he was going to thump us. So when Mr Farthing told us to run away from the scene of the fight otherwise he'd grab us we didn't hang around.'

The ultimate lengths Ken and his team would go to get the realistic shot they wanted, would take many bluffs and guises. The assembly scene was not going well. 'Mr Hesketh had singled out McDowell two or three times,' explains Padgett, 'but it must have looked false. By now we all knew he was going to be pulled out of the crowd for coughing and it must have shown on our faces. We overheard Ken Loach telling Mr Hesketh that in the next take he should leave McDowell and instead pick on somebody else nearby. We all became very nervous. Rob Naylor (McDowell) relaxed. But of course it was McDowell who was pulled out again and the shot worked. The ploy looked really clever at the time.'

Padgett's part in Kes, as he was about to leave school, had been one of the most significant events of his life. It was all so incredible and yet Barry Hines, his teacher, had written a book that had been made into a film. All the kids knew him. And here was Barry working side by side with Ken Loach, Tony Garnett, Chris Menges and those other important people from somewhere near London, with their posh accents and expensive camera equipment - making a real film about them. 'They were filming our lives and we were living the film,' comments Mike, philosophically. 'When the film was shown and you saw yourself and your mates up there on screen, it really did shrink the world a little bit. But it sort of disturbed you. Made you feel less settled. Being involved in the film was a big factor in me leaving home at twenty-one to travel round the world. And feeling for the Caspers of this world and underdogs, pushed me into a satisfying job in Employee Development and still drives me today. When anyone finds out you were in Kes they want to know what it was like. And they're always smiling when they ask.'

Duggie Brown – *Milkman*

Duggie Brown, born Barry Dudley and brother of Lynne Perrie, was born towards the end of the Second World War in 1944. He was a natural comedian and staked out the Northern clubs before getting his break on television with *The Comedians*.

When I tried to track Duggie down I had little luck. Then while I was doing an interview for Radio Sheffield with Wendy Middleton – they were going to get Duggie on the show to surprise me. Unfortunately they found out he was working on a cruise ship in the Antarctic. I suppose the budget did not stretch to *ship to shore?*

Eventually I caught up with this workaholic comedic thespian, who had about as much free time as the laughing clown in Blackpool centre. His movie casting debut was connected to his vocal sister. 'Both Lynne and I were with the same agent,' explains Duggie, 'it was ATS in Leeds where Ken did most of the casting for Kes.'

Loach kept with his unorthodox techniques and offered Brown little in the way of guidance or dialogue. 'At the beginning there was not much direction I don't think,' says Duggie 'Ken basically gave us a scene to ad lib through.'

He could not recall how long the scene lasted or how many takes - but he remembered he enjoyed every minute. 'I played the milkman and I think I remember a few pints of milk and orange juice getting stolen or should I say lost!'

Duggie Brown has always been busy – life for the comedian and actor has constantly been sweet before and after *Kes*. 'I had been with a rock group for 12 years from 1956 to 1968, then left to work in the local clubs and theatres, I was driving every day to the Kes set from Morecambe where I was appearing at the Morecambe Bowl. Kes started my drama career which thank goodness is still blossoming today.'

The cast and crew were always one happy family, but Barnsley was Duggie's town. *'I remember taking Tony Garnett and Ken to a local night club in Barnsley called the Baba,'* smiles Duggie, *'and the bouncers wanted to shave Tony's side burns off before they let him in. It was a rule - no long side burns, but when I explained who he was they reluctantly relented.'*

All classic movies hold a total fascination for the public. Duggie still gets recognised – even the people who have booked him! *'I get it all the time, and lots of big executives I work with on golf days etc all remember doing* Kes *for their school drama studies.'*

On the eve of finishing the final draft of *Life after Kes*, Duggie is busy filming *Heartbeat* and *Doctors*; for the BBC. He is a jobbing actor, in the minority of his profession – he has full employment. Duggie Brown thinks himself very fortunate – I was lucky enough to catch an after dinner speech at the Midland Cricket Conference. Luck, in my opinion, does not come in to it – Duggie Brown is a fine actor and a damn good after dinner speaker!

Bernard Atha OBE - *Youth Employment Officer*

Bernard Atha was born in Leeds. His dance career started when he trained as a ballet dancer at the Royal Academy of Dramatic Art – up until his mid twenties he was a speciality dancer. He was a club entertainer, who lectured in humanities at Huddersfield Technical College, was on the books of the Joseph Brothers – who ran a theatrical booking agency ATS.

The agency knew of the director, Ken Loach, and his forth coming project; *Kes*. At that time Atha was with The White Rose Players, who were a professional repertory company. *'I was asked to audition,'* remembers, Atha, *'for the possibility of doing one or two parts, actually. They asked me to read for the Headmaster as well as the Youth Employment Officer.'* Due to Atha's former relationship with student counselling and vocational guidance, the latter part seemed more appropriate.

Atha explains, *'Loach offered me the part of the Youth Employment Officer… it was dilettante acting, really, while I was teaching and on the council* (since 1957) *as well. But it's a very important role in the film, because he's the character who throws Billy on the scrape heap.'* The role fitted Atha like an old key in a well-oiled lock. The pleasing smile, the air of authority, the disenchantment of his job. The rehearsed phrases delivered beautifully and the obvious ironic dissociation with youth.

It reminded me of my experience in front of the Youth

Employment Officer or Careers Officer I think we had, on leaving Edgecliff Comprehensive School back in 1978. I knocked on the door, unlike Casper, entered and sat down. He was younger than I had imagined. I wondered what he had been like in his leaving school interview. He was obviously impressed by his interviewer – after all that was the career he chose.

I had not got a clue as to a career in all my 16 years building up to that 15 minute meeting - so I was pretty sure he was not going to come up with something. As he spoke, I leaned back on my chair; he had the same monotonous monosyllabic voice that teachers save for disinterested kids or unruly ones. Or more likely ones they can not rule. I thought to myself if this guy is the link between childhood and adulthood, there was not much help for me.

He kept shoving these brightly coloured pamphlets my way, trying to gauge my reaction, hoping I would suddenly jump up in the air shouting eureka! I kept hearing words like apprenticeship, college, night school, tech etc. as I drifted in and out of controlled consciousness. I had the feeling, looking down at a green file with my name on it, sat on his desk, that he had already made his mind up about me – and he was probably right. At that time I did not want to listen. I had been under the educational regime for over 10 years and at 16 - I did not want to play the game any more. Nothing he said or was going to say would inspire me in any shape or form. I left the room quite deflated and let down. I knew at that point, it was all up to me. I could have guidance if I wanted, but as far as the school was concerned – that was it. After all they had another year of fledgling pupils to look after. So, I was being kicked out of the nest – it was time to fly totally free! I threw the pamphlets in the bin – I could always go and work for my dad I thought.

Bernard received much criticism from the Youth Employment Services for his portrayal of the dissociated officer. *'I got a lot of letters on the council from people saying I was showing the Youth Employment Service in a very bad light. But I'd been a teacher, so I could reply that that was exactly what happened in poorer areas, that they did give up on people... it was a true depiction of the life as it was then.'* Not only had Atha seen this at first hand, with secondary modern boys being offered either pit work (9 out of every 10) or a menial job at a low wage, but also for the girls.

'I can remember as a teacher in Shipley, very bright girls being told: "You're very clever – you can be a burler and mender." And the less bright girls went into the weaving sheds. It was an automatic rule.' A burler and mender were considered a better job. They used to go over the

cloth, after it was made, looking for any imperfections and if found, mending them with fine needlework. The room where they worked was quiet, allowing the workers to talk or listen to the radio and was also relatively free from fluff. The weaving sheds, in the mills, with the spinning looms, was a different story. The atmosphere was choking and noise was actually harmful to health.

Bernard was made Lord Mayor of Leeds from May 2000 until May 2001 as well as his long service as a Leeds councillor (Holbeck ward) and was awarded an OBE. But *Kes* is what everybody wants to know about. *'I've done nearly 200 films and television shows over the last 30 years, but the one everyone knows about is Kes. I was in Sydney, Australia a while ago and a young man came up to me and said:"Weren't you in that film, Kes?"'*

'The appeal of the film is that it reaches so many different levels. People who just want to have a good laugh; have a good laugh. People who want to have a good cry, can cry; emotionally, and people who want to see a serious political message in it – can see it. Kids want to watch the film and adults can watch the film – they keep showing it on television and audiences keep watching it. Funnily enough, it's the only film I have ever been in where I don't receive any royalties.'

Ken Loach's reluctance to rehearse before the camera rolls was highlighted by Bernard Atha. *'Ken just keeps shooting the scene over and over, letting you do it like this or like that, he never shouts or gets excited – he just suggests different ways of doing it. So you don't rehearse and shoot, he just keeps taking different shots of what you are doing. It was a standing joke, because Ken would always say:"Just one more." And from that he got tremendously realistic performances. I remember them filming the sequence outside the Youth Employment Officer's room; before Billy comes in to see me, in the waiting room. The dialogue, the conversation, between mother (Mary Southall) and son and between Billy and the son; was just so right. All the kids were marvellous. But Ken is a genius at eliciting great performances. And that's why his films will last a long long time; they are socially real, like watching real people.'*

Robert Bowes - *Headmaster – Mr Gryce*

Bowes, a former Doncaster town councillor, as the headmaster, brings a weary irascibility that could only be mustered by a genuine and no doubt sorely-tried headmaster. As he was in fact the real-life head of Ashton School, and one of St Helen's own masters teaching secondary English and History. A graduate of Sheffield University and South Willton College. Where Robert Bowes ends and Mr Gryce begins may be wider than first thought – but there is a perception, an understanding. It may be Mr Bowes on an off day. The fact that he was the genuine principle at a near-by school may be the only ones to truly testify are his former pupils. It is quit piquant to know that some of the most offensive masters are portrayed by actual teachers from the school. This is obviously what Loach was striving for and nobody let him down. Sadly Bob Bowes has passed away.

Desmond Guthrie - *Billy's friend*

In January 1973, four years after making *Kes*, Gordon Burn from the Sunday Times tracked down the boys from *Kes*. Guthrie, who plays one of McDowell's mates, shies away from going nesting; *'I'm takin' me girlfriend to Sheffield,'* he informs. When Burn caught up with Guthrie he was down the pit; working the same face as his dad, collecting his fare share of blue nails and black scars. When asked why he became a Barnsley miner, he quipped, *'There's nowt else, or nowt else that pays.'*

Like Guthrie's father and Dai Bradley's father; Desmond worked the face at North Gawper colliery, where he thinks Bradley would be if Ken Loach had not turned up. Guthrie did not stay on at school, to further his education. But he says he had no regrets at the time, commenting back then, *'Eight of my mates stayed on for CSE and five of them are next to me down the pit now. I tried for a clerk before I went underground but it were dead boring, and no money.'*

At the time, in January 1973, Desmond was picking up £28 a week and £35 after he had finished his training.

Peter Clegg – *Goalkeeper* - *Spurs*

Peter Clegg, Cleggie in the film, played the Spurs goalkeeper who saved the first penalty from Sugden's alter ego; Bobby Charlton. The second attempt, after Sugden deemed the goalkeeper to have moved, he pushed it to Clegg's right – and the game was 1-1. We then see the plump games master strutting up the pitch, commenting, *'And that, boys, is how to take a penalty. Look one way and shoot the other.'*

Clegg, like Bradley, was a keen footballer and actually played in goal. *'Of course I saved the first penalty,'* remembers Clegg, *'I mean they didn't tell me to; they didn't say anything about saving it. It was a penalty and that was it – I'm a goalkeeper and I'm going to try and save it. The second one I knew I had to let in – although I could have saved that one.'*

Peter Clegg and Dai Bradley were very good friends. They were both pupils at St Helens; both enjoyed football and shared the same classroom. They had also both starred in the annual school pantomime.

'I'm not sure if it was Dave Dyson or Betty Corner who put my name forward for the audition at the Queens Hotel? Mr Dyson was the metalwork teacher and Corner was the chorus mistress – they ran our school pantomime. I know Kenneth Loach came to see one of the pantomimes David (Bradley) and me were in.'

Peter Clegg was also in the classroom scene where Billy is prompted to speak by Mr Farthing. *'That scene where he talked about the bird, that was amazing to me, to all of us. That was the first time I'd heard that speech. It was the first time any of us had heard it and everyone said how interesting it was. It wasn't rehearsed or anything. Bang and it was out there, and although a few things I've noticed were added after filming, ninety percent of his speech was as it happened that day on the first take!'*

During another take Clegg was heard but not seen. *'When Freddie Fletcher (Jud Casper) came to the school looking for Billy, because he hadn't put bet on, I was the lad in the toilets. Freddie is seen kicking the cubicle doors in along the row until he comes to mine. "Seen our Billy?" to which I sarcastically reply, "Aye. He's in here wi' me."'* Jud then violently moves forward, out of shot, and threatens Cleggie, and the scene ends with his strangled cries. *'I got a busted lip that day off Freddie Fletcher. What they did was shot it three times. The one that you see on the film, the second was from the washbasin looking over the top of the cubicle and thirdly right over the toilet door. And in this last scene he came rushing in and gave me a wallop – I finished up with a bloody mouth. It was an accident. I didn't mind I got extra money for it.'*

George Speed – *Billy's friend*

It is not very often you have the chance to appear, albeit a supporting role, in a major film production – but for Speed it could have turned out a lot different. It was between Dai Bradley and George Speed who would play Billy Casper. *'It was Barry Hines, my gym teacher, who asked me to go and audition at the Queens,'* remembers Speed, *'I actually auditioned with David for main part. He got it – he spoke broader Yorkshire than what I did. When I didn't get it, to be so close, it was crippling – a big shock to me.'*

The cutting room floor was host to another piece of film, which Speed remembers very well, about a travelling group of actors who descend on St Helens and put on a show for the kids. The scene was filmed by Loach but it never reached the completed print. *'It was the last bit of filming, but I'm not sure at what point it would have been shown in the film. Some travelling company of actors are performing on our school stage – an opera scene. We were sitting in a huddle and laughing about them on stage. Someone said something; I think it was lad playing McDowell, like: "which one o' lasses do you mean?" And I say "Ere we' tits hangin down to 'er kneecaps." I can't remember too much about it, it was last night of filming and crew had taken us over the pub and bought us a few pints. From start to finish it was a fantastic experience.'* The scene, opera for all, was a travelling company of actors who perform special one-act operas, actually written in the 18th century. Ken Loach initially included the scene because he was told he needed more music in the movie.

The young actor was also involved in the trip to London to re-dub the shower and classroom scenes. *'We stopped in a hotel and we were due to go back the next day, but we all finished so quick. We spent the next day at Tony Garnett's house and watched the cup final.'*

It was George Speed, one of three from Railey School – using his own name, who starts Casper's famous narrative in front of Mr Farthing and the rest of the class. Following the teacher's instruction for Casper to stand and tell a story, Speed chips in, with hand raised, *'He's got this hawk. He's mad over it. He just goes wi' t'hawk all t'time. He's crackers over it.'* At which Casper replies, *'Better than thee, anyroad.'* Up until this point there is a wonderful boredom that is evident amongst the pupils, that is probably indigenous with the world over – a midweek class of government branded no-hopers being dictated to by authority. Even the kindly, caring Mr Farthing cannot maintain his energy through a whole lesson.

A legacy of *Kes*, that time has not diminished, is that people will either recognise you or get to know that you had a part in the film. *'I was recently in Cyprus on holiday and a stewardess came up and asked me for my autograph. She actually came from up north and had seen a recent article about Kes. She had probably been born 10 years after the film had been made.'*

Joey Kaye - *The comedian in the club*

The first time I spoke to Joey Kaye, the man who sang the great double entendre song about a marrow, was on the telephone; it was a hot sticky Sunday in August. There was a wasp in our house that had terrorised the whole family for a few hours, as I was making notes I could here screams as it moved from room to room, intimidating my young family. It finally reached my office – this was rapidly becoming harassment, as Joey, in his soft Liverpudlian accent, answered the telephone. Within seconds, the heat, the humidity, that damn wasp, was all gone and I laughed out loud and listened as if I was sharing a pint with a trusted friend.

Ken Loach, when filming and gathering his players and crew, does naturally attract an ensemble of dedicated, loyal and real characters. Joey Kaye was not only an exception to the rule, but he was a man of extreme kindness and charm. As well as being one of the gifted few – he could make people laugh, effortlessly. Our first chat lasted an hour and I laughed more in those sixty minutes of ad-lib humour than two episodes of *Porridge*.

The notes I made, bullet points to pick up on – to steer the conversation, I screwed up and threw it at the wasp. This was a time to listen and learn.

Joey Kaye, born by the docks in Liverpool, has been seen many times on film and television including the movie *Betta Betta in the Wall, Who's the Fattest Fish of All?* (1970) and TV parts including *Scully* (1984), *Days Of Hope* (1975) and *Another Sunday and Sweet F.A.* (1972). This latter outing, a TV movie by Jack Rosenthal, Kaye appeared with Freddie Fletcher. There was another *Kes* veteran who also appeared, Duggie Brown (milkman). Alas the David Bradley halfway down the cast list was not Billy Casper, but the one who beat the actor playing him to the name and forced Bradley to change his name to Dai when registering with Equity.

Kaye had worked with Ken Loach a few times and most notably in *The Golden Vision*. It was a football drama about Everton Football Club. 'We all worked on and off for Ken over the years,' remembers Kaye, 'There was a few of us. Most of us were doing the cabaret circuit, that's how we got our equity. When I first auditioned for Ken, it was The Golden Vision a Wednesday Play; I was one of the last groups to go in, the agent was sending in all his favourites first. And they were no good, they were trying to do the acting bit; instead of being themselves. Ken was looking for natural, out and out football supporters. He called us in in groups of three. All he said was "Right, I just want you to chat about Everton football club." And that was it, he just listened. So the ones who went to watch Everton play, like me, knew all the terminology – the nicknames of everybody. He just weeded out the ones he didn't want which just left a bunch of us for the film.'

Another film Kaye worked on was Loach's *Days of Hope*. '*Loach has the patience of a saint – I saw it on* Kes. *That man has never slammed a door in his life! We filmed* Days of Hope *in Durham. They had loads and loads of local people dressed in the old clothes. They had all cultured the accents, but they were very unruly. Some of the adults were mucking about and the kids were running everywhere and climbing over everything. And I could see Ken Loach in the middle of all this madness and he was just so relaxed.*'

Joey Kaye had hit on a golden rule when auditioning for Ken Loach. Ken does not want you to act or react – he wants, quite simply, a natural performance, a performance that is both believable and above all, real.

Often the threads of *Kes* are picked up, when actors meet up at an audition or two actors may share a stage or dressing room. '*I haven't seen Ken Loach for years, I was away performing summer in Jersey, The Isle of Man even Australia, so I was always missing castings – I also changed agents, so you lose touch. But I was doing a summer show and I was back stage. There was this old fashioned door with a circle of glass in the middle, what you looked through. And I saw this face pressed against the glass, tapping. I'm walking past, thinking it's nothing to do with me. It doesn't happen to anyone else but when I walk past the door, tap, tap, tap. Anyway, it was Tony Garnett, it was really great to see him.*'

Like all true professionals and the ones that work and keep working, the ones that recognise their agents voice when they call, Joey Kaye adapted his act when the business changed course. In the seventies there were plenty of cabaret clubs and plenty of jobs for a jobbing stand-up Liverpudlian comic. As the working-men's clubs diminished the club scene tired. Eventually there were hundreds of stand-ups fighting over the same piece of bread. Many hung up their frilly shirts and velvet coats and drifted back into the audience. Others, like Joey Kaye, transformed themselves and offered something different. For Joey this was a simple mixture of humour and music – or as Joey puts it *comedy at the keyboards*.

Following the practised delivery of The 4D Jones band, it was a slice of northern humour that transcends dialect and localism. Any club, certainly in England, following the start of the Carry On tradition of the double entendre in the late fifties – recognised this risqué genre and lapped it up. The Marrow Song emerged from impromptu jamming sessions.

During Kaye's time as a stand up comedian he would often do TV extra work and speaking parts, making use of his equity card. '*When I was doing some of these plays for Tony Garnett and Ken, when we* finished shooting we'd end up in the pub, sitting round having a few beers and having a laugh. I used to carry a little ukulele in the boot of my car and I used to go and get it and play. Ken and Tony used to love it. One of these nights, they were both talking about Kes, the film they were shortly to make. Tony Garnett was discussing the set in the pub and said they really needed another act that would go on during the playing of the band. And Ken said: "We'll get Joey to do it." And that was it. A few weeks later I was in my car bombing over to Barnsley with the ukulele in the boot.'

Incredibly, Joey Kaye never recorded his most famous piece, The Marrow Song. 'That was a great song, I got it off an uncle of mine, my Uncle Tom. He used to always play it. It was actually an old music hall song. Because of the double meaning — I said to Ken I thought it was a bit strong, but you know Ken Loach! You have to give it to Ken, he knows what he's doing.'

Following the movie Joey Kaye has often received requests to play The Marrow Song. 'Everywhere I go, even now, there is some request for it. It's amazing the interest — it was just one take in Barnsley, with no rehearsal. It's a funny thing, when someone has been on TV or appeared in a film, something that has a wide appeal, even if it's a small part, people will focus upon it. I did a small part for Alan Bleasdale's, Boys from the Black Stuff. I was the electricity man who had come to cut Yosser Hughes's supply.' I remembered the part vividly and confirmed Kaye's thesis by quoting his few lines back to him. It appears to be a theme that has run through Kes and other exquisite productions — a spotlight shines down and aluminates and levitates certain performances. And it is these unique layers that burn the image into the minds of the audience. This enlightening phenomenon is often attributed to music — where events and often mundane happenings are frozen in time by a few bars of music. The Marrow Song, for me, has the same effect.

My last comment to Joey Kaye was one he had heard many times — when are you going to pen a biography. He is a natural — the text comes out his mouth, he doesn't need editors. Somehow, very funny things are still happening to him. Or certainly stories that he can make sound very funny are still happening to him. When you write you almost stop living in the real world and shut yourself away for a few months. I do not think we should be deprived of Joey Kaye for a minute.

Trevor Hesketh – *Billy's form teacher*

'Fisher?' blasts out Mr Hesketh, reading from his morning register. 'German Bight.' calls out Billy Casper, lost in thought. Of course he is talking about the shipping forcast; Fisher. German Bight. Cromarty.

Trevor Hesketh was cast as a pompous teacher, who was Billy Casper's form teacher. Amazingly, Trevor Hesketh was Dai Bradley's form teacher in real life. He was also given the job of looking after the young screen kids, most of them he actually taught at St Helen's.

The script had Trevor playing Mr Crossley. Due to the fact that Trevor Hesketh was not in Equity, and having problems getting Equity status, someone had the great idea of Trevor using his own name! He was therefore playing himself – and needed no Equity card. A practise that became very useful throughout the film.

When I met Trevor Hesketh and his wife, Hazel, at the Brooklands in Barnsley, the years had been very kind. In fact, minus the black-topped glasses he wore in the film, his own pair, he appeared rather less threatening. As I thrust out my hand and muttered something about coffee and pointed to reception, I half expected him to shout: 'What are you babbling about boy, and stand up straight!' The warm smile and easy manner developed into a quite friendship. His knowledge and enthusiasm shone through. The memories were as vivid and as vibrant as they were over 37 years ago. Trevor's delight in recapturing that most unusual summer of 68' flowed through his dialogue and shone through his eyes.

Trevor Hesketh was in an unusual position as it was he who had liased with the production team, all those years ago, right from the start. 'I remember the Headmaster, Clarence Hirst, coming up to me waving a letter from a production company, which he said, wanted to do a documentary about St Helen's. His final words were: "Trevor, sort it out." And that was the beginning of all this.'

Trevor saw at first hand the process from script to screen. 'When Ken had finished filming at the end of the day, somebody on a motorbike would courier it to Wakefield and then it would travel on the train to London. It would then be printed and returned to Wakefield and then back to the location – within a very short time. Then when the cinema in Barnsley closed at night, the crew would meet up and show the rushes.' Trevor Hesketh was privileged to go and see some of these late night film shows. A vary rare situation when working with Loach – for the rest of the cast, the first time the actors saw themselves was at the premier at the A.B.C. Cinema in Barnsley. Most actors had not even seen a script, or if they did, it would either be incomplete or had sections blanked out. Trevor had an up-to-date completed script. It may be due to the fact that he had liased with Kestrel Films from its embryo stage and Garnett and Loach viewed Trevor in a different light – possibly as one of the crew. In those young days they had certainly formed a relationship as the many pages of correspondence (Tony Garnett Productions) testify.

Hesketh, who had amateur acting experience at the town's Wishing Well Theatre, and the now famous school pantomimes; along side the young Dai Bradley, was offered a role in the early part of 1968. Trevor was informed he would appear in four scenes and filming would commence on Friday 12th July 1968 (Assembly scene 22, 24). At that time the working title was taken from Hines's book – A Kestrel for a Knave.

'The film unit rapidly increased in size,' explains Trevor, 'and both staff and pupils began their education in the craft of film making, it being a stipulation of the local authority that this should be part of the school curriculum during the time of the filming. The unit, paradoxically, resolved itself into teams. The production team, the camera crew, the sound, the artistic crew, lighting, finance and feeding.' Initial enthusiasm did wane a little, as the nature of the business is slow and methodical. Time can pass quite mundanely while the heavy camera is hauled from one position to another, while the lighting was being rearranged and the microphones adjusted, and by the constant repetition of the action. 'The director's words became a stock phrase, "Very good – we'll just do it once more." They did it again and again and again.'

'However, the lighter side will remain in the memories of the children. A statement such as: "This morning we will shoot the whole school, and this afternoon we will shoot the Head Master," caused a great deal of mirth.'

When it came to the dream sequence, when the assembly are all standing; chanting the Lords Prayer, Casper's mind wanders and he misses the queue to sit down. He is of course left standing and the school is all seated on the floor, he slowly comes round as the repeated shout of his name by an angry Mr Gryce. Loach thought it a great idea to walk around the busy Barnsley market with hawk on wrist, receiving non-believing glances from its occupants. 'The camera, which was in a shop; ready to catch the reactions, was following Bradley with the kestrel and NOBODY took a blind bit of notice,' says, Hesketh, chuckling. 'He was just walking around and not even one person looked at the bird. They actually filmed it three times before they got a reaction.'

At one point Trevor mentioned a boy from St Helen's that Barry Hines had taught and he was initially who Barry envisioned to play Billy Casper. In fact during the time Barry was both at St Helen's and writing A Kestrel for a Knave, the lad was very much on the authors mind. Whether the young lad in question was truly cut out for the rigors of film life – he had problems with time keeping. 'Of course they were all up for the part of Billy Casper,' points out Hesketh. 'The thirty or so boys who went to the Queens Hotel for the initial auditions, they were all potentially Billy Casper's. But this lad was one who Barry Hines knew and wrote about and he is in the film. It's certainly not obvious who it is. I'm not going to mention his name, but the lad knows who it is.' A second cup of coffee and the offer of a cream scone did not loosen Trevor's tongue.

The World premier of *Kes*, Wednesday, March 25th 1970, at the ABC Cinema, Doncaster, was particularly memorable for Mr & Mrs Hesketh. Their car would not start and they had to go up in the next-door neighbour's vehicle – which was a builders van; complete with tools and cement bags. It must have been quite a sight, between the assortment of black and white stretched limousines, who pulled up to drop off its occupants at the entrance to the cinema – to suddenly see an old builders van deftly pull up before the customary red carpet.

Another premier, this time for the press, again Trevor Hesketh was chaperoning the young Dai Bradley. 'We spent quite a bit of time together,' comments Hesketh, 'obviously before, as his form teacher and all the pantomimes, but also looking after him on publicity outings after the film had been released. He was a little bit of a rebel was David. On this one particular occasion, it was the press release of *Kes* at the Dorchester, and he hadn't got a tie. Always resourceful he borrowed one from one of the reporters as he went through the gate of the hotel.'

It must have been quite surreal to mirror life so closely. In the space of a few months lives would change dramatically for some. There was no-one closer than Hesketh, who with in a few months, went from being Bradley's form teacher to chaperoning him on huge press launches for United Artists. The lad sitting in front of him answering the morning register to the name Bradley, would probably never be the same again. 'To teach David,' smiles Trevor Hesketh, 'he was very very good. He was a very intelligent lad as you can tell. And of course, at fourteen, he was younger than most of the screen class.'

Following Bradley's success in *Equus*, Trevor Hesketh went to see the play at the National Theatre. 'His performance in that was absolutely superb, I went round the back to congratulate him, but before I had chance to say anything, David ran up to me, saying: "Hey, Barnsley have won two nil!"' It was a Saturday matinee show and the football results would be broadcast as they were all on stage. 'I said how on earth do you know? David said: "You know that scroll that's passed round in the second act, it's got all the football results of the casts teams.'

Trevor Hesketh, who looked after the pupils when not filming, felt the whole experience totally benefited the children who took part and most absorbed enthusiastically the sights and sounds of that unusual summer. *'There was an opera scene in* Kes, *which unfortunately did not make the final cut, few of us could ever forget the sight of an opera singer, dressed in 18th century costume and sporting dressing gown and cloth cap, while eating his lunch at a trestle table. Some kids will recall being taught for a few days by a former member of the Z Cars TV series, or dressing in exactly the same clothes, when required for filming, for eight weeks. Some remember the gigantic lights shining from outside the school windows; of the huge polystyrene sheets to deaden sounds and reflect light; of the frustrating weather conditions and the over-all dedication of the director and his team.'* Towards the end of filming everyone was feeling the effects of movie making. It had been a gruelling eight weeks. *'David (Bradley) was really tired at the end,'* remembers, Trevor Hesketh, *'The scene with Bernard Atha* (Youth Employment Officer) *was one of the last scenes to be shot. If you look closely at his eyes, they are drawn and dark – the lad was exhausted. But it fitted into the scene.'*

When the cameras stopped rolling and the film makers packed away their equipment in their pantecnicons, they departed to go back to their own lives and onto new projects, Trevor commented at the time, *'At some future date, when the film is released, the children involved will be thankful that they have had the opportunity of taking an active part. They have learned the technique of film making and will see films in the future from a new viewpoint. They have become more critical, more observant and have met interesting people from various parts of the world, with jobs not as glamorous as they formerly imagined. They have mixed with technicians, actors, television reporters and press, learned new technical terms and have gained confidence in themselves. Fortunately, they have been carefully screened from personal publicity and so their egos, in general, have not suffered. Some have had to learn bad habits, for use in the film, but the harm done, should be only temporary, we trust.'*

Jean Palmer – *Bible reader*

It was a strange coincidence how I tracked down the girl who read out the bible passage (Matthew 18: 10-14) in Kes. I had been talking to an extra who was in the playground fight scene. The Yorkshire Post was running an article about the book and Anne Goulding had agreed to take part. A couple of days later Anne telephoned me excitedly and I assumed it was because the interview with the paper had gone well. It turned out that on Anne's return home from a short break, she was on the North sea ferry, she recognised fellow cast member,

Jean Palmer — who had stood on stage at St Helen's - while filming the assembly scene and read out the bible text. The girls had not seen each other since the late sixties. Anne bought Jean up-to-date with regards my book and I received a telephone call a few days later.

Jean Palmer was 14 years old when she took centre stage, on the creaking boards at her real School; St Helen's and delivered the words, 'This mornings reading comes from Mathew chapter 18, verses 10 to 14. See that you do not despise one of these little ones...' Ironic words delivered to the little ones sitting on the cold floor, with the teachers in a row looking down upon them.

Jean was actually in the same class as Dai Bradley at St Helen's. 'I can't really remember why they chose me,' says Jean. 'I think there was three of us, one was Julie Shakespeare, and we all had to read a passage from the bible — and they chose me for the part.' Julie did get into the movie, not large on female roles, when she was selected to tell a story during Mr Farthing's class, just before Casper's speech on falconry.

Jean Palmer is quite unique when you study Loach's technique — nearly all the actors are kept in the dark about what they are to say and do — and there is not a script within a mile radius of the set. But not only did Jean know her exact speech — she was even given the script in the shape of the bible.

Even the shot was not pure Loach, his developing skill, which started during Kes, setting the camera unobtrusively out of reach of the actors. 'I can remember Chris Menges the cameraman,' laughs Jean, 'he was right in front of me while I was reading my lines, this big camera. It was a bit nerve racking at fourteen, I don't know really how I did it?'

'I must watch it because I haven't seen it for so long,' admits Jean. 'I've also only got it on video. My friends all say, "You cheap skate, why haven't you got it on DVD?" I will get it one day.'

Eric Bolderson - *Farmer*

I spoke to Eric's son first — he had seen the Ay Up web site; who had kindly ran a recruitment drive for former cast and crew members from Kes, and said his dad would be pleased to speak with me. A week later I rang the number I was given. A friendly voice greeted me. A voice that was full of honesty and contentment. Eric had a lovely Yorkshire brogue that was all warmth and understanding. He had experienced a lot in life and was happy with his lot. Out of all the people I spoke to, even my heroes like Loach, Garnett, Hines, Menges,

Fletcher, Welland etc. he really sticks out in my mind. A gentle man, a man of integrity, the type of man you would talk to in a strange pub and know you would be made to feel welcome. In the true sense a man of the world - he may not have experienced everything in it, but you feel what he has seen he understands and what he does not understand does not bother him. A Yorkshireman that could teach us all a thing or too.

The part was not major, but he made it his own. There was no doubt that Eric Bolderson was as much a Farmer as he was a Yorkshireman – or so I thought. In fact I could not have been further off the mark – at the time Mr Bolderson was working as a bookie in Leeds. *'I worked for a firm of book-makers and our personnel officer knew a book-maker, who was doing business with our firm, who had his betting office in the City Varieties of Leeds yard. City of Varieties was conducting interviews and castings for Kes. They basically sent people who they thought appropriate to the production company making the film and they would then audition them. My name was simply added to the list. When it came to the audition it was with another chap and Colin Welland from Z Cars – I was quite surprised. In front of Colin we had to act out a scenario – I was to pretend to take a shirt back because it had ridden up after a wash and other chap played shopkeeper. I had never done anything like this before. I started off and we just sort of chatted, back and forth, obviously without any script.'*

After about half an hour of add-lib chat Colin Welland called an end to the audition explaining that someone from the production team would contact either if a part was offered. Eric Bolderson went back to his job at the betting shop and thought little about it. *'A while later I received this letter through the post saying I was to take the part of the farmer in* A Kestrel for a Knave, *and not* Kes, *as it would later be named.'*

It was Loach and Garnett's idea to put a bookmaker, for realism, either in the shop where Billy does not place his brother's bet or the man (*Ted Carroll*) Billy chat's to about Jud's bets – Tell Him He's Dead and Crackpot. It was Colin who saw a farmer emitting from Bolderson's delivery, build and sturdy gate. This is even more incredible when you learn that Eric broke his neck well before making *Kes*, when he was 21. *'It was actually while I was playing rugby,'* says Eric. *'I was paralysed on my twenty second birthday; I couldn't move my arms or legs. Eventually over a period of four years, wearing a plaster jacket and leather collar, I got back to normal health.'*

Bolderson was born in 1927, in Castleford; twenty miles from Barnsley, was 43 when he appeared in *Kes*. It was a nice time to divert from the mundane – he found the experience both refreshing and exciting. '*There was several times we got on call,*' explains, Bolderson, '*it was all new to me. But they explained I'd have to be ready, costume on whatever day it was. They said they wanted an early morning shot, with early morning mist about. Many times it just wasn't satisfactory and they cried off. Then one day it all came together and we just started filming.*'

'*The very first line, I had to say, I fluffed. I got a script in the post some weeks before filming was to start. But I was living on my own – I wasn't with anyone. So I'm rehearsing on my own. The first words I spoke were: "Now, then. What's tha doin'?" to which he (Dai Bradley) replies: "Nowt." But to me, I'd never met David before, or heard him speak, it came out like 'nought'. It just didn't register with me and I froze. From then on I didn't have any problems at all.*'

'*At one point we ran out of script – David kept on adding bits and they kept filming. So quite a lot of my dialogue was not scripted, like, "They're hard to train. If they're not kept properly, it's criminal." There was one or two phrases I use that was not in the script. I think if I had kept on talking they would have kept on filming.*'

'*Originally my sister's daughter was going to be in it, because the farmer had a little girl with him and she was the right age. But due to all the postponements, when we actually started filming, my little niece was on holiday – she's only just started talking to me.*'

'*I think I got paid twenty-five pounds in all. I was always interested in photography myself, and some how I felt I was cheating, taking a part in it and getting paid. I was just grateful to be doing something different. I wasn't nervous – how did I know at the time it was going to be so big? Although, I'm pretty level headed. When I broke my neck and I couldn't work for nearly five years – on the sick all that time, wearing a solid cast jacket and neck brace – and I review my life now – I just feel God's been very good to me. My life at 77, coming through all that, is so wonderful. Although I don't do a lot – I'm surrounded by nice people.*'

For an ex-Kes man living in Yorkshire it's not an easy secret to keep. '*Last week I went to a neighbours 100th birthday party, actually it's only a centenary celebration I can go to where I am younger than the principle by over twenty years. My next door neighbour was there and he had just learnt I took a part in Kes. He was absolutely amazed he's been next door to me for 10 years and didn't know. I don't like talking about it because it looks like your bragging. They want me to take the film round – my son and daughter bought me a copy a couple of years ago.*'

The 4D Jones – *The Band in the club*

The 4D Jones Band, played at the club, The Cudsworth Hotel – now the Dards, where Mrs Casper and Jud enjoy their night out. The line-up was John Stenton; vocals, David Hargreaves; lead guitar, Les Stokes; rhythm guitar, Alan Lodge; bass guitar and Geoff Hollin; drums.

They were a professional band that had been playing for about 4 years before they got their gig on the *Kes* set. They mainly played the working men's clubs of South and West Yorkshire – performing around 5 nights a week – with a good reputation and a strong following. '*At this time the club-land scene was thriving, vibrant and expanding,*' explains lead guitarist, David Hargreaves. '*We opened many of the new clubs and played along side many of the top artists of the day.*'

'*We were playing on stage in a club known locally as the Buff Club, when a group of people came and sat at a table near the front. They stood out because they were not dressed as typical for the area. When we returned to our table after doing our spot we were approached and asked if we would like to be in a film.*' The band accepted the request with nonchalant shrugs, assuming it was some sort of wind-up. They finished their other spots and nothing more was said about it.

'*It was only at the end of the night when we were getting changed,*' says David, '*the club secretary came in to pay us, and said that the committee room had been made ready for us and that the film people were waiting - that we realised they weren't kidding.*' The producer, Garnett, had received several recommendations from different sources when he was trawling for his screen band. Both he and Loach liked what they saw and booked them there and then.

Once the details of how much notice the band would require to be at a location in Barnsley, Tony Garnett and Ken Loach and a couple of the crew, together with the band, finished the evening off with a few drinks and a lot of laughter. '*A short time later we were contacted and told to meet at the Cudworth Hotel for filming,*' remembers David. '*We set up our gear and then put on our regular stage wear, but were informed that this was not the image they were trying to portray and we must change into something much more northern working class.*'

'*We then had to play as normal for about 1 hour and this was all recorded together with the filming of those in the hotel audience.*'

During the big night out for Mrs Casper and her boyfriend (Joe Miller), and Jud and his best mate; John Grayson, together with The 4D Jones band was the comic Joey Kaye. Hargreaves takes up the story, 'We were then told that a comedian had also been booked and could he use our microphone and PA system, which we agreed. Joey Kaye, who I did not know, told some jokes and then did a comic song with us playing along as backing.'

According to David Hargreaves there was a fight scene shot when they were filming at the Cudsworth Hotel.

'So that dialogue could be filmed,' explains David, 'we were asked to mime to what we had already played, a playback was set up at the back of the stage so that we could here what we were miming to. As I best remember, the older brother Jud was filmed trying to pick up two girls standing at the bar, their boyfriends returned and a fight broke out between them and Jud. This was no stage fight as they all just had a right go at each other. Chairs were smashed, proper solid ones, tables and glasses knocked over and all those fighting ended up with blood over them and bruises. There was loud applause when the director closed the scene. All this time we were trying to mime, we had been told to carry on no matter what.'

At the end of the days filming Tony Garnett told the band that he would make sure they received plenty of publicity. 'Unfortunately it was 12 months before the film came out and the group had split up and we had gone our separate ways.'

Les Stringer – *The butcher*

Les Stringer played a wonderful cameo as the kind, nicely rounded butcher, who you felt ate three hot meals a day. With his brilliant white overalls and his worn blood-stained stripped apron, he was every inch the family butcher. I was somewhat shocked to hear that meat was not his profession. 'I was secretary general manager of the colliery social centre; we used to book many of the acts and put on shows. I met a gentleman called Claude Hunter he was the general manager of ATS. The company was owned by the Joseph bothers, Stanley and Michael. They just added me onto the list – the next thing I was accepted – I didn't have to audition for the part and there was no rehearsal. I actually went on four separate occasions to film my part. I had not met the young David Bradley before. Also I was not given a script. I remember I was paid fifty a day, well half days – 10 till 2, and received two hundred pounds at the end of filming. I enjoyed the whole experience, my only disappointment was the ending to the film – I like happy endings.'

Due to his capacity as secretary general manager, Les used to book and know personally many of the acts. And a few made their way into the movie. 'I knew Lynne Perrie personally and her brother

Duggie Brown. I used to employ them both as artists.'

Although Les has moved out of Yorkshire, he now lives in Shropshire, he still gets associated with *Kes*. *'Don't tell me how they know or find out – but most people know I was in Kes. I've been living here for the last 14 years. I'm disabled and am not capable of driving, so I find it quite difficult to get back to Yorkshire.'*

Stringer, now 85, started his working life at 14, down the mines, and finished up as director of a brewery in Hamburg. After some television-extra work, mainly in the series *Hadleigh,* starring Gerald Harper (1969 – 1976), Les stringer melted back into Yorkshire life. Few will forget the cheery butcher, Billy did not see very many smiling faces, and few cannot believe Les Stringer was not a butcher!

Geoffrey Banks – *Billy's maths teacher*

Geoffrey Banks was a newsreader at BBC radio in Manchester, who also acted in amateur dramatics and taught French. He has enjoyed 13 TV guest appearances including *Heartbeat, Juliet Bravo* and *Coronation Street.* He has also been in 3 television roles, his most famous to date *Poirot: Dumb Witness* (Starter) in 1996. Banks was also seen fleetingly, credited as Lycra Cyclist 1 in *Calendar Girls* (2003). Unfortunately, Mr Banks declined to take part in the book.

Joe Miller – *Mrs Casper's boyfriend*

Joe Miller, a South Wales-born comedian who had appeared in the television show *Blackpool Night Out,* played Billy's mother's date in the pub scene. Loach found Miller through the Variety Artists Federation, which was affiliated to Equity.

20

The Crew – The professionals

Penny Eyles - *Continuity*

It may be of interest that Penny Eyles, who has worked closely with Ken Loach on a few films, has had plenty of continuity experience notching up five Monty Python films including *The Holy Grail* (1975) and the *Life of Brian* (1983) – which may be the subject of a book on its own! One of the first things that Penny warned me, as I was to go back 37 years after her stint at continuity on *Kes* that she only ever remembered the meals and terrible weather.

With heavy influence from Hollywood around the mid 1980's the profession continuity was re-named script-supervisor, which was a small step forward, I was about to learn, in describing one of the most under-rated occupations in cinema.

Penny Eyles originally met Ken Loach in the early sixties while working for the BBC. '*When you worked for them you did everything,*' explained Penny, '*secretary work, general dog's body, arranging meetings etc. And they used to just hire you out and send you off to work for another director. This one day I was asked to work for Ken Loach, who I had heard of. I went through a labyrinth of corridors and found this tiny office where Ken was working from.*'

When I suggested my first face-to-face meeting with Ken; he reminded me of a kindly uncle who would let you have his last humbug or a gentleman that would get off the bus and walk rather than sit next to a woman with bare arms – Penny vary quickly corrected me, '*Ken is totally ruthless,*' she smiled, adding, breaking into a laugh, '*and Chris Menges, who you thought a softly spoken, friendly, sincere gentleman – is equally ruthless, who would drive the camera over his own baby if the shot required it!*' We both laughed, but I did not doubt her views for a minute.

There is only one continuity girl, or should I say script-supervisor on the set – although you can sometimes be granted an assistant by a friendly producer. *Kes* only had Penny!

The job description in the late sixties, continuity girl, sounds a little incidental and perhaps the sheer magnitude of work during those wet Barnsley days and nights has eradicated it from Penny's mind. *'I don't actually remember much about my job as continuity girl on Kes,but the food was ok and the terrible weather - it was freezing and it rained – and this was the beginning of August!'*

I often aimed the question at actors – if they watched themselves on the big screen – and the reaction is always different. The crew I assumed would watch in the hope the actors did a good job and had not let them down. But Penny seemed to be right in the middle. If she pulls it off with out a hitch – the director, the actors, the crew, everyone gets the credit. Get it wrong and the spotlight can fall unflatteringly on the script-supervisor. *'I can't really watch films I have worked on,'* explains Penny. *'I mean I have done it but it's not an enjoyable experience. I think some of the magic has gone from a movie you have been intimately involved with.'*

The one thing that kept coming back to me was the relevance of *Kes* – with issues being raised in the late sixties depressingly still around nearly forty years on. *'I think Kes and* Cathy Come Home,*'* says Penny, *'both I worked on, and they have both stood the test of time.'* Four decades have passed and kids are being squirted onto the street with little or no prospects and Loach's powerful piece of film, *Cathy Come Home*, dealing with homelessness – there are more homeless people around today!

All the cast and crew had praised elf-like Bradley for his naturalistic playing of Billy Casper, the gap between the real Bradley and the fictitious Casper is unimportant – what matters is that you can not see the join. *'I think it was a funny thing with David Bradley,'* comments Penny seriously, *'I actually met him again some years later on another film,* Absolution *with Richard Burton. Both times he didn't seem very happy, he never appeared at ease with it all or himself. It was all a bit of a strange metamorphosis for David.'*

Every millimetre of film or every second of movie time increases the chances of mishaps and also increases the work load for the script-supervisor. *'Ken has a tendency to over shoot,'* explains Penny, *'that is his style – which does not help continuity, I am really a second pair of eyes to the director.'* Inevitably the more feet of film you use – the greater the possibility while in the editing suit to make or assemble mistakes. This habit of re-shooting – to give him the best chance at the editing stage – the more takes you have – the more performances you have.

'Ken really does not want us around (incidental crew) *he would prefer*

us to be in holes in the ground.' Penny must have done something right – putting aside her work at the BBC, Ken has used her professional services four times on film.

Penny's incredible history is down to her straightforwardness – and I wonder about her ruthfulness although she has the ability to see it in others. Penny certainly has an abundance of spirit – it is not easy looking over the shoulder of Terry Gilliam and comment that the shot including Michael Cain and Bob Hoskins holds a continuity flaw.

I had to mention this fascination, especially in the USA, with continuity problems – or goofs and gaffs as they call them. There are several books that catalogue each one and giving the exact time slot so you can zip forward and find it. You can see Judy Garland in *The Wizard of Oz* as her stunning red shoes change colour (the original ones used to rub her), you can see Richard Dreyfus as Hooper in *Jaws,* digging out the Great White shark tooth when suddenly the mutilated head of Ben Gardner appears (I still jump) – with no apparent reason why or how Jaws could spit the head, through the hole, back into the boat? And in other movies you can see Henry VIII wearing a Rolex watch and a Centurion solder with a mobile phone!

To Penny this was all very annoying. I had to mention the couple of continuity problems during the football match (see page 210 – continuity problems) – where players swap sides in mid play. I was very smartly bought back to reality. What I had not considered, especially in the case of working with Ken *'Now just one more time'* Loach, who shoots and re-shoots, once ALL the film is in the can, once it is a wrap – what Ken and his ensemble do in the cutting room has nothing to do with the script-supervisor. The next time Penny will see it, if she can be persuaded, is at the premier. Also there are genuine mistakes, which Penny and any continuity girl or boy worth their salt should immediately point out - but sometimes the scene has worked so well they are left in. So you really cannot win.

I remember listening to the director of the superb *Shawshank Redemption (1994),* Frank Darabont, discussing the scene where the embittered warden Norton (Bob Gunton) discovers Andy Dufresne (Tim Robbins) has escaped from his sell by digging to freedom. The warden peals away the Rita Hayworth poster to discover the escape hole. The question was – how did the escapee replace the poster – when he was already in the hole? But the director stated he knew all this – but wanted the shot because it was more dramatic. All the crew were advising him to change it – but he assured them that nobody would notice, but they did notice. People always do.

I was relating this to a fellow film buff. There had been an old man half listening to my narrative while playing a fruit machine – we were in a pub. He shook his head, in disbelief, and I wondered if he was bored with all this film talk? *'That film drives me crazy,'* he said eventually. *'For a start Federal Income Taxes were due on March 15th, not April 15th as they are today in the USA. And when Red follows the instructions to find the box under the Oak tree near a New England hay field, there is the clear song of a cactus wren in the sound-track. The nearest cactus wren would be in central Texas!'* He laughed smugly, scooping his golden nuggets from the centre of the machine, adding, *'And it wasn't an oak tree either – it was ash!'* The Ornithologist, botanist, accountant, ceremoniously left.

Penny would have strangled him with a piece of film from the cutting room floor, taken a picture of him with her continuity camera – and show the world what happens to people who dissect the art too much.

Shawshank... is a great film, and one of mine and my dear friend; Harry's, who is no longer with us. I still cry when I watch it – but in different places. Places we both enjoyed and both used to talk about. It is not a morbid self-indulgent experience but a mutual admiration of all things great – especially films. I always thought film buff was rather trivial for an art form I rank with the greatest painters the world has known. In a way when you are painting with words, actors, locations, lighting, editing, directing and so on – I understood Penny's professionalism and realised how many things could go wrong. That is why I celebrated *Kes*, and whether it really was all to do with what the modest producer, Tony Garnett, called serendipity?

Getting to know the different director styles is part of the job for Penny. *'Ken is really not interested in incidental continuity or continuity as a whole and I must say, and it may seem strange, but neither am I. There are certain things you lookout for and this is all part of the job. Every director I have ever worked for, they all have different obsessions.'* And Penny has worked as a second pair of eyes with the best directors in the business; including Altman, Schepisi, Potter, Joffé and remains a Stephen Frears favourite.

At times the director is paying for an opinion – continuity during a movie is not always an exact science. Everything can change on set in an instant, however much you prepare. *'Sometimes continuity can be very difficult, you don't know what the director's thinking – you often have to second guess with rushes – not seeing the end result. Some times when I have a worry about a particular scene and mention it to the director*

– sometimes the performance is so great they keep it in. Sometimes they can cut round it – but if they don't and people pick up on it at the cinema – you feel everyone is looking at the script-supervisor. After all I can only advise. You don't want to put actors in straight jackets. Sometimes it is not that the actors have made a mistake or I have made a mistake it can be down to a choice in the cutting room. I must say it is not something I lose sleep over!'

I wondered if there was some sort if inner spiritual payment for the un-sung heroes of continuity? 'No I don't always enjoy it. It really depends on your relationship with the director. If you're just sitting there doing the continuity it can be mind bogglingly hard work and you have no say in anything. I worked with Robert Altman on Gosford Park, (laughing) that was interesting.'

I do not think I would swap jobs with Penny Eyles – and yet I thought I would do almost anything to get on a film set. 'I think script-supervisor and the focus puller, are incredibly under-rated jobs, they are both tough professions – they are both thankless tasks, nobody notices the work we do until something goes wrong. I worked with Chris (Menges) when he directed A World Apart, he works with a very low light level which means you have a very minimum focus – it can make your work very challenging.'

There is an intense feeling on a movie set. The nature of the beast is big and ugly. The arc lights, the bank of crew members, the actors centre stage and a director often high above the action like some god-like creature dictating and controlling life. 'You are there every second of the film and you have to record every second of the film. Something that happened months ago – people want to know what lights were used, was it raining, where the actors were, even what lenses were used etc. – this is information any member of the team can ask you at any time. I mean everybody is doing their thing, the make-up, wardrobe, operators – but you're really at the sharp end – the buck stops here. And if something goes wrong with the number of shots and nobody is sure what has happened – I have the record for the camera – it may be just a common fault with the lens – but I have the information.'

Penny Eyles was a wonderful, charming parson to speak to – her cut glass pronunciation was a delight and I was told off several times – but like an experienced teacher, I was unaware at the time – but heeded everything that Penny said. It was a total revelation to me – I was going to fill a few lines for Penny's piece – bathing in my glory at tracking down the continuity girl from a film that was made over 37 years ago. My self induced slaps on the back receded as I began to understand possibly one of the most hard working and underrated jobs in the film and television industry. There were no days off, the script-supervisor had to be there every single day of the shoot, even when the second units were going out. I had mocked this profession. I had waded through the many catalogues of disaster, and blaming one aspect of the profession – I even did it in *Kes!* I was slowly coming to terms that it was often NOTHING to do with the continuity girl. Yes, there are bad script-supervisors, but Penny Eyles is at the top of her game.

Another testament to this quite remarkable woman – my narrative kept breaking off as she caught up with the gossip from the rest of the cast and crew. Penny's thirst to keep up with her former colleagues proved she cared.

There is a large movement at present that wants to see mistakes in great movies – there is almost no lose of pride in picking these so called faults from your favourite film. I cannot think of any other business that attracts such negative interest that wallows in criticism of something the admirer holds dear. It is hard to imagine selling a video with all the mistakes made by Manchester United – to there own fans. Although I could see Manchester City buying a few copies! I have been instrumental in promoting this unconstructive hobby, although Penny has completely altered my prospective.

Penny made it quite clear to me that if people were to discover she was a script-supervisor dealing exclusively in continuity, and they wished to discuss the humdrum aspect of topics like in Star Wars, although Tatooine has two suns, the angular distance between them is quite small, so only very large objects would cast two distinct shadows. Penny is adamant at her stance, *'I would walk away from them – if they wish to know aspects of my job or the film making process – then I will talk to them.'*

During *Kes* Penny logged all the information she is trained to do. It is a highly complex technical process and the mind is your most powerful tool. *'I am logging information with a Polaroid camera. I log data and can also have a monitor and the director records it. Stephen Frears who I have worked with half a dozen times doesn't want to record it – he doesn't want to look at playbacks. Actors can often see the playbacks and alter their performance.'*

You have to be observant. To me it must be on the level of a combination of Sherlock Holmes and Columbo with a touch of my mother – I never got away with a single thing!

'You have to record and observe a lot of stuff that nobody else wants to know. So you do have to be very observant. You have all this stuff in your head that is completely useless after a film hits editing.'

I will think again before I complain about the knife Rambo (First Blood Part 2) is cleaning on his Levi fatigue jeans, made 11 years after the time it was set, and mentioning there was more blood on the weapon before this scene. Also the fact that the green lake warble frog is not indigenous to that part of Vietnam. I will remember Penny's voice, the sound of utter condemnation and sit in silence. After all, does it really matter?

Ray Orton – *Camera Operator*

Ray Orton left school and worked in Rank Labs for eighteen months in order to get a union ticket and then joined Eyeline Films in London. Ray worked as loader and focus puller on commercials, CFF films, documentaries, music videos and whilst there met Chris Menges. Orton assisted Chris on a nine-week documentary for American Broadcasting Corporation which involved travelling to Africa and Zaire. 'The following year,' remembers Orton, 'Chris asked me to be his focus puller on Kes. During shooting I closely observed Chris's approach to natural lighting, which is echoed in my work today. Having worked on commercials, films and documentary it was good to see the fusion of cinema drama and documentary on the big screen. It was certainly unusual and a wonderful opportunity that the whole camera crew were under thirty, also very much enjoyed working in Yorkshire.'

Orton was constantly amazed and intrigued as the movie started to develop. 'For me the greatest bit was to see Ken Loach approach a scene and give one set of directions to one artiste and a conflicting set of directions to another, with the result that it was impossible to know what would happen in front of the camera when the scene started, hence it created a sense of anticipation amongst cast and crew alike. Typically the little lad (Martin Harley) who comes in with a message for the headmaster, whilst the boys are waiting to be caned, had no idea of what would develop in the scene.'

Kes made statements that criticised the whole ethos of the political education system and with the air thick with acidic views and opinions, pointing the working class finger at the governing power, Ray recalls the establishment's reaction to the film. 'We all appreciated that the film was politically left of mainstream cinema and were not surprised at the right wing reaction.'

Like true professionals all the crew worked well together and many helped each other on the next rung of the occupational ladder. There are many facets to the industry. In film a Camera Operator points the camera and frames the shot. Lighting Cameraman/Director of Photography (DOP) will direct the lighting and photographic style. 'Working with Chris on Kes led to me working on Gumshoe (1971),' recalls Orton, 'I was engaged as camera operator with Chris planning to light and operate, but after a few days Chris realised the workload of the lighting was not going to allow him to operate and he tried me out on a few scenes; having seen the rushes I was allowed to operate the rest of the production.'

Ray, having proved himself on Gumshoe as operator, it opened the door to his career as Director of Photography (DOP) with BFI productions with Peter Smith. 'With the opening of C4 and S4C (Welsh Channel 4),' explains Ray, 'I became a founder member of Teliesyn, a film production co-operative making programmes for C4, S4C and BBC.'

Since BAFTA Cymru started Ray Orton received several nominations for Best Cinematography, and has twice won Best Cinematographer for Gadael Lenin (1993) and Tair Chwaer. Ray Orton's career has spiralled upwards and he is now a respected cinematographer in his own right. After working on the well-respected Hedd Wyn (1992), it went on to be nominated for Best Foreign Language Film at the Oscars.

Over the years Ray Orton has shot countless productions and has even wound up developing florescent light heads, which have become part of his lighting style.

Richard Hines – *Technical Advisor*

It was a real thrill to talk to Richard, days before the final draft. He certainly was a major factor in the creation of A Kestrel For A Knave, and without his struggles and passions I am sure we would not have had Barry's novel, and subsequently Ken's film.

Richard Hines had lived and breathed Billy Casper. Many of the stories in Kes were from Richard's own experiences, 'When Casper goes to the library and ends up nicking a book on falconry – I did that in real life. What I did, I didn't steal the book, I was so obsessed I ordered a book and it was that long in coming – I went to the reference library and copied the whole book out in long hand – word for word!'

'I told him (Barry) about Fisher - German Bite, during morning register– it happened in my school. The innocent lad that got the stick – I actually witnessed that – we, me and my mates, gave the cigarettes to a young first year to hold – and he got cane as well,' laughs Richard.

Franco Rosso - *Filmmaker*

Franco Rosso was just another filmmaker on *Kes*, but has now been elevated through editor to director and writer. In 1982 he won an Evening Standard British Film Award. Franco even directed a *Kes* favourite in the shape of Freddie Fletcher (Jud Casper) in *The Nature of the Beast* (1988).

Daphne Dare - *Wardrobe*

Daphne Dare was wardrobe on *Kes* but had worked as Costume Designer on *Doctor Who* at its birth in 1963. Daphne subsequently worked on several of Loach's productions including *Carla's Song* and *Hidden Agenda*. Sadly Daphne passed away in September 2000.

Gerry Humphreys - *Sound*

Gerry Humphreys was sound recordist on *Kes*. Gerry is a prolific worker and has been a sound mixer, dubbing mixer and sound recording mixer on over 224 films and 15 TV movies. He has worked on such classics as *The Lion in Winter* (1968) with Peter O'Toole and Katharine Hepburn, *The Italian Job* (1969) with Michael Caine and two *Superman* and *Pink Panthers*. Gerry has received two Oscar Academy Award nominations for a *Chorus Line* (1985) and *Gandhi* (1982) the latter losing out to Spielberg's *ET*. BAFTA's came thick and fast with nominations for *A Chorus Line*, *Blade Runner* (1982) and *Sunday Bloody Sunday* (1971) and won with *Cry Freedom* (1987) and *A Bridge Too Far* (1977).

21

The Extras – The People of Barnsley

This chapter is dedicated to all the un-credited cast that blended into the background. Jim Ryder, a key player in the football match and Anne Goulding who featured in the fight scene and many many more. Even the climber who first tackled Monastery farm wall, so as Dai Bradley could follow and retrieve the hawk from the nest.

Julie Goodyear MBE – *Woman in betting shop*

Julie Goodyear's stepfather ran the Bay House in Heywood and Julie helped behind the bar. As art once again would imitate nature the actress would spend many years behind the bar at the Rover's Return public house on the set of *Coronation Street* as buxom Bet Lynch.

Julie came to my attention via Freddie Fletcher. He maintained that every time he bumped into or spoke to Julie she maintained she had a speaking part in *Kes*? Freddie asked me if this was correct – as it had been a standing joke. I quite smugly said, being the great aficionado on the subject, that there was no way Goodyear was in *Kes*. 'Right,' said Freddie, '*I'll have her about that.*' It was sometime later I was talking to Trevor Hesketh, who played Casper's form teacher in *Kes,* he told me about a trip to Granada Television. At the time Trevor was chaperoning Dai Bradley and taking him to castings not associated with the movie. This time he was up for a part in the series *A Family at War* (1970), playing Alfred, which he secured. Trevor told me that after the audition he and Dai were sitting in the Granada canteen when Julie Goodyear came over and made a great fuss of Bradley. When he asked Dai how he knew her – Bradley replied, '*Didn't you know, she had a part in Kes.*'

Before I rang Freddie and apologised I watched the part where Billy Casper enters the betting shop and walks up to the counter. There is a woman in silhouette behind the grill. '*Can I help you, son?*' There is no mistaking the voice of Bet Lynch.

When I finally had the chance of talking to the actress, Julie set the record straight. 'Yes it was me. I remember being behind a bookie's counter. And yes it was just the one line.' This was not, like most of the cast, her first acting appointment. 'Kes was in 1968, although I first appeared in Coronation Street two years earlier in 66. This was for about 6 weeks and then they chucked me out because I'd had no formal training. I then went to Oldham Rep to get training. It was after that that this tiny, tiny part in Kes came up. Which of course to me was a huge step on the ladder of what I considered acceptance into what I so desperately wanted to be my career for the rest of my life. It was very, very exciting'

Julie was born in Heywood, Lancashire – where she still resides today. 'I heard about Kes, like all local people did, by word of mouth. The next thing I was up for an audition. Lynne Perrie had the really big part.'

Careers can hang on a single performance but in Julie's case, shielded from view, uttering the one line, it is doubtful the appearance had any positive effect. 'The film came out in 1969, locally and I rejoined Coronation Street in 1970, where I stayed for the rest of my career. I would love to work with Ken again, but not in silhouette this time.'

Actually, Kes was very kind to Coronation Street, it gave them, as well as Goodyear's Bet Lynch and Perrie's Ivy Tilsley/Brennan – they had Geoffrey Banks' Herbert Townsend, Freddie Fletcher's Bob Whitely, Brian Glover's Fred Henshaw and Harry Markham's Handel Gartside. More recently Duggie Brown has been spotted as a Corrie regular playing George Freeman.

Julie Goodyear deservedly collected an MBE from the Queen in 1996. Julie finally quit Coronation Street on 2nd October 1995 after walking away with a lifetime Achievement Award at the first National Television Awards.

Ann Goulding – Extra (playground fight)

Ann Goulding is still living in Barnsley, and in 1968 was a 15-year-old pupil at St Helen's school, Ann featured in the playground fight scene. She was not classed as an extra and did not get paid. Her younger sister, who appeared in the ballet scene when Casper was trying to evade brother Jud, received £5.

'We were told about the fight scene at playtime. We were just told what was expected of us, which was to do as kids do and run to the scene of a fight, and to act natural. I was in that scene – it took me a while to find myself – but there I am, in the last frame as Mr Farthing scatters us kids.'

'It was an amazing experience to have all film people about; most of the girls had crushes on the crew. I must admit I was quite taken by one of the sound recordists, I think – he was named Tony. I mentioned I was good at sowing and he had ripped his trousers while filming. I offered to sow them – until I found out it was in the crutch area – I refused to do it. I was very shy and naïve back then,' Ann laughs heartily adding, 'I'm not bloody like that now!'

When Mrs Goulding viewed the premier in 1970 she was shocked, 'I thought our accents were chronic! But we were kids and all rough. I really enjoyed the film.'

She felt especially privileged to watch the football game featuring Brian Glover. 'I remember watching from the classroom, it was absolutely hilarious.'

Jim Ryder – Footballer

I think out of all the extras, un-credited extras, I was amazed that Jim was not mentioned in despatches – e.g. the credits. He had a few lines during the football match and in the changing room, most famously, 'Tha's had it now, Casper', as Sugden disappears to get a pair of oversized shorts for Billy to wear. Ryder was also one of the reluctant guards preventing Casper from coming out of the showers, as the evil Mr Sugden turns the water to cold; as he believes he deliberately let in the last goal.

'A lot of the lads in the film still live in the area and I see them from time to time. I haven't seen Freddie Fletcher or David Bradley for many years, but I would like to see them both again. We all had some great times.'

'Funnily enough, both my daughters did Kes for their GCSE's and they asked me loads of questions about it, and I seem to remember I got a few wrong!'

It was a strange world to be cocooned in for those seven weeks in Barnsley. Life was imitating the film as there were so many genuine friendships mirroring screen friendships and teachers playing themselves. 'It was actually quite confusing. Most of the lads in the movie were my mates in real life, and Mr Hesketh, who played Mr Crossly (Later changed back to Hesketh,) was my form master and English teacher – then after filming we all had to try and go back to normal.'

Mr Addy - (Rock Climber)

Mr Addy was a colleague of Barry Hines and took his place at St Helens as PE teacher, when Barry required more free time to concentrate on his writing career. He remembered one days filming very well. 'What was quite remarkable was the climbing sequence,' recalls Addy. 'At the time I did a lot of walking and climbing. The scene where Casper climbs up to the hawk's nest, which was about forty foot up, the wall was all crumbling.' The actual location was Old Hall Farm; re-named Monastery Farm in the film. 'What they did was to send a crew up with a camera first, before filming started. The kestrels were ready for flying. I put on some climbing pitons and went up and left a few pegs – it was sheer and very slow going and that was in the light. We also had to cover the pegs up so you could not see them. There was a cherry picker with the main camera in and young Bradley started climbing up – there was no messing he went straight up. By this time it was quite dark in the evening – there was no ropes or harness. I think this was one of the most remarkable things he did.'

In the film Casper makes the climb in the morning and it looks and feels hazardous, as it actually was. 'As we were standing at the bottom,' continues Addy, 'just watching the filming, a crew member came up to me and my mate, who had done the climb with me, and gave me £25. I really couldn't believe it, we both couldn't.'

22

The Caning – The Boys Who Volunteered

Realism was everything for Loach, who used the element of surprise to elicit natural performances from his young cast. When Billy is sent to the headmaster's office to be caned for not concentrating in assembly, he is joined by four others - three from the smokers union and McDowell; wrongly selected by Mr Hesketh for coughing in assembly. The fifth boy to join Casper, making six in all, was an innocent youngster who had been told to take a message to the Headmaster.

None of the young ensemble expected a real caning to be administered, which it was, least of all the twelve-year-old, Martin Harley; his tears were as real as his protestations. Barry Hines, who was present for most of the filming, recalled, *'Ken said to Bob Bowes (Mr Gryce), who played the head: "Every time that little lad opens his mouth, tell him to shut up. Don't let him get the words out." You see the panic on his little face, but afterwards Ken explained to all of them why it was necessary and they understood, so they didn't bear any grudges.'* Or so everyone thought. Martin Harley may have laughed off the incident at the time, but the film is now a reminder of a traumatic period in his life – a time he believed he was let down by the crew.

As with the moment in *Cathy Come Home* when the children are taken away from Carol Ward (Carol White), Loach justified such realism, effecting screen children, with the need to portray reality. *'They were going in for a caning but weren't sure what was going to happen and it stung for a minute or two,'* said Loach. *'Kids were getting the cane routinely every day and it's a very important scene because the headmaster is going on about the collapse of standards and how people don't respect authority in the way they used to, but he's so blind to the fact that he canes the wrong boy. The young lad got a couple of strokes, but we gave him extra pocket money afterwards and, within seconds, he was smiling through his tears.'*

The boy, Martin Harley, was quite an infectious giggler and this caused problems. When Casper is talking to Mr Farthing; after the fight with McDowell, he hints about this particular scene. *'And this little lad, sir. He'd only bought a letter from a teacher, and he got t'cane,'* explains Billy, emotionally, adding, *'It's nowt to laugh at, sir. Afterwards, he was as sick as a dog.'* Loach decided to film this scene rather than let it come out through dialogue. *'He was constantly giggling, all through the caning scene he would start, in the end they had to get quite tough with him, although the crew found it funny as well,'* remembers, Hesketh, *'Afterwards they wanted to show Martin being sick in one of the school drains. One of the crew gave him some salt water, he leant over and was sick — but all the time he was laughing. He did this about five or six times and he got worse. The more he was sick the more he laughed. In the end, because they really wanted the shot, the crew had all got their backs to him, as they were crying silently with laughter. Anyway, whether they got the shot or not, it never went into the finished film.'*

There was one lad who was upset about the caning, Michael Joyce, but because he did not get it! *'I was as mad as hell about it, I was Naylor's (McDowell) mate and his best friend in the film. I was supposed to get caught with the others smoking and get the stick, by Gryce. Only I missed one day's filming due to an interview at Fox's — for four quid a week and I didn't get it! I missed out on £3 for the day plus extra other lads got for each swipe — I would have made a fortune.'*

For the people who remembered when the cane was legally used in schools and the wrath it demonstrated, it all works beautifully in this scene. In a recent interview with Bradley he revealed that the caning part of this scene was not in the script.

'Ken and Tony had assured us that we wouldn't really get caned,' said Bradley. *'So we didn't put our hands out how we knew they should be put, lowering your thumb as much as possible and gently flexing your fingers so that the cane hits flesh, as opposed to bone, when it really hurts. When we were actually caned, we were really upset, not in terms of tears, but angry we had been lied to. So we decided that we wouldn't do it again and went on strike. Ken and Tony got together, then came back and said a couple of the caning takes could be done from behind and we could wear gloves, but they would have to do the actual shot from the front one more time and would pay us an extra ten shillings (50p) for each hand caned, which would include those with gloves on. In total, the rest of us made £3 10s (£3.50). We realised that it had to be real, but it was the shock of having trusted these people over several weeks and, suddenly, we were told that we didn't have to worry about the scene because we wouldn't really get the cane, but we did.'*

Director of photography Chris Menges was also prepared for the shot. He recalled, *'Ken whispered in my ear, "They're going to be walloped." I thought: Christ! We're going to beat up children what happens if I miss it! It's a scene that millions of people have lived for real in schools, though.'*

One of the most dominant film moments of *Kes* was when the all-powerful head master, Mr Gryce, or as he is known by the pupils; Gryce puddin', canes the innocent young boy, played by Martin Harley. I can still see his naïve, virtuous countenance and trusting pool brown eyes - it must have been like shooting a spaniel!

Tracking down Martin Harley tested all of my journalistic and detective skills and the help of a few un-tiring cast members. Although Martin was one of the first names I added to my want list – he remained there until the very end as others were being ticked off around him. It slowly dawned on me that Harley did not have the same feeling about the film as other cast members. There were no romantic memories of that mad summer of 68' when a bunch of un-trained school kids in the art of acting from Barnsley made a Hollywood funded movie. For Martin the whole experience left him feeling used, exposed and exploited. He felt the principle crew members had let him down and his humiliation was there for all to see.

His reluctance to talk to me was not born out of rudeness; simply a desire to keep the past buried in the further recesses of his mind. Time had gone some way to shroud these negative images, and the last thing Martin wanted was to bring them all to the surface and share his anxieties with a total stranger and then, when the book hit the shelves – a few thousand readers. Over a few months I called Martin and we chatted, when he was not on shift work, about everything but *Kes* and I like to think we formed a trusting relationship. In fact Martin came to realise that I was an ideal tool to set the record straight. He wanted his say.

Harley's movie career started and ended with *Kes*, the role was not very big – but the cherubic twelve-year-old did make an impact. He was in his first year when the film crew swamped the Barnsley school. On every ones lips the chatter was all to do with the new movie that was being made on their very doorstep.

Martin Harley, with a few first years, did an audition and received the usual phrase *'we'll be in touch if we need you'* – slight deviation from the stock-in-trade movie buy-off; *'don't call us, we'll call you.'*

Martin began his summer six-week break playing football in the fields and riding his bike. It was a warm drizzly Thursday evening when his mom and two production staff traipsed across the park, beckoning Martin towards them. *'My mom eventually found me, stuck me in my school clothes and I was driven to the school. Nothing really happened that Thursday, but we started filming the next day; Friday.'*

It turns out a teacher from St Helen's had put Martin's name down and suggested him for the part. *'I think Trevor Hesketh put my name forward,'* remembers, Martin, *'because I think he liked me, he knew my background, my family. I wasn't the best English student, but I enjoyed the subject. I wasn't from a rough family. My mother, although we had no money and there were four of us, always took pride in our appearance. Having said that, a silly thing happened, because they more or less dragged me from the park, I put on a sweater, I happened to have some black trousers on, and I went into school. The next day I was asked to return in the same cloths, during filming outside the head's office, the lad gives me the packet of cigarettes to hide – and they drop straight through my pockets on to the floor – I had holes in them – they were playing trousers. They had to staple up the holes for me.'*

There was disparity and contrast with the line-up of boys. With Casper's awkward sinewy figure hunched in boredom and the bullying MacDowell's impressive wiry physique, flanked by equally scruffy defiant friends, Harley stood; small, quiet and polished. The pack of older boys - arrogant, cocky - street urchin types, certainly street-wise teenage survivors – with the pristine, gleaming Martin Harley – clean jumper, cute hair cut, you could not see his shoes but you knew they shone. He almost appeared like a bird, perched on the far boy's shoulder. *'Yes there was certainly contrast,'* laughs Harley. *'My mom used the word angelic to describe my appearance back then.'*

You knew this twelve-year-old lad was not smoking behind the bike sheds or fighting the local kids on the cobbles – this lad did his homework and crossed old ladies over the street. And I think this was Martin Harley and this is what the production team saw.

Early on the Friday morning it was all *'lights, camera, action'* (although Loach refuses to use the phrase). Although there was very little action as the heavy camera was moved around for the next shot. *'I filmed in the head masters study – about half a day. Overall, with the other scenes, I was filming for two and a half days. I remember there was quite a bit of hanging about, as they were filming other scenes. They filmed the bit where Bradley climbed naked over the showers and I remember watching that.'*

It would be a fair assumption that using inexperienced actors, moving around cramped locations, actors ad-libbing because of unscripted text - that breaks in concentration, forgetting words, would be expected. *'Not really.'* Martin explains. *'We only filmed a bit at a time. The main problem why we had to stop was aeroplane noises, by flying overhead.'*

For a twelve year old, for two and half days work, the money was not to be sniffed at – it was 1968. *'I received forty-five pounds in total. I don't think we got much for the actual filming, about a fiver a day, but we did get extra for each stroke of the cane. That made up the money.'* Normally this would turn any child's head and the movie business might be considered a career one could start straight away. *'I did go to one casting at Granada Television, it was* Family at War *(1970) – which David (Bradley) also went for and got,'* says Martin. *'I never really wanted to pursue acting as a career. I always knew all my life what I wanted to do. Originally I wanted to be a car mechanic or an engineer. My great uncle told me if I became an engineer I could always come down to be a car mechanic – but it doesn't work the other way round. I straight away took an engineer apprenticeship in Leeds and have never looked back'.* Martin now works in a large bakery in Swinton near Rotherham. He is now engineering supervisor, covering the whole of maintenance at a bakery which is the largest bagel factory in the world.

As usual in a Loach film the script was as scarce as a rabbit at a stoat's reunion. *'There was certainly no script to read from,'* comments, Martin. *'You were just offered what to say and made it up from there. As each scene developed it was almost out the blue – on the spur of the moment. We filmed a little bit, then another bit, although phrases were offered to me.'*

The boys were to get a bigger shock as Gryce Puddin' lifted the cane and started to dish out the punishment to the line of boys. *'None of us ever expected to get the cane,'* comments, Harley, seriously. *'I just felt total amazement I think. I don't think I felt angry, not at the time. Just total amazement – I couldn't believe they had done it. They kept filming, kept going.'*

Ken Loach had not finished there. *'Six times on each hand I received the cane,'* explains, Harley. *'The first one – which was straight on each hand and then round the back for the other five, with us all wearing sheepskin mittens.'* All the swipes were painful, even with the mittens, as the angry wheal was repeatedly hit. *'On the DVD, I have been told, if you look closely, you can see the black mark left by the first swipes.'* I automatically glanced down at his hands, somehow looking for a scar or faint indentation – of course there were none - not after 37 years! As my gaze returned to his face, his pained expression, as his mind re-visited that claustrophobic head masters study - I realised there was a mental scar, albeit not serious.

I could see the cane coming down on the innocent boy on

screen, the shock, the amazement — that adults could be so unkind. Of course that particular piece of film ceased to be a cinematic moment and I would forever watch Martin Harley being cruelly caned. Of course as Ken Loach has said, it was only what other kids were being put through, in schools — throughout the land, on a daily basis. But it didn't make it any easier for me — and I'd like to think that the madness stopped there. It did all change for the better. Corporal punishment is a Victorian, out-dated tool that only breeds resentment and distance for the guilty culprits and bitterness and injustice for the innocent victims.

Giving a man thirty lashes or the cat-o-nine-tails is not that greater leap from swiping a child on both hands and six of the best on the buttocks with a wooden stick. Deriving pleasure, as I assume some masters do, has to be an even greater crime than most of the victims ever committed.

Martin Harley, up until that summer evening in July, had never received the cane. I knew the answer but asked him if the tears were genuine? 'Believe me those tears were real — I think it was the shock more than anything.' I wondered what the effect was watching the film today. 'I avoid watching it,' said Martin, sadly, 'It's an episode in my life I want to forget. There was no enjoyment in it and no pleasant memories — I felt exploited.' All these negative feelings, it developed, were not all to do with the caning scene. 'It was the way it was all done — how I was treated, everything. Once the film was made — they forgot everybody.'

These disheartening thoughts did not manifest themselves, totally, at the time of filming, but shortly afterwards. 'Within months of making the film,' states Martin. 'I and many others just assumed the film was not going to be released — it took that long for anything to happen. The first I knew was when I was contacted to go down to Pinewood Studios, with half a dozen others, to do the re-dubbing. Actually, not just our scenes — we also did some dubbing for other characters. My mother came with us, actually she chaperoned the six of us.'

Many people have hailed the movie a classic, but there was obviously a price to pay — certainly in Martin Harley's experience. 'For me personally, I think it was very expensive,' says Martin. 'I think it was very expensive to everybody who was in it. I think we all felt used and abused. No production team contacted any of us to say what was going on. To me it's disgusting and I think it sums up the film industry.' The problems appeared to be a lack of communication between the production staff and the young cast, although Dai Bradley was enjoying a wave of publicity as the film began to get noticed. 'There should have been some kind of rapport,' states Harley, bitterly. 'The production team should have continually kept people informed at what stage the film was at – just a call or letter. We all thought it had been made and dropped.'

I think it is probably indicative of the whole movie merry-go-round, and to a point understandable. There is not much after sales service. Ken and his men swept into a small community, and lavishly handed out attention and boundless enthusiasm. Then one day they are gone forever, never to return, and the people are left behind. But not necessarily forgotten, as a previous meeting with Loach proves. He personally asked about several cast members and was genuinely concerned about their well-being. I think the strangled start of *Kes* to secure a regional release date, which was down to Rank, kept everyone in the dark – including the crew! The general release only happened because of the success *Kes* received during the Academy run which no one could have foreseen.

Of course the finished film is there for the world to see. 'Whenever they show a clip of Kes, that caning scene is one of the most used, it's probably the most dramatic.'

Unfortunately, Martin was one of the youngest on set. 'The film crew were alright to me and some of the other lads in the cast weren't too bad, but of course they didn't know me,' says Martin. 'I was two or three years younger than them – I was a stranger to them and they were all school mates. I was really a bit of an outcast. Then things started to add up and I just felt used. You're lucky I'm talking about it - at times I won't.'

There was no doubt who the young actor felt responsible. 'I think the main crew were to blame – the director, although I was embarrassingly young and naive then.'

It appears Harley was not present during many of the press launches for the film. However he did appear in one with Brian Glover. 'It may have been a picture taken at the premier? I don't remember doing any press stuff at all.' Martin was invited and went to the premier at Doncaster. 'I remember it coming up to my scene in the movie and I just wanted to crawl under the seat. I just felt very uncomfortable'

Without the pride and natural euphoria usually connected with appearing in a cinematic release, Martin faced fans of the film a little humiliated and miffed. What with the whole film industry voting, permanently securing it as the 7th best British film of all time and the release of the DVD it did nothing to quell public interest. There is always someone that will mention it, especially in Barnsley. They say in England you are never further than 10 feet away from a rat. In south

Yorkshire you are never further than 10 feet from someone who knows a person who was in *Kes* or was in it themselves! Martin can run but he cannot hide.

'Yes, they get to hear about it. Every time I go into town I have that nagging thought – who knows and who is going to come up and talk to me,' comments, Harley. 'Some people shake my hand and admire me for it - others take the mickey out of me. It's been over 35 years ago and people still recognise me for it. I've just come back from Crete and a mate must have mentioned I was in Kes and these two lads, who'd seen the film, knew straight away which character I played. It started, while I was still at school, when the film was released – and they really took the mickey. I am just embarrassed by the whole thing.'

Ironically, during the films release, Martin Harley's mother had just started at teacher training college, as a mature student, to become a teacher. 'My mom is actually very proud of it,' smiles Harley. 'She's not proud of what happened or how it was done. But the fact I was in a film - she tells everybody and anybody.'

What had happened to Martin was very unfortunate. It was tragic that he could not look back on this part of his life with any affection. For nearly all concerned it was an exciting and invigorating time. The crew all seemed to put themselves out to make the young screen kids feel special. Ken Loach is a film-maker first, and as Penny Eyels has previously pointed out, Ken is totally ruthless when it comes to film making. Whatever decisions he makes, they are usually well thought out and ultimately, for the good of the film.

Nina Hibbin, for the Morning Star, after seeing the film in 1970, with regards to the innocent caning scene, wrote, 'The fact that caning is still legal is a clear condemnation of one aspect of our education system. But do such cases of injustice really occur? And how deeply do they scar? I thought back to my own schooldays when, at the age of six, I was slapped and stood in a corner and made to wear a dunce's cap for a crime I didn't commit. It was my first conscious encounter with social injustice, and it has stayed with me ever since.'

23

The Kestrels – Freeman, Hardy and Willis

Just two weeks before the cameras were set to roll, Richard Hines found a baby kestrel, which the team called Freeman, in a nest at the Old Hall Farm – Monastery Farm in the movie. When they filmed Casper climbing up the crumbling face to get to the nest, it was the real nest that contained Freeman and it was Bradley who actually liberated the bird – all on film. Again Loach wanted realism and needed that look on Bradley's face – it was the first time he had seen the nest and it was the first time he had met his new co-star.

During filming, he was to look after the bird, as well as two other hawks supplied by a gamekeeper on an estate at Wentworth, near Doncaster, to act as understudies in case of loss, illness or poor performance. They were then named Freeman, Hardy and Willis; after the chain store. To capture and man these hawks the Hines brothers had to apply to the Home Office for a licence, to comply with the Protection of Birds Act 1954.

The training of the kestrels was lead by Barry Hines's brother, Richard, a falconer as a boy and technical advisor on *Kes*. Richard looked after Freeman, the main bird, although all three were seen. Bradley looked after Hardy and Barry; Willis.

'Although I didn't know anything about kestrels, I did marvel at them,' said Bradley. 'They're such stunningly beautiful birds. Freeman would fly straight at me, very low, perhaps eight to nine feet off the ground, whereas Hardy used to fly high and then swoop down. These were the two main birds we used in the film. Willis, unfortunately, was completely neurotic and psychotic and we couldn't use him much, eventually we had to let Willis go.' Tony Garnett spoke of Willis's attitude, 'I've heard of temperamental artists, but this kestrel beats the lot.'

Richard Hines, an expert in the handling of birds of prey, admitted total defeat with Willis, saying 'I'm not sure what happened with that one. You just couldn't train it to do much. It was weird, in all my years of training and rearing - he was a one off.'

Eventually all three birds were released back into the wild. 'They call it hacking it back,' explained Richard. 'You go out in the field, feed them up and then release them. You then come back the next day and if they haven't caught anything they'll take some meat off the lure. They gradually get wilder and start to miss a few days. Eventually they just don't come back.'

'With regards to Willis, we made the mistake of releasing him too early. We would be filming and he would suddenly appear, swooping down attacking the other birds - trying to take the meat. A nightmare bird that was.'

Freeman, the main bird, is a long winged hawk, with a wing span of 2 ft 7 ins., a weight of eight ounces and brown eyes. Like a true star its weight had to be monitored very carefully; a quarter of an ounce over or under can make a crucial difference in flying form.

Richard Hines took the youngster, Bradley, through the training process: attaching a swivel to the jesses (leather straps fitted to the falcons' legs to hold them) and a leash to the swivel; the manning, to get the falcons used to humans by carrying them on the glove; flying the falcons to the glove, first on a creance (a long, thin line), then freely; and, finally, stooping the falcons to the lure (a string with a leather pad with a pair of bird's wings and meat fastened to it). Critical to the filming was the fact that these falcons fly only when they are hungry, so the weight of the three kestrels had to be monitored carefully and they could appear before the camera only for a short time each day.

It was stated by the director that at no point should Dai Bradley read the book. This was the beginning of Loach's practise of handing out pages of script as filming progressed – with some lines blanked out.

Like the caning scene the director was looking for a similarly realistic reaction to the killing of Billy's kestrel by Jud, the result of Billy's failure to place a bet for his brother. In reality, a dead bird was found by the British Falconers' Society, with the help of veteran anthropologist John Murray of the Royal Edinburgh Museum, but as much as possible was done to convince Bradley that this was one of the kestrels, Hardy, he had helped to train. 'David had realised that, somewhere along the line, there would have to be a dead bird,' explained Barry Hines.

But Bradley insisted he never believed the bird was one of those with which he had formed a bond. 'Barry and Richard tried to prepare me for the fact that, come the end of the film, they would have to put my kestrel, Hardy, down unless they could find a dead one,' Bradley explained. 'Then, suddenly, about a week before we were to shoot that sequence, Hardy went missing, so training during the last week was purely with Freeman; Willis had already flown back to the wild. I interpreted it that *they were trying to make me believe my kestrel had been killed, but I didn't believe they would do such a cruel thing. When I saw the dead kestrel, I couldn't tell that it wasn't Hardy, but I was convinced that they couldn't do something so nasty.'* There is collaborative evidence to suggest that this was not the case that Dai thought it was his bird laying in the bin. Freddie Fletcher has always maintained that as he lifted the dustbin lid – he one hundred percent thought it was Hardy. *'There is no way, no way, Dai didn't think I or Richard had killed his bird and if he says different he's a lying little shit,'* smiles Freddie.

Dai Bradley believed other sinister tricks were being woven around him. *'What actually gave me the feeling of great grief or anger was not the kestrel, but what had happened before shooting the scene. After filming something else in the morning, I arrived at the canteen caravan late for lunch; they had my favourite meal on the menu, shepherd's pie and apple crumble with custard, and hadn't wiped it off the blackboard. When I asked for it, I was told they had run out and they hadn't put any by for me. I was really pissed off by that, so I elected not to have any lunch and went to pig out on fresh fruit. As I ate it, I thought about what had happened and concluded that they were trying to upset me, and realised I had to go along with their wishes.'*

Although Richard Hines confirms Freddie's story about the suggested killing of the hawk - in ear shot of Dai, he is still unsure of Bradley's true feelings. *'We had this hawk which had died of natural causes. When it arrived it was in a block of ice. I thawed it out and put jesses on his feet and placed it in the dustbin. I'm not sure that David was all that bothered about the kestrel. I know Ken thought if he trained it he would probably become very fond of it, but I don't think that happened. The training is very hard and David used to try and wriggle out of it. I never felt David was into or moved by the natural world, but having said that I think he did a brilliant job.'*

It was Richard's skill as a youth that gave his brother, Barry the nucleus of an idea, which matured into *A Kestrel for a Knave*. The opening quotation from *Boke of St Albans*, in Hines's book – states that the kestrel was the one animal in medieval society that the lower echelons could freely own. Loach quips, *'Exactly. It's the bird for the riff-raff of the world.'* It is an ideal bird for Billy Casper – because he is a knave in both the fifteenth-century sense of the word, meaning at the bottom of the social and economic hierarchy, and in the twentieth-century sense of being a rogue or a thief. Billy was a loveable rogue and a little bit of a thief.

24

The Awards – BAFTA and beyond

After breaking box-office records following its gingerly start, *Kes* has also won golden opinions at the Cannes festival where it was shown in the programme organised by the French critics. Which is ironic as the only films that come close in sympathy and perception, showing a sensitive small boy whose life is blighted by oppression on all sides, we must turn to France and such rare masterpieces as *'Poil de Carotte'* or *'Les Quatre Cents Coups.'*

It was generally thought it would have won the Cannes Grand Prix had it been entered into the main competition. United Artists refused to enter it, and the reason why has never been satisfactorily explained.

Kes won two BAFTA's – Best Promising Newcomer: Dai Bradley and Best Supporting Actor: Colin Welland. It also received three BAFTA nominations - Best Film, Best Screenplay and Best Direction. It was also nominated for a UN and National Board of Review award.

At the Karlovy Vary International Film Festival 1970 it won the Crystal Globe for Ken Loach. It also won the Writers' Guild of Great Britain 1971 award for The Best Screenplay, for Ken Loach, Tony Garnett and Barry Hines.

Had United Artists been bolder and had the conviction and confidence many critics and public had who knows what heady heights *Kes* would have soared. You should never peck the hand that feeds you.

25

The Goofs and Gaffs – Continuity problems

With regards goofs, gaffs, flubs etc there were very few mistakes or continuity problems on *Kes*. When you think about the relatively small budget, in film terms, of £155,000 even in 1968 – the 8-week shoot and the high proportion of untrained actors not hitting their marks – it is surprising there were not more. I'm not sure if it was Penny Eyles, the continuity girl, day off, but they all appear during the football scene?

Of course after speaking with Penny I have had to eat my words here. Having put me in my place and enlightened me on the whole continuity process – I am certainly not pointing the finger of blame at the continuity girl or should I say script supervisor, as they are now referred to. Who am I to criticise a profession which their whole survival balances on their ability to juggle every aspect of the intricacy of the complex movie industry. I am particularly bad at observation and lateral thinking, two of the key ingredients needed for a successful career in continuity. I have as much chance at winning the Krypton Factor as at winning Mastermind answering questions on early Hungarian cabinet makers.

The main visual mistake (not Penny's fault) was when a technician was seen at the beginning of the football match. A bearded member of the crew is visible in the scene where Mr. Sugden is selecting the football teams.

The other was probably down to the way Loach works – letting the actors take a natural feel for their prospective rolls. Again this particular goof or gaff took place during the football match where Jim Ryder was selected to play for Sugden's team but ended up protesting about the allowed goal his captain, Mr Sugden, had scored. Jim, whose real name was used in the movie, remembered the scene, *'Yes, I was chosen to go in Brian's (Mr Sugden) team – he clearly shouts out Ryder when we are lined up waiting to be picked. It wasn't till watching it back recently that I am seen protesting against the goal my captain has scored – I actually stand in front of him with my arms up.'*

Again, during the game, when Sugden is dancing down the pitch, in the early part of the match, he kicks the ball, incidentally without looking up (which is in character and not a gaff) – which has obviously gone astray – and he shouts out, 'Come on Speed. What you playin' at, Lad?' Followed by admonitions from Speed, 'What do you think I am sir, a whippet?' Sugden quickly responds, 'You should have been on the move, lad. It was at yer feet.' Unfortunately, Speed was on the other side, Tibbutt's team, for Spurs and was his first choice.

There also seems to be a lucky escape. The scene where Billy is fighting on the coke with McDowell nearly led to a serious continuity problem.

The two boys are roughly man handled by Mr Farthing, who separates them and then bellows at the watching kids dispersing them to the four corners of the playground. Filming had finished for the day and a couple of grips moved in to secure the site, for continuity, as the spewed coke was being used in a shot first thing in the morning. Michael Joyce takes up the story, 'We were all watching the fight, as many extras and pupils were in the scene. Afterwards everybody drifted off. Bradley went straight home without changing his clothes – which were being used in the shoot the next day – which were obviously all covered in coke stains.'

'Bradley got home, changed, hung up his clothes and went to bed after a long day. When he got up in the morning – his mom had washed all his clothes.' When the continuity girl, Penny Eyles, realised what had happened she nearly had several litters of kittens. After a brief discussion with the director a couple of lads were called for – one of them was Joyce. 'We had the job of dragging him through the coke – to get all his clothes torn and dirty as before. Bradley was very uncomfortable as we really went for it. We must have done a good job because I don't think you can tell the difference from one scene to the next.'

26

The British Film Institute – 7 Of The Best

The history of the British Film Institute, which was set up in 1929, can be seen as a succession of great achievements and innovations – the true word in British films. When the institute voted *Kes* 7th Best British film of all time – *Kes* was knighted a classic.

It is one of those classic pub or dinner party arguments. *'What is the best British film ever?'* The debate is, of course, never-ending. At the beginning of the new millennium it was an ideal time to reflect on a full century of British film-making. Not to try to answer the unanswerable question of which is the best, but rather to poll the opinions of those involved in British film, who have seen more movies than most, for an indication of where their professional tastes lie, what their favourites are.

Early in 1999, the British Film Institute produced a selection booklet and sent copies to people embracing all strands of the film, cinema and television industries throughout the UK - producers, directors, writers, actors, technicians, academics, exhibitors, distributors, executives and critics. Participants were asked to consider culturally British feature films, released in cinemas during the 20th century, which they felt had made a strong and lasting impression. Altogether, more than 25,700 votes were cast, covering 820 different films.

The final selection makes compulsive reading. It spans seven decades, from 1935 to 1998, accommodates the work of 70 film directors and much international talent.

The Top 10 of favourites certainly features some names to be reckoned with. Three films from David Lean, others by Alfred Hitchcock (whose centenary was celebrated in 1999), Nic Roeg, Ken Loach, Carol Reed, Robert Hamer, Michael Powell and Emeric Pressburger, while intriguingly in 10th spot is that very '90s film *Trainspotting*, directed by Danny Boyle.

The British Film Institute – TOP 10

1. The Third Man *1949*
2. Brief Encounter *1945*
3. Lawrence of Arabia *1962*
4. The 39 Steps *1935*
5. Great Expectations *1946*
6. Kind Hearts and Coronets *1949*
7. Kes *1969*
8. Don't Look Now *1973*
9. The Red Shoes *1948*
10. Trainspotting *1996*

When Channel 4 ran a major campaign to find THE 100 GREATEST MOVIES of all-time, *Kes* came a very respectful 28.

27

The Child Star Syndrome – When the Spotlight Goes Out

'Steer clear of temptations. Keep your feet on the ground. Don't believe all the hype. And, above all, enjoy fame and fortune while they last, for they can be fickle. I know, I learned the hard way.' Jack Wild – Actor

Quite early on, as I was tracking down the credits, and searching for the lead; Dai Bradley, I was aware of this powerful force that can twist reality and turn lives upside down and inside out. *Kes* briefly illuminated many young performances, but the spotlight stayed on its star for slightly too long. At times I am sure Bradley wanted to step back into the shadows, giving him chance to re-group and re-evaluate his aims and aspirations. The publicity bandwagon can catapult you into a world of fame and riches – it can also run you down and trample any dreams you might have had.

It certainly revved up the young people of Barnsley, who dared to dream about a life in the movie business – even if they were just extras, happy to rub shoulders with the stars. The cruel reality, when Ken and his men moved out, the mundane shadowed innocent thoughts as life drifted back to normality. The bigger the dreams, the farther there was to fall. Some I spoke to wished they had never glimpsed the illusory affect of the swollen world of the movie industry.

Darryl Hickman once commented, *'To survive in Hollywood, you've got to have a shaft of steel right up your back. It must be flexible enough to bend but not brittle enough to break.'*

How many individuals have not envied the celebrity status enjoyed by child performers as they masquerade on the silver screen – adults rushing around pandering to their every need. It is hard to comprehend armies of kids and adults paying to see you and asking for your autograph. What is it like at age eight to earn more in a week than your father or mother earns in a whole year? Or by the age of 12 you never need to work again – like the big box office young stars of Hollywood.

On the other hand, how often has one pondered the enormous sacrifices made by these talented toddlers?

Jackie Cooper readily admits that psychiatry helped repair the damage of having been a famous child star, *'I lived in an adult world, studied at the studio and seldom met kids my own age. I wasn't given an ounce of responsibility or taught the value of money. It makes you emotionally ill to be treated like an enlarged infant.'*

Hayley Mills, as a child star, was Disney's biggest money-maker since Mickey Mouse. Haley, who declined to contribute towards the chapter without a substantial consultation fee (I'm still a big fan), has made that tricky rout from child star to adult performer.

One of the biggest and most famous child stars was Shirley Temple - Little Miss Moneybags, who once said, *'When I was three I was a nobody.'* Although she was admired the world over by age six (Temple was making 3 or 4 movies a year and managed 8 in 1934) – carrying movies and making movies work – but as she matured nobody wanted to look at her anymore. The swan had turned into an ugly duckling or certainly a bland duckling. At age 12 she was a has-been and washed up.

The biggest crime with regards child stardom, it appears, is the stolen years of youth. Shirley Temple stated bitterly, at age six, *'I stopped believing in Santa Claus at an early age. Mother took me to see him in a Hollywood department store and he asked me for my autograph.'*

In the early days the odds against any child becoming a star was estimated at 15,000 to 1. That statistic was worked out many years before British actor Radcliffe playing *Harry Potter* (2001) had cast his first spell and USA born Macaulay Culkin had been *Home Alone* (1990). Culkin, who retired at fourteen-years-old because he was burned-out, and Daniel Radcliffe, were not the first kids on the block to have it all. Radcliffe, who has clocked up over 6 million for playing Potter, is high up in the British wealth stakes – although Prince Harry and Charlotte Church can still give him a run for his money. There were plenty of young performers willing to strut their stuff. Who could forget the great performances from a clutch of early stars fighting in the shadow of the Shirley Temple years.

There were many pocket-sized dancers, singers and actors treading the boards. Some had special talents such as Margaret O'Brien who could cry on cue. She once asked a director, *'When I cry, do you want the tears to run all the way down, or shall I stop halfway down?'*

In a ruthless industry, with equally ruthless parents of some kids, desperately trying to bathe in the reflected light of their offspring, some, you might say, have taken a step beyond decency. One report from America had an embittered and twisted parent, crushed by the failure of his infant, and had sent out poisoned candy to various busy child stars.

I desperately wanted a balanced view. I wanted to hear it straight from the horses or foals mouth, kids who had lived and breathed it. All their emotions, there experiences – whether it be good, bad or ugly.

So I decided to look at other actors who like Bradley had been projected into the public gaze to find out how they had managed their own period of fame and what changes if any this had caused during their adult years. Had their young talent and the tremendous success they had enjoyed enabled them to survive the industry?

Mark Lester – *Child Star*

I was very excited about meeting Mark Lester. I had watched his films as a young boy; Mark was actually just a couple of years older than me. I drove round the beautiful town of Cheltenham, Mark's home town, tall elegant buildings, and leafy streets; dotted with immaculately dressed young girls, carrying shiny leather satchels and lacrosse rackets.

When I finally found Mark Lester's clinic and home it was as impressive as I had seen. I walked into reception and was immediately greeted by Mark, who was both relaxed and charming. He showed me through a short warren of corridors; of the busy house and we ended up in the main room; the heart of the house – as tall as it was wide. Over tea we chatted about passed films. I asked some questions relevant to the book, others the ramblings of a film buff; happy to be in the company of actors.

Eventually we discussed the serious business. Things like how did he feel having his career taken away from him at eighteen? How had the industry treated him and how had it affected him personally? I certainly could not see any scars.

Mark Lester was born in Oxford in July 1958, the son of actors Michael and Rita Lester. Mark made his professional debut when he was only two-and-a-half, playing in a TV commercial with his father, who was the featured player. *'Having theatrical parents did help, it certainly helped in regards the way things in the industry worked, as far as auditioning etc.'* remembered, Mark. *'Knowing that when you were up* for an audition the chances were you were not going to get it. I think a lot of the time, they - parents and children, almost expected to get it. I was very lucky; if ever I went on an audition most times I got the job. At the time when I was experiencing all this success I didn't really know what was happening. One day I would go to an audition and the next day having got the job was a day off school — which was great.'

Mark Lester's early employer, at around two, was Marks and Spencer's. Here he modelled everything from short trousers to woollen jumpers. '*I must of done about 150 of them in the sixties including Fairy Liquid, Reddybreck, Percil you name it — everything!*'

He was later enrolled into the Corona Stage School in London, where he studied acting and mime. '*At stage school the morning was normal lessons,*' explains Mark, '*with the afternoon dedicated to drama, speech, mime, ballet; whatever.*' Mark made his film debut in *Allez France* (1964) at the age of six. '*A very small percentage makes a career out of the film business or even can make a living. I often think about all the kids I was with at stage school and what happened to them and of course I have no idea.*'

He made countless TV appearances and became very well known in England. Fame abroad developed as a result of his portrayal of a stuttering child in *Our Mother's House* (1967). As the pathetic, blond, tousled haired cherubic waif who tremulously asked, '*Please, sir, can I have some more?*' in *Oliver!* (1968), this British child star charmed his way into the hearts of international movie audiences everywhere.

The producers of *Oliver* auditioned 2,000 child actors for the title role, which took two months, and finally chose Mark Lester — this film turned out to be the pinnacle of his career; he was just nine-years-old.

The cast of *Oliver* included 84 boys between 8 and 15 years of age, and one Member of Parliament suggested they were being exploited just as the depicted orphans had been. The filmmakers replied that they needed protection more than the boys did, due to the rowdy nature of the production during the summer.

'When I landed the lead part in Oliver we had to do 3 hours of normal schooling a day,' explains Mark. 'There was a special school set up for all the kids. The day-to-day acting moved along quite nicely — we weren't really pushed a great deal. That was the brilliance of the director Carol Reed where he appeared to elicit a performance without you working too hard for it. Having said that, I remember Carol during one scene with me, doing 130 takes just to get the expression from me. That was all day and the actual shot only lasted 3 seconds. But that was unusual, most of the *time, in my case, the director usually let me get on and do it with little interference.'* When you have young minds that have long lost the initial excitement and the novelty of the film world - it can have a negative effect if kids are pushed too much — they are more likely to rebel against the figures in authority.

The production was seven weeks old when Oliver Reed joined the cast to play Bill Sykes. Meeting Oliver after nearly two months of *'happy and enjoyable'* filming was a frightening experience for the young Mark Lester. The day's shooting would be in Fagin's rooftop lair and included a violent disagreement in which Sykes grabs the Jew by the throat. *'Oliver arrived on the set fully made up and mentally into his part,'* recalls Lester. *'He terrified the living daylights out of me. I think we were all frightened of him. I remember looking into Ron Moody's eyes during the fight and, even at my age, seeing real fear.'* The end result was that Mark Lester and Oliver Reed became very good friends.

Speculation which dogged the production was centred on the angelic voice of the young orphan, Oliver Twist, who sang the piping lyrics given that Mark Lester admitted he could not sing a note. It was the Mail on Sunday newspaper who finally ended the rumour when they tracked down Kathy Green, daughter of the film's musical director John Green, who 36 years after the event said she was the voice of Oliver! *'I knew nothing about lip synching,'* commented Kathy, adding, *'But I did the lot in a week-and-a-half. I was 20 and got paid about 400 pounds.'* The film of the Dickens classic which won six Oscars in 1969, including best picture, cost $10 million and grossed close to $17 million - a phenomenal amount at the time.

A definite direction change came up quite early in Mark's career as he played the lead, Philip Ransome, opposite John Mills in *Run Wild, Run Free* (1969). This was no Disney 'pet' film with a cute kid and tame horse and kestrel. The horse was wild and untrained and the hawk would have given the *Kes* trio; Freeman Hardy and Willis a fly for their money. *'All the roles, throughout my acting career were chosen either by my agent or my dad,'* adds, Lester. *'A lot of scripts came flooding in after* Oliver! *And it was decided what I was and what I wasn't going to do. I didn't really have a choice in that.'* Mark plays a ten-year-old mute who eventually buries the dead kestrel in the very same silent way Casper did. Unfortunately the public and critics failed to admire Lester's shift in gear and range, and either did not go see it or review it favourably. *'I remember the film* Run Wild Run Free; *it came very quickly after* Oliver! *I think it was a couple of months after. I enjoyed making that film. It was an interesting film to make and I had a lot of fun* making it. The cast and the director, an American director called Richard C. Sarafian who directed Vanishing Point – a completely different movie to Run Wild… I played the main part and was filming everyday – it was great. The working environment was just very relaxed and you just got on with it. I also got on very well with John Mills, in fact all the cast and we all jelled very nicely together.'

Like the character in the film Mark had to learn a couple of skills. 'I had a couple of months bareback riding and a lot of training with the falcon – I actually had some nasty claw marks from the kestrel – they are very powerful birds. I was actually taught by the writer David Rook, who wrote the screenplay, who'd taken his experiences from his novel The White Colt.'

Mark Lester, who is rarely lower than third credit and usually the first has worked with Telly Savalas (*Senza Ragione* 1973), Brit Ekland (*Diabólica Malicia* 1972), Dirk Bogarde (*Our Mother's House* 1967) and Julie Christie (*Fahrenheit 451* 1966). By the time he was 14 years old he was starring in an average of 2 films per annum, and earning £100,000 a year.

The decline started with Kirk Douglas's film (he starred and directed) *Scalawag* (1973), an inept pirate's story set in 1840 Mexico, but filmed in former Yugoslavia, one British journalist reported, '…(Douglas) so mishandles Mark Lester that his "Englishness" looks like embarrassingly bad acting.' Plans for Mark to play Jim Hawkins to Orson Welles's Long John Silver, in a new version of *Treasure Island*, disintegrated a couple of days before Lester was to sign the contract. Also a picture called *A Dream Time* closed down production after the young actor had already filmed a portion of the movie. Mark was no luckier in his next foray into acting with the Italian made *All' Aperto* (Dance under the Elms -1975), in which he was miscast as the intellectual son of a Viennese professor. Variety magazine were quick to point out that Lester looked very 'uncomfortable' in his screen assignment.

Mark Lester's last film was *The Prince & the Pauper* (USA - Crossed Swords - 1977). On the first day the cast met at the impressive Gellert's Art nouveau lounge in Hungary. Oliver Reed was with his drinking partner Reg Prince. 'They downed a bottle of vodka between them,' remembers Mark. 'It was the first time I had seen anyone pick up a bottle of spirits by the neck and empty it straight down, in the films, yes, but never in real life.'

Reed and Lester were partnered again and the gorge was as wide as Oliver Twist and Bill Sykes. Nothing to do with ability, but Reedy was his cavalier self and Lester was either the snivelling pauper or the arrogant young prince. *'I have worked with Oliver Reed, a very powerful actor, a couple of times and he is very professional, fine when he is working, it's when he is not working that it's a problem. All the stunt men before they did a scene with Olly were all vary wary – which is unusual situation with stunt men. But Olly would give it his all. He always gave that impression, as the character was, fighting for his life. During the Prince and the Pauper, I was surrounded by an awesome cast and I was aware of that, obviously. It was just fantastic, Rex Harrison, Charlton Heston, Raquel Welsh. Ernest Borgnine also had a nice cameo, he always played evil bully type rolls and he was wonderful to work with – so was George C. Scott.'*

They were all huge people. But Mark was bought up in the business so he was never star struck. With all the heavyweights acting around him, Mark steers his two leading parts unselfishly, but to viewing producers puberty had stepped in and robbed them of their juvenile lead.

Manhood was reached while filming was still in progress. Mark began celebrations of his eighteenth birthday with the whole cast, minus Oliver Reed, who turned up drunk with Lester's present, an equally new member of adulthood in the shape of a well-endowed prostitute. She was wearing a white shirt, and very little else, with 'Mark Lester – Private' scrawled, in shaky hand, across her generous breasts. As Reed fell amongst bottles and glasses with thunderous energy the young girl fled in tears. Oliver Reed realising he had failed to impress the established guests of the movie world and botched his present for his co-star Lester, staggered towards the kitchen. When he returned he held a huge gateau unsteadily balanced on his outstretched hand – with a sharp flick he plunged it into his face. As the guests and Lester looked on at the sorry sight, Reed offered him another present in the form of advice. *'Never take yourself too seriously, Mark,'* said Reed, grinning through cream and pudding, adding, *'in this business you have to be able to laugh at yourself.'*

Mark Lester's eighteenth birthday marked not only the end of his childhood but also his acting career.

Since *Oliver!* Mark Lester had made fifteen films, sometimes three a year, all under the guidance of his parents. Coming of age, Lester rebelliously demanded control of his financial affairs. Finding himself with access to his teenage earnings he soon squandered most of it on high living and drugs. *'The Prince & the Pauper was meant to be my transitional film,'* explains Lester. *'Instead it was my last. I never worked as a movie actor again.'*

Mark left the spotlight, as his film career ended, but entered the lime-light (a lime-light follows the lead actor in theatre) starring in legitimate theatre. *'When it stopped I did a bit of stage work. But I was never really into that – it was too monotonous. I did enjoy the stage work initially – it was good fun for the first week and after that it becomes very repetitive. I can't understand how anyone can go on for a sixth month run – night after night would drive me potty. And then I decided to bow out.'*

Mark was left with little but a sharp wake-up call to re-evaluate his life. *'To be honest I never really thought acting was going to be a lasting career,'* explains Mark today. *'Like when I made* Prince and the Pauper, *you never really know its over – there's always a gap between every film. There is always that nagging thought – what is going to happen next?'*

Producers did not let Lester develop or grow into more mature roles. On the release of *Prince & the Pauper* Mark was handed a cheque for the money he had earned, and there seemed little else for him to do, than go wild and spend it all. Things soon turned sour, however, since the money disappeared fast. *'I did go a bit mad when it all stopped,'* smiles Mark, *'I think that was inevitable and if I had gone back and had the life again I would have done the same thing.'*

When I asked if he enjoyed it Mark broke into a monkey laugh and said yes of course. *'I was nineteen and driving a Ferrari around and enjoying myself. It was good fun while it lasted but it didn't last forever. Then there came a point when I realised I had to do something about it.'* It took a short two years for the money and friends to finally disappear, and for his girlfriend of 3 years to tire of his dissolute lifestyle, and the relationship to decline, as he entered re-hab.

To break the vicious circle that wants to pull you down further into the murky depths, strength of character, a purpose in life and of course a desire to stop the self-destructive nature of addictive binges of drink and drugs. In mark Lester's case it was attending a class to learn a respected discipline. *'It just happened, I picked up the local paper and saw a karate class. This was when I was living in Chelsea and the gym was close by in Fulham. I turned up one day and started training. I originally started going one night a week, then two and eventually three; towards the end I was almost going every night. It sort of focused my life.'*

Getting fit – he was now a black belt in karate, making new friends, and breaking the mould of previous haunts and regurgitated habits Mark looked towards a career that was close to his new found hobby. *'At the time I was working for my dad's restaurant in Covent Garden. That was Ok but I wanted to do something in sports injury. I'd been into karate about four years then and felt it a natural progression. I knew I had to have a profession – and that's how I found osteopathy and in 1996 I qualified as an acupuncturist. It is regular work and it totally fulfils me.'* At the age of 27, having kicked his addiction to hard drugs, Mark went back to school and sat A-levels and went on to qualify as an Osteopath. He founded the Carlton Clinic, which is a successful osteopathy and acupuncture centre. He very occasionally makes an appearance in a TV programme or short film and would rather leave his past behind him.

What is well documented and something Mark is very proud of is his 25 year friendship with Michael Jackson. *'Michael phoned me up in the early eighties,'* explains Mark. *'He was doing a show in London with his brother and he wanted to meet me because, and latterly with Macaulay Culkin, we were child stars. Michael just wanted to meet me because we did share something in common.'* Mark is godfather to two of Jackson's children and vice-versa. Lester was actually at the superstar's Neverland Ranch home in Santa Barbara, California at the time the prosecution claims Jackson assaulted minors, and immediately offered his sevices to help the defence. *'Michael is innocent,'* claims Mark, *'The allegations against him are complete and utter nonsense. I would totally trust my children with him. He is their godfather, why shouldn't I.'*

Mark Lester is in a good position to make decisions about his children entering into the entertainment business – and it is a confirmed no. *'If my kids wanted to go into acting, and they range in ages from 5 to 14, at a later stage, not while they're at school, it's too disruptive, but as adults that's fine. I mean they all do drama at school and if that is their chosen profession in later life then so be it.'*

Lester's screen appeal did not survive puberty, although he appears to have past over to civilian life relatively unscathed. *'It is like another life (Hollywood child actor) – I have sort of detached myself from it... I am out of show business now although I often may give an award, or be on some programme or be invited to a premier – a peak from the past, but I don't actively involve myself or have friends from the business.'*

Mark, who has four children (one called Olivia) from a previous marriage, was getting ready to fly off to California to get married to his second wife. His life is as far away from Hollywood child stardom as Mark wants it to be. Life has moved on from that golden unreal era and what is more important is that Mark Lester has moved on too. Onwards and upwards and developed into the mature, respected adult and father that mid-seventies film producers never envisioned. Mark Lester has had at least two fantastic lives where most of us would settle for just one.

Adrian Hall – *Child Star*

Like many generations before, during and after – I watched in my small years the unfolding magical story *Chitty Chitty Bang Bang*. The year was 1970, roughly the time *Kes* started its slow jog towards cinematic history. They were both financed by Hollywood dollars, both distributed by United Artists – *Kes* was made for the modest sum of $400,00 and Chitty... was bought in at $10M. At the time the biggest budget for a British based musical.

On my first screening at age nine I wanted Grandpa Potts (Lionel Jeffries) to be my Grandfather, Caractacus Potts (Dick Van Dyke) for my father (although Jeffries was 2 years younger than Dyke), Truly Scrumptious (Sally Ann Howes) as my mother and the two beautiful children; Jemima (Heather Ripley) and Jeremy (Adrian Hall) – who had to be my brother and sister. Oh and Benny Hill (toymaker) could make all my toys!

When I eventually tracked down Adrian Hall who played cute blond mop haired Jeremy – the well-spoken son of Caractacus, he was Head of Production at the established acting, musical theatre and production school; GSA Conservatoire. The Conservatoire has built an international reputation for excellence in training for actors and technicians in all areas of theatre and recorded media. Brenda Blethyn OBE, Michael Ball, Gaby Roslin and Bill Nighy, to mention a few, have all attended the academy.

Adrian Hall, at age eight, was doing the odd commercial here and there, usually on a Saturday morning, when suddenly his world was turned upside down. He never even considered acting as a job and had little or no training or experience. *'I sort of drifted along and suddenly – with landing Chitty... it was like winning the lottery,'* says Adrian today.

Unlike many young stars that share stardom through a ground breaking movie, and then disappear into civilian life, Hall went into legitimate theatre. *'I have been very lucky and have had about five runs in the West End. The last one I did was at the Ambassadors which lasted around 18 months.'* After 12 years he decided to put away the grease paint and look for a more stable job. *'I absolutely loved theatre work. I moved away from that line of work because I wanted a mortgage – some form of stability.'* Adrian has not looked back and does not miss the roar of the crowd. *'No. Not since I have been doing this job at Conservatoire. I love the job I'm doing now, very challenging.'* The contentment comes from working close with new talent. Watching it mature and hopefully develop. This is theatrical farming, replenishing the soil – breathing new life into baron souls.

It has been nearly 37 years since *Chitty Chitty Bang Bang* first premiered in London on December 1968 and still people come up to Adrian and want to chat about it. *'Yes, people still want to talk about it – it's usually a pattern of about twelve questions. It comes up because most people have seen it and heard it.'*

Initially, Adrian was asked to go to an interview, which produced an audition, followed by a screen test at Pinewood studios. Heather Ripley who played his screen sister, Jemima, had already been cast in a movie that would carry a huge budget for a musical at that time. The production team were having difficulty casting the young son and Hall was one of the last youngsters to audition.

It was all Hollywood razzle-dazzle, block-buster stuff with impressive names up and down the credits. Hall was credited a much respected 10th – he was eight years old. *'You have no context of it,'* says Adrian, *'it's so unreal – and of course it is.'*

The film was from a story penned by Ian Fleming, the creator of James Bond, and was produced by 'Cubby' Broccoli – the producer of the Bond films. The music was composed by Disney greats Robert B. Sherman and Richard M Sherman. Dick Van Dyke was at the top of his game together with an incredible ensemble cast including the legendry Benny Hill.

Everybody in front and behind the camera conducted themselves admirably and showed only patience and affection for the two young stars. *'Fabulous, absolutely fabulous,'* comments Adrian, enthusiastically. *'To be honest I can't remember anybody, cast or crew, and we were filming for 15 months, being other than charming; with happy cheery faces.'*

With a producer of 'Cubby' Broccoli standing, which at that time had already produced four Bond movies, was a force to be reckoned with. If Cubby says jump – you say how high! *'I think that the nice thing about it was they realised they had to deal with that side of it quiet carefully – in order to get the best out of us – me and Heather,'* says Hall. *'Everybody was very very attentive, made sure we had what we needed and made sure all we saw was smiling faces. And that made sure there was little pressure on us.'*

The whole process with rehearsals at the beginning, dance training, post production work, recording and filming the movie, from start to finish, lasted a year-and-a-half. At eight years each and both moving into their nines – it was important times academically for the two children. *'There was a private school on the lot at Pinewood,'* explains Adrian, *'specifically for kids in films. We all had private tutors – working with us for around three or four hours a day.'*

One of the lingering images of Chitty... is the entrance of the Child Catcher played superbly by the famous ballet dancer Robert Helpman; who was pricipal dancer at Sadlers Wells ballet from 1933 to 1950. He still visits me some nights in my tossing and turning nightmares – he is one of the reasons I have given up cheese. His long thin nose, haunting black shark eyes and his tapering spider fingers holding those lollipops, even today as I am writing, sends a frisson jogging up and down my spine. I wondered if Adrian suffered the same fate as me, and had given up eating Cheddar – after all he had stared into the face of the Child Catcher, been within his spidery grasp. 'Not at all,' laughs Adrian, 'The exact opposite in fact. Hellpman was such an easy-go-lucky, friendly, jokey person. It's actually the first thing people say – it's the image they remember.' Well, I might risk a cheese omelette tonight!

Adrian Hall still keeps in contact with his screen sister, Heather Ripley, and they speak on the telephone every couple of weeks and swap emails back and forth. Heather also left the business and now lives in Dundee, Scotland, an eco-warrior, who currently creates and sells art made from driftwood collected from the beach at Broughty Ferry. Both can put the experience behind them and get on with their lives. Adrian, now 46, certainly has affection for those mad eighteen months in locations such as Bavaria and France, Buckinghamshire and on the lots at Pinewood. He now has two sons and would not mind if they went into the business. 'No, not at all, as long as you've got someone behind you, someone who can guide you, give you the right instruction, then there's no problem.'

Hall had been through the Hollywood mangle and had come through the other side perfectly adjusted. What is it that makes some people take celebrity in there stride and enjoy it for what it is and for how long it lasts, and others torment themselves until the next possible fame fix? 'I think it's what's in you naturally,' comments Adrian, seriously. 'You must remember that everything that happens to you, while you're in that position, is completely false. A chauffer comes to pick you up in the morning – that doesn't normally happen – so forget it. You often see it with famous people's lives – when it stops, when it ends – that's where the shock is. For a child performer – he goes back to school, back to normality. The problem comes when a person is not equipped to except that. That's when they struggle. They constantly want the false reality. They then try and make that feeling last or get more of it. Somehow you need a mechanism that allows you to think well that's finished, that's over. And get back to normal stuff.'

The ability to readapt seems imperative, almost chameleonic

qualities that not only lets you adapt to a new environment, but also to revert back to a previous one. For young kids - the going back to school can be like entering a hostile foreign country, where jealousy is rife. Hall was lucky due solely to geography. *'I lived around half an hour from the studio lot,'* he explained, *'so when I was not filming, I could pop back and play on my bike with friends – normal stuff kids enjoy. Everyday was a return to normality for me. It wasn't quiet such a big thing. I mean if you are living in a hotel for six months – well that's not real is it. If you want a sandwich you pick up the telephone and order one, where normally you go into the kitchen and make one – or you get your mother to do it. And that's where the problem is.'*

Paul Petersen – *Child Star*

'Scratch a show business parent and you're likely to find a past association with some form of entertainment, be it high school plays or elephant training. Show business parents have a lot in common with rabbits on a dark highway. Bright lights blind them.'   Paul Petersen

Paul Petersen started out on his acting career in 1955 on *The Mickey Mouse Club* and followed up his success to play the good son, Jeff Stone, in *The Donna Reed Show* from 1958 until 1966. During this time Petersen starred in many television programmes and series. His film career, which includes *Journey to Shiloh* (1968) with James Caan, *A Time for Killing* (1967) with Glen Ford and Harrison Ford, *The Happiest Millionaire* (1967) with Fred MacMurray and *Houseboat* (1958), playing Cary Grant's son, started in 1957 and fizzled out towards 1968, although he has appeared in *Mommy II: Mommys Day* (1997).

Capitalizing on his fame following the *Donna Reed Show*, Paul had hit records with, *My Dad* and *Lollipops and Roses* along with magazine covers, screaming fans, fast cars, and girls all followed. Petersen is also an author who has written numerous books on various topics. His first book written in 1972, *High Performance Driving* focused on auto racing. Petersen has always had a passion for the automotive industry. Paul also wrote the challenging *Walt, Mickey and Me, Confessions of the first ex-Mouseketeer.*

Paul Petersen, after going through the lot, gambling, booze, drugs and sex, founded *'A Minor Consideration'* (www.minorcon.org) which is a non-profit, tax-deductible organization formed to give aid and support to young performers - past, present and future.

'Children in the Entertainment Industry are subjected to unique pressures,' says Paul, *'and many times the images they create outlast*

the money and the fame. Americans make a habit of resurrecting and reattempting their dreams through their children.'

The odds are heavily against landing a part in a movie or TV series. There may be 300 children up for the smallest of jobs. Paul says, 'Most parents lose there determination after a year of useless auditioning. Most kids are delighted when they do.' Failure every step of the way can be crushing to the young performer, but in some cases catastrophic in the eyes of the parent. 'The adults in charge of auditioning did their best, but a dismissal, no matter how gentle, is still a rejection. Crying and parental recriminations filled the air. Lord knows what happened in the parking lot afterwards.'

In some cases near misses can extend the torture as the young performer is asked to re-audition. Petersen explains, 'The call-back is what every professional craves yet dreads. It means you're on the border-line, almost, but not quite right for the job that you have to prove yourself.'

In the early day's kids with promise and a career in the movies had to have the elusive Presence or more fashionably, due to Simon Cowell, having the X-factor. There was no definitive answer and sometimes it took time for a star to shine. A solo audition could appear quite ordinary and a child may be picked to make up the numbers in a chorus line – but suddenly, amongst the group, the individual swells and grows in stature.

Paul Petersen comments about the Mickey Mouse Club, 'The kids claim that early on they had no idea of who was the real star or who was most favoured, but there in the theatre the older and presumably older and wiser parents and guardians, many of whom were professionals in their own right, could hardly fail to count close-ups and lines, seeing for themselves the pattern that emerged from the raw film.'

There could also be a negative effect on the people closest to the young performer. How does the new earner fit into the family dynamics – where a son or daughter of eight may earn 10 times more than their father or mother?

Fame also had a depressing influence on the wider family group. A former Mouseketeer, recalls, 'I was suddenly a big deal in my family. An uncle or aunt would want to have me sing at the wedding, or if not sing, at least turn up and of course, if I didn't then the family started calling me stuck-up, too big for them. How could I explain that I was tired from six days of work or that I had other commitments?'

Walt Disney, was, and still is an institution. It has a huge industry built from the vision of its founder member uncle Walt. Like all big conglomerates – they had their successes, but alas also failures. The studios built up these young performers. 'It was tough adjusting to the *dishonesty of the real world after being told you were great, marvellous, and all that other crap studio people throw at you,'* a Mouseketeer recalls. They say you should never bite the hand that feeds you, but if the owner of the hand turns hostile and the hand is extended empty – is it not time to snap? *'I had to find out if I was real or a sham. That's what happens to a kid who gets success too quickly. You wonder if it's all real, if you deserve it. So you try to find out, like I did... for four years.'*

Paul Petersen remembers very well when he was fired from the Mickey Mouse Club and had to give back his ears. *'With my quick temper well known and my aversion to nicknames - a part of Mouselore, casting director Lee Travers persisted in calling me Mouse. Finally I'd had too much of him, too, and I forgot myself. This "full-grown" adult, whose belly preceded him everywhere, had called me Mouse once too often and, calling him fatso, I punched him in the stomach.'*

The axe fell that Friday night, just eight hours later. Mrs Petersen took the call. The voice explained that Mr Walter Disney had witnessed the scene and Paul's services as a Mouse were no longer required. Petersen would agree that Disney had not shaped him. Paul was what he was. *'I was rambunctious and confrontational and undisciplined. Heck, my third-grade teacher said: "While Paul was one of the smartest boys in his class his behaviour is abominable." And that pretty much explains why I was fired. I didn't know that kid actors aren't supposed to be children.'*

It has never been proved that child actors grow up quicker because they are around adults. Paul Petersen maintains the opposite is actually true. *'Kids who work do see more of adult behaviour and may be called upon to conform with more adult rules of conduct, but the truth is they are outsiders in the process, largely protected and catered to, and thus more likely to carry away false impressions of adult behaviour, which has been altered in their presence.'*

Whether the question comes from the young actor, parent or guardian – it is usually the same – how long will it last? *'In all but the rarest cases, it is impossible to continue a career started too young,'* comments Paul Petersen. It is very similar to a long distance race, with the horse hitting the front very early on. In most cases the same horse does not win or even finishes. Such stayers like Liz Taylor, Mickey Rooney, Haley Mills and Dennis Waterman are rare indeed - the vintage bottles of wine that improve with age.

Paul Peterson at the age of twenty-one had a financial turning point. *'I had set up my life to the point where after the age of twenty-one, I needed to work 13 weeks each year to keep everything I had.'* Everything he had, at one point, included twenty cars, five homes and thirty state of the art television sets. 'The reality for me was that in the first year, after the Donna Reed Show, I worked sixteen weeks... then eight weeks, then four weeks, then not at all. And, you know, without the cash flow, everything came apart.'

'An adult has, well, hopefully a rather more mature understanding of the fleeting nature of work in this industry, an understanding that actors are mostly out of work. But for a kid, you don't get those messages. What you get is not preparation for the future, but an intense focus on the now. They say children in the Hollywood acting industry are protected. Bullshit. Hollywood would save Bosnia before the life of a single child actor.'

Mickey Rooney was Paul's influence in leaving Hollywood after his career crashed and burned. Through Rooney's guidance he got an education. Paul eventually earned college degrees in English and History. He even served the United Nations as a delegate for the World Safety Organization, and represented 300,000 film workers as Vice President of the Hollywood Entertainment Labour Council.

It does not take long to become accustomed to fame. Petersen states, 'It is a privileged state, while it lasts. When fame begins to evaporate, however, the first hint of self-doubt begins to creep in. Contrary to the ordinary experience of maturing adolescents, the circle of effect and influence shrinks rather than expands. For the young celebrity this is an awesome period, one which creates distortions in the personality.'

Maybe fame should be controlled or at least there should be clinics for people who can not obtain it any longer. Perhaps love and fame should be on prescription. Aptly, Paul Petersen says, 'Fame is the hardest narcotic known to man.'

www.notapushymum.com - Help for Performing Children

Not a Pushy Mum was set up in April 2004 (and the forum in May) by Sarah Culverhouse and Sandy Knight. The site is aimed at giving parents of performing children as much advice, information, and help as possible.

'The site was set up to inform, and support, all the parents of today's young rising stars,' says founder Sandy Knight. 'I felt that the better informed they were, the better prepared they would be and more able to protect their children against the emotional roller coaster they were about to ride!'

With the growing popularity of Minor Consideration in the USA, the UK was rapidly catching up and by early 2005 boasted an average of 40 new members per month. Sandy states, 'Too many parents, in my experience, knew too little, and all the information was too hard to find *unless you knew exactly what you were looking for.'*

Support was never going to come from within the industry, these young minds constantly exposed to the hard drug of fame, often found washed up before their first teen birthday, even if it was just unbiased information about casting, training or contracts. *'I have performing children of my own, and have constantly come up against brick walls when trying to find things out. Since starting this site, there have been a growing number of people visiting, and more importantly, the numbers of parents (and children) have been growing on the Forum - all offering support and further information from their own experiences, in their quest to help each other.'*

The magic of the performing industry is a hypnotic dream that encapsulates the imagination of youth. Roddy McDowall reflected on his fundamental philosophy when he said, *'I enjoyed being in movies when I was a boy. As a child you're not acting – you believe. Ah, if an adult could only act as a child does with that insane, playing-at-toy-soldiers concentration!'*

To sum up the illusion is a true story promoted by the site…

When he was 4, Jonathan noticed that on the TV, Dr. Who and Worzel Gummage were the same person. His mother explained that the man (John Pertwee) was really an actor playing the two parts. Some months later, little Jonathan started school. *'What do you want to be when you grow up Jonathan?'* asked the teacher, *'A policeman? A train driver? Or maybe an Astronaut!'* *'No,'* the boy replied, *'I'm going to be an actor - so that I can be all of them!'*

Ultimately, our children need looking after. Whether your young daughter or son's debut is on page 113 of the new Littlewoods catalogue or taking centre stage in a West End play or appearing in a blockbuster movie opposite Johnny Depp, it is nice to know that the cavalry is just over the next hill.

Sarah Culverhouse adds, *'I don't know where the site will go to in the future, but it defiantly helps those of us who are part of it.'* Let us hope that www.notapushymum.com continues to grow and expand – with that comes enlightenment as experiences are exchanged and parents, guardians and children are better equipped to handle the spotlight; when it is shining in their faces and of course when it goes out.

27

The Teacher – Today's View from the Classroom

I desperately wanted all the answers to help save young children from falling into the Billy Casper Syndrome – and a million questions also whizzed around my head as to the state of our current educational system?

Some months previous, through my publisher, I was introduced to a smart looking, athletic young man, who I warmed to immediately. Neil Reed proved to be intelligent and caring – the ideal person to give me my *view from the staff room*.

Neil came from up North in Middlesbrough, moving to Berkshire as a child, before eventually settling in my home town of Bridgnorth.

He had left school, as I did, with little or no qualifications. But unlike me, Neil being a great adventurer, used his valuable young years to travel and see the world. Having quelled his thirst for adventure he decided to enter the teaching profession. With his life skills and new found proficiency in outward-bounds activities he would be a useful, inspirational member. Unconventionally, he joined Teacher Training College as a mature student. On becoming a teacher he has taught at primary and junior schools. Extra curricula activities followed, where he worked with young people and ran Youth Clubs.

Neil Reed is a balanced, level-headed, inspirational teacher, in the mould of *Kes*'s Mr Farthing. He has a vast experience with youngsters and teenagers who are stereotypically Billy Casper's.

* * *

I have never let my schooling interfere with my education. **Mark Twain**

Before reading any further take a minute to think about Billy Casper the person. How would you describe him? Can you sum him up in three words? What feelings were invoked after following his life for a short time? Do you really care about him?

The general consensus is that the immediate response is to feel sorry for a lonely young boy who is unloved - having been affectively abandoned by his family, labelled by society and rejected by the education system. His mother has little time for either of her sons - more concerned with finding a replacement for her husband and the life style she feels she is due at her time of life. The shop keeper is wary of him just because of where he lives and his reputation. As far as the school and his teachers are concerned he is a failure due to poor academic standards, a lack of ambition and poor prospects. We follow his daily trial of being mocked, cast out and bullied and suffer with him at the tragic end to the film. But is that it? He is by no means the perfect citizen or pupil; we witness him lying, stealing, practicing deceit and bullying others - so should we feel sorry for such a child? We find it easy to make allowances for him as in the scale of things his crimes are not too serious; not everyone enjoys games, he was only stealing breakfast for himself as his mother does not provide it, it's only a second hand book and he did try at the library first - and the reason is to educate himself after all and if he didn't join in the bullying he would probably have been on the receiving end. We are able to tolerate his frustrations, anger and need to rebel and empathise with his desperation. Why? Do we feel that his misdemeanours are a fair response to the way in which he himself is treated and are therefore justifiable? But which came first the chicken or the egg?

Looking beyond the anti-social behaviour Billy also demonstrates a great deal of other qualities and traits, the key one of these being self-sufficiency. He is a survivor who is independent and extremely resourceful. He has a sense of humour and a quick wit but the qualities that stand out are those of caring, love, enthusiasm, passion and respect. Despite the way in which he himself is treated he has not lost these traits and is able to demonstrate them – even if they are directed towards a bird.

A substantial part of the film highlights the difficulties Billy has at school. The focus is on the problems he faces as a pupil who is considered by the education system to be a failure. Again there is the question of whether his behaviour is the cause of the teachers' attitude towards him or vice versa? Either way, it is clear that he is not happy at school and his energies are not being channelled in a way that meets his needs. As a result he has become disinterested, his strengths are not recognised and an uncertain future lies ahead of him. The reasons for Billy's disaffection with school are not completely clear as the film only offers a snap shot of his academic career and not a full history. Domestic factors and low self esteem can be taken into consideration but do not give a full picture. While not demonstrating his abilities within the school setting he is clearly able to read, comprehend and understand texts so despite his self confessed inadequacies he is clearly not as poor as is first made out. This suggests more that he has been failed by the education system rather than the other way round. Whether Billy found some form of employment, where he went and what happened to him are questions we will never know the answers to. Should we be asking though whether the present education system is still letting students out of its doors with such low prospects for the future?

Does the modern education system cater for the likes of Billy Casper and would he have been better off in the classroom of today? The answer we would hope for of course is a triumphant 'Yes'. This would be demonstrative of the fact that the film had had a significant impact in altering our attitudes to children and the way in which we educate them. Whether a political agenda was intended or not the drawing to public attention, in such a direct, honest, no punches pulled manner, of how cruel the education system of that time could be, had to raise questions. The injustices were there for children, parents, teachers and government to both recognise and comment on. As with the issue of school dinners we have all known and complained about the lack of quality in the majority of school dinning rooms but it has taken a TV chef to highlight these issues and initiate actions to be taken. The fact that a generation on, people can still relate to the characters and especially identify with Billy, pointing out examples in their class or children that they know, suggests that we have not eradicated this problem. Is the education system to blame, society possibly or do we just have to accept that we will always have the likes of Billy Casper in our midst?

Kes is a bleakly realistic film… It tells the story of Billy Casper, the product of a broken working-class home who has been in trouble with the law for stealing and who is also the victim of bullying at school both by the teachers (particularly the gym teacher) and the other students and at home by his older brother Jud who is a miner at the local pit. His mother seems more interested in going to the pub with a boyfriend than in either of her sons. Billy's only interest in life is reading comic books like the Dandy.

www.filmeducation.org

Are characters like Billy still to be found in the modern day school? The frightening answer is 'Yes' and even more worrying in some schools it is more the norm. The issues relating to bullying in schools thankfully have been addressed and it would be unwise and unlikely for such blatant bullying to exist between adults and pupils within the school setting and with the recent national news stories concerning the extreme actions of victims of pupil led bullying it is a key issue for schools to address and is no longer swept under the carpet. The home life of some children though is far worse than that described above with a disturbingly large proportion of children coming from broken homes or living in single parent families. It is not uncommon in the staffroom to hear stories of parents taking part in criminal activities, with drug and alcohol related problems or of children observing and receiving both sexual and physical abuse. Are these concerns that schools should be dealing with and are they able to? Where is the line drawn between social worker and teacher?

This point was highlighted early on in my teaching career - actually while at university when we were on our final teaching practice. Talking with a fellow student one night she told me of a boy in her class who was only eight years old but got himself up in the morning and made his and his younger sisters breakfast and got the two of them to school. This was while his dad was serving a prison sentence for dealing drugs and mum slept off her hangover.

How do these children deal with the school environment? For some of these children, school can be a place of refuge, security and consistency in their traumatic lives. For others it is a place of conflict where one set of standards clashes with another. The former will blend in wanting to be lost in normality while the latter rebel seeking attention and dealing with matters in the only way that they relate to with indifference, rudeness or their fists. The feeling at the moment is that no one wants to take responsibility for these children. Teachers can manage children and the situations within the school setting but education has to come first and with increasing workloads it is difficult for teachers to provide all the support that is needed. There is also the opinion filtering through that some parents are giving up on their children and want to pass on the onus of behaviour and standard setting to others - they do not feel that it is their responsibility or are unable to cope for whatever reason. This has been highlighted by the controversy over making parents punishable for truanting children and more recently accountable for the supervision of pupils who are excluded from school due to improper behaviour. Social Services obviously have the difficult job due to funding and manpower of ensuring the welfare of those children at risk but how much can be put on them and where is the line drawn as to those who have priority? Finally there are the children themselves are they helping their own cause with the types of behaviour that have lead to the issuing of ASBO's (Anti Social Behaviour Orders) – do they not have to take responsibility for themselves?

Children have particular rights additional to those that adults share, who is it though that is going to stand up and be accountable for making sure that they are achieved? Is the breakdown of the nuclear family and community living – due to increased mobility, economic factors, rising house prices and employment issues turning us into a less caring society? Or is it that the blame culture not only has financial implications but moral ones as well?

If we can accept that we have not yet overcome the cause of the situation are we any better enabled to deal with the results? How are children seen by society? Do we accept their need for a childhood and to be children – is provision made for children to play and explore. A recent survey has shown that children would prefer to play - predominantly on computers and games consoles – in their bedrooms than outside. The main reason given is fear for their own safeties whether this is from the inappropriate behaviours of certain adults or from other youths and gangs who either just want to cause harm or steal possessions. There are also the considerations of a lack of maintained amenities and the attitude of those adults who just do not want children playing outside *their* door. With the increasing rates of divorce, single parent and step families – we have probably more children coming from the type of 'broken home' that Billy grew up in - the children at the centre of them are often the ones who are emotionally neglected. How often are children's views taken into consideration with decisions being made about them or for them by the adults concerned? The children often become the pawns in parents' personal arguments with inappropriate affection and gifts thrown at them as means of manipulating partners. Even those parents who mean well and have good intentions can over compensate and cause just as much harm by spoiling the child. Within all this the children concerned can pick up conflicting signals and standards of behaviour and when school is thrown into the mixture the confusion is heightened. Is this lack of consistency and stability good for the child and is it any wonder that they can find school difficult? How much time do children spend with parents particularly during the week? There is an increasing need for childcare and the extension of the school day as both parents or single parent are forced to work to meet current economic pressures.

With increasing demands on their time is it not the children who are suffering?

Would Billy have felt as abandoned and alone in today's school? Within schools there is the growing popularity of Emotional Literacy where the emotional state of the child on the day or for that lesson is taken into consideration. This can be monitored in several ways – one is to have a scale on which children can refer to their emotional state at that particular time – i.e. 5 being on top of the world and -5 being down in the lowest of dumps. They may also refer to posters depicting facial expressions associated with emotional states of mind both to help understand how they and others are feeling. The desire is to produce an Emotionally Literate School. Will the school of the future be any better for the likes of master Casper? Here are some thoughts and views of what the ideal school of the future may be like;

- *a vibrant active school where everyone respects and values each other their rights and their surroundings,*
- *confident children with high esteem willing to ask when unsure and to engage with others,*
- *stimulating interactive displays which value what is being done,*
- *positive statements displayed around the school,*
- *appropriate use of language and how to talk to each other and greet strangers,*
- *strong relationships,*
- *an enthusiasm for learning,*
- *an environment which has areas of calm and areas for reflection,*
- *and a feeling of safety and fairness.*

Cotwall End Primary School, Dudley

This sounds the perfect place for Billy. Is it new or a radical development or is it just a scheme devised by the powers that be to provide 'jobs for the boys' and raise awareness and standards in poorer schools so as to emulate what is happening naturally in good schools anyway?

So much for the school of the future, would Billy and his fellow pupils recognise the schools of today? Modernisation has taken place but a majority of schools are still based in the buildings of their era and the physical layout of the actual classrooms would have varied very little and the decoration may even be in a worse state. The tools for teaching may have altered. Chalk boards were replaced (though some still exist) by dry wipe boards and screens for overhead projectors. But even these have been superseded as technology advances with interactive white boards that are networked and 'Broadband' enabled – providing the teacher and children access to the most current information quite literally at their fingertips. But the main emphasis is still on direct communication between the teacher and the pupils. It would though be expected now for this to be more of a two way process with pupils taking a more active involvement in discussions rather than the draconian process of the teacher imparting his or her wisdom for students to take onboard verbatim. Does this style suit the more disruptive children? Is there something to be said for the stricter discipline policy? Can corporal punishment ever be justified - because as the headmaster (Mr Gryce) himself stated before dishing out the punishment he had reservations about its effectiveness as he knew the same culprits would be before him again the following week?

Are schools still as bleak and dour? The atmosphere of the modern school is generally more relaxed and friendly. Better lighting provides brighter work and recreation areas. Furnishings are softer and more colourful as are displays. Notice boards are more informative all this adding to a warmer, more secure and more inviting learning environment. Security has a much higher profile with restricted access to most schools now. Key coded or electronic locks guard entrances to the building, access for visitors is by means of a buzzer and adults are required to carry identity badges. What sort of sub conscious affect does this have on the occupants of the building do they feel safer or is it an annoying rigmarole that actually leads the adults into being suspicious and educates children to trust no one unless they wear a badge? At least modern day Billys are safe from irate siblings chasing them through school.

Has the balance of power also shifted within schools? Children and their parents are almost seen as customers and if the old adage is true then can they always be right? There has certainly been a shift in the feeling of pressure – teachers and schools can be affected just as much as the pupils themselves by SATS and exam scores. The results of which, directly relate to how the school is reflected in league tables. As part of the recent and seemingly becoming annual criticism of national tests when the results are published - accusations were made that especially in Key Stage 2 the children were being coached and groomed on how to pass their tests. This we are informed, suggests that we are not obtaining a true reflection of the children's knowledge and ability. It is not unusual in Year 6 for the focus of the work to be on the core subjects and in extreme cases there is an almost restricted timetable of Literacy, Numeracy and Science.

In the autumn term I went as a supply teacher for an interview for an assignment at a school where I learned I would have been working with groups of Year 5 and 6 children just doing Literacy and Numeracy. The aim being, to boost their learning by - levelling their work and setting individual targets each day. I fortunately was not offered the position as I do not wholly agree with the ethics. Improving children's learning and understanding is great but it has to be for the right reasons.

At a cost of five thousand pounds this was quite a financial risk for the school to take but demonstrates the pressures that schools find themselves under as with the headmistress a couple of years ago who altered papers so as to improve the scores of weaker pupils and secure the schools position. There is the conflict with this complaint however - that the powers that be see it fit for children in the UK to be amongst the most highly tested in Europe. Is it therefore fairer to the children to teach them how to pass exams and achieve higher scores? But do we fall into the trap of training children rather educating them? A decision then has to be made on how we value and assess children. Is it just and proper to judge people solely on their academic qualifications?

Those on the *shop floor* as it were are coming under more performance pressure and being deluged with paperwork generated by senior managers, LEA's and the Government. While this is going on children's rights have come to the fore and pupils are very much aware of them and how they can be used to their advantage. It is now more likely for the teacher to feel physically threatened by the child than vice versa.

A female colleague teaching in a secondary school would lock the door to her room when alone after suffering sexual oriented verbal abuse from pupils and having her e-mail provision hacked into during school hours. Also a fellow student from teaching training was threatened with a knife while teaching in a primary school in London.

Standards of behaviour are now becoming an important issue not just in localised schools but at county and national levels. Long gone are the days that teachers were 'respected' - quite wrongly in a lot of cases out of fear.

However saying this towards the end of the summer term I was informed - at the end of a particularly long day with a very disruptive class - that was in fact about the only thing they responded to and it way to deal with them.

Respect is something that as rightly quoted should be earned but in a lot of staffrooms it is felt that this something that many children have lost altogether and not just for the teaching profession it includes other adults, children and in a number of cases property. This attitude combined with inclusion policies means that a small number of children and in certain cases an individual child can dictate the learning environment of the classroom often to the detriment of all children and the frustration of the teacher. How would Billy have managed in this classroom? Would this have given him the opportunity to hide away even more or would he have been able to avoid the attention of his bullies as attention was drawn else where?

What would tracking Billy's performance at school have shown? Would he have been labelled with a condition or specific learning difficulty - have an IEP (Individual Learning Plan), would he be on the School Action register would or could he slip through the system? It is now not just the school SENCO (Special Educational Needs Coordinator) who is expected to identify and manage those with learning difficulties but this responsibility has been passed down to the teachers. Through attending courses and In Service Training they now have a wider understanding and knowledge of a range of conditions that can affect pupils behaviour and learning abilities in the classroom – ADD (Attention Deficit Disorder), ADHD (Attention Deficit with Hyperactivity Disorder), Autism, Aspergers Syndrome, Dyspraxia, Cerebral Palsy, sensory and physical impairments and many others. If these conditions have not been identified at an early stage then when children do not perform to expected standards considerations have to be made. Initial assessments are undertaken, requests for assistance put forward, professional observations and assessments carried out and if you are lucky and the child is considered to be severely hampered by their condition then assistance – in the form of one to one support and or withdrawal from the class for short periods is provided. If this is not the case then the teacher is left to manage the situation and ensure the best learning conditions for the child within the classroom situation. If energies are focused on those with specific needs is this fair on the remainder of the class?

Once a parent complained that she felt her son - who had behaviour and learning difficulties – was not getting enough support from me. So I sat down and calculated that during the week he received over an hour of direct one to one contact with me. This at first does not seem significant but if you take into account that at the time I had thirty five children in the class if I gave them the same attention then there would be very little time in which to actually teach the class. When this was pointed out she thanked me for my honesty and was appreciative of the help that he was receiving.

As it was with Billy it is not always the case that just because a child finds school based learning difficult and does not perform to the expected standards that they are less intelligent. Billy demonstrates this with his knowledge and understanding of falconry.

I have had this point highlighted on a couple of occasions the first with one pupil who like Billy was disaffected with school which influenced his behaviour and learning ability - but when you talked to him about football his depth knowledge and understanding was astounding. He was able to recall transfers and league positions over several years gather and collate information from a number of sources, give you stats on individual players and teams, he could calculate the scores and goal differences required to move teams up or down the table. The contrast was incredible it was just a shame that he was not able to transfer these skills to academic work or the school could not engage him in a similar way.

The second was a young lad who came to me in year five with a medical condition that led to learning difficulties these had not really been addressed in a previous school and he was not even on the bottom rung of the ladder with regard to reading and writing but his scientific knowledge was excellent. A written exam would have stressed him out and shown nothing but talking with him showed a very advanced understanding of concepts.

There used to be an adage '*I hear -I forget, I see - I remember, I do - I understand.*' Is this the case for all children? As well as the above considerations of Special Educational Needs, teachers are also being asked at this time to be aware of the different learning styles of all pupils including the average and higher attaining pupils. Shortened to VAK this stands for Visual, Aural and Kinaesthetic learners. This suggests that individuals have preferred learning strategies i.e. those who gather information by observing and reading, those who are stimulated by sounds and voice and those who enjoy the more practical hands on experiences. This can then be combined with other aspects of emotional intelligence including which side of our brain we use and whether we are logical or creative thinkers - bring in gender differences, racial and cultural issues and stages of cognitive development and it is clear that it is impossible to cater for the needs of every child despite the fact of knowing what is actually better for them.

What part have the children themselves got to play? Many teachers share the views of the Head teacher in *Kes* when he proclaimed *"Yours is the generation that never listens"*. Whether subsequent cohorts did in fact pick up their ears to be attentive to their masters voice is debateable. This comment stands true in many of today's schools and while not applicable to all pupils it can be honestly aimed at many of those who under achieve.

When recently given a document, generated from tracking and assessment data, of children who were not performing to expected standards I went through the list initialising 'DNL - Does Not Listen' along side the majority of names of those children who had been highlighted.

Why? This view was shared by a fellow colleague and was also attributed to a general air of apathy emitting from the children who left you with the feeling that they had no wish to take an active part in their learning hoping instead to be spoon fed and acquire their knowledge and understanding with the minimum of effort. They can not wholly be to blame for this though when little else in their lives requires effort – electrical devices in the home take the effort out of the majority of household tasks, they are driven almost everywhere out of either fear, safety or convenience and all they have to do is flick a switch to be entertained.

Attention has also be drawn to the effects of health on learning ability the old maxim of '*A healthy body for a healthy mind*' has been proven to have some grounding. It is painfully obvious for all who work in schools that the general fitness levels of children has dropped dramatically and that childhood obesity is a national concern. Recent documentaries have highlighted the fact that the high levels of poor quality and artificial ingredients, combined with high fat content and preservatives contained in the majority of school dinners has added to this problem and can also contributes to levels of poor behaviour. Schools have been aware of this for a while and healthy eating initiatives have been operating over the past few years and balanced diets are taught in science but recent publicity has made this more of a critical issue. But are the children responding to it and will parents back it up with good quality meals at home? Effects on the brain of dehydration have also been researched and children are now encouraged to drink water regularly during the day to counter this. *Brain Gym* breaks are also becoming part of the norm in schools allowing children to stimulate their brains particularly the sides not generally used.

Kes is also critical of an educational system that tends to uniformity and restriction.

www.filmeducation.org

Is the education system of today any less uniform or restrictive? There has certainly been an increase in the number of schools requiring pupils to wear school uniform even at primary level. This is for many reasons – to bring unity to the school to prevent extreme fashion statements and to prevent the snobbery associated with wearing or not wearing the right labels. This fits in with the concept that in a politically correct society we should all be treated fairly and the same. There is a contradiction to this though especially at primary level where as a means of reinforcing cultural, racial, religious, gender and weight issues to mention a few - we are teaching children that they are all unique, all special. We should be celebrating our differences - rather than using them as reasons for abuse, ridicule or harassment.

The week following the bombings in London I taught in a different school each day and three of the assemblies were based on this theme – not only as a response to current events but as a means of subduing possible tensions in ethnically diverse schools and communities.

It is not what is on the outside that matters but the individual within that counts. In a recent documentary 'My Teachers a Monk', when asked to comment on the comparatively relaxed dress code adopted by Ampleforth College and in particular a couple of the students - the Headmaster suggested in his reply that it was a poor situation when society judged people purely on how they dressed.

As far as the curriculum is concerned the extreme example of days when teachers focused on what they enjoyed and taught that at times to excess have long gone. The National Curriculum focused the requirements to be taught but still allowed for flexibility despite encouraging at Primary level subjects to be taught discretely, rather than being topic or theme based as had previously been done. Recent government documentation though suggests a return to the more creative rather than rigid timetables. The introduction of the NLS (National Literacy Strategy) and NNS (National Numeracy Strategy) has to a certain extent regimented nationally what is taught in English and maths and to an even greater extent dictated the daily time table – in the majority of schools - with literacy and numeracy being taught in the morning and the afternoons being left for the foundation subjects. There have always been published schemes of work for schools to buy into for these two core subjects but especially with the unit plans provided for Numeracy there has been a broad take up by teachers pushed for time. As a result the odds on being able to predict what maths lesson is taking place in a particular year group in a random school are fairly short. There is also a growing number of web based schemes especially those provided by the Hamilton Trust that save teachers time and as result of this are in growing usage. With the foundation subjects the trend - as means of ensuring the OFSTED inspector cannot complain about the quality and content of planning – is to use QCA (Qualifications and Curriculum Authority) units of work. Although not directed to follow this government led planning the pressures on teacher workloads is leading to uniformity with regard to the curriculum and a restriction in the variety of teaching being offered. Is this good for teachers and more importantly the children? Are we heading towards an education system that is centrally directed? Would not individuals drawing on their own experiences, enthused by their passions, using their strengths be more useful, stimulating, engaging and enjoyable?

The behaviour that Billy demonstrated was and is not that unusual; either from personal experience or recounts through the media - whether it is in news, documentary, narrative or dramatic form - life is full of similar examples. Do we share the same feelings for the culprits of these activities and are we as sympathetic and understanding? If not, why not? Is it because we don't *know* these children have no connection with them and therefore cannot relate to them? Are we not interested in the person but solely in their actions?

Where do we go from here? Since the film was made the views, values and standards of society have changed and are still evolving as is the education system. It is still possible though to identify the Billy Casper Syndrome within communities, youth groups and schools so it is unlikely that we are ever going to be without these characters – for better or worse. So the suggestion is that we are going to have to learn how to manage these people both within education and later the workforce. Systems are now in place that will identify at an early age children's learning abilities and potentials but rather than use this information to either label or as happens in some cases write off these pupils should we not be opening other avenues of progress for them to follow? As was mentioned earlier we are all different and not everyone is academically minded so why should these children be put at a disadvantage and made to feel failures or below standard from such an early age.

When people are interested and enjoying what they are doing then their learning increases as does their confidence. As their enthusiasm grows then they are more willing to develop skills that will enhance their performance and progress. We seem to approach learning in schools from the opposite end and teach unrelated skills that they can hopefully use in later life if and when necessary.

I remembered being informed during a maths lecture whilst teacher training that there is only one profession that actually still uses the written method of long division – teaching?

Billy may have lost interest in schooling but the possibilities for learning based around his passion for birds is endless and he would have been more willing to take this on board due to his enthusiasm.

We need to start talking *to* children more rather than *at* them and more importantly listening to them – as quite often they actually do know what is better for *them*. Concepts such as Child Initiated Learning in the foundation stages and a growing diversity of specialist secondary schools and colleges allowing more favourable options show we are working towards this process. There will always be academics and the current education system works fine for them but not all children are that way inclined. The issue though is to change the mind set of the academic institutions, employers and the public. There is already a trend towards looking for more than just academic qualifications on CV's and application forms as a means of distinguishing between candidates. But a step needs to be made towards levelling out the playing field with regard to exam passes, vocational qualifications and experience.

Rather than feeling sorry for Billy and those like him we should be looking for ways to support them and give them the opportunities they deserve.

Education is not the filling of a pail, but the lighting of a fire.
William Butler Yeats

28

The Billy Casper Syndrome

Throughout all the interviews and mountains of research if I have learnt one thing it was that *The Billy Casper Syndrome* is far bigger than *Kes*. Exactly how big the problem actually is may never really be known. Some schools are churning out a percentage of kids who have no idea of their true potential. It happened yesterday and it happened today and I have no doubt it will happen tomorrow. This is not a direct criticism of teachers or even the educational structure – it is more far reaching than that – it is what the angry young men were complaining about in the sixties – the system.

I am not even sure at what age the syndrome raises its ugly head. I have a two-year-old daughter, Summer, waiting in the wings ready to step off the guarded and secure merry-go-round of safety and parental control; into a world of strangers and learning.

Life After Kes forced me to reflect on my childhood years and at times I was back in the classroom of yesteryear. I fixed my time zone around Billy Casper's age, 15 years old. I froze my image and looked around the classroom. Disregarding the future six form, for most of us leaving school was very exciting. But as I remember, leaving school was exciting – but work or the possibility of work was not. Like most Easter leavers, somehow we all knew, although nobody mentioned it, that we were totally ill-equipped to join adulthood. I felt a bit like a fawn (no not Bambi), who was wandering too far from its mother. Occasionally, when I lived in Kinver; near to my old school, I would bump into those frozen images. The one signature that was apparent in these random and disjointed meetings – there was no pattern. Ambitious raconteurs who would strut up and down the halls of Edgecliff School, would be seen executing some mundane low paid job with little prospects. I remember one lad who used to sell his sandwiches at lunchtime, his mum used to make plenty for his own consumption. He would take orders on a particular day and his naive mother would prepare them that evening – happy that her son had such a large appetite and wide pallet. When our eyes met, after so much time, he was working in a dowdy, greasy café – I wonder if his mother was still innocently doing the catering.

On the other hand I bumped into Edgecliff window-starers; who, during class, mumbled answers and struggled with reading - driving gold Bentley's and silver Porsches; with the confidence of ownership, as opposed to the arrogance of hire.

Of course not every child is a fragile soul who drifts through school, an empty vessel that the teachers and masters can pour in knowledge and hopefully their experiences of life, there are kids who know who they are and what they want to be. The Billy Casper Syndrome has no such go-getters in its ranks. Not that the founder would in anyway be described as fragile, but as I have said before – it is not about that Billy Casper – it is about all the Billy Caspers up and down the country. They may not even know who they are – which in a way is a bigger tragedy.

We have great innocence in youth and somehow that can transcend puberty and manifest itself as denial in latter life. It is not a blue print because we are all different, thank God or whoever is watching – and like most of the grown ups growl, 'The young don't know their born.' And unlike most of the stock-in-trade sayings; that are past down from parent and guardian to child, it is probably true. It is meant as a negative slur – what the new-wave experts would call aversion therapy. The sound bite of the millennium, although it started much earlier, seems to be praise the good and ignore the bad. A way of communicating and promoting positive behaviour – it all sounds wonderfully simple – I just hope it all works. Unfortunately, we may see the results of such timid discipline in later years – when the experimental child may turn against authority and once again bite the hand that feeds him or her.

At one time, during my earlier career as a writer, I was negotiating with Oliver Reed about penning his biography; his agent at the time was distancing himself from his client. We discussed the financial aspects and the physical criteria Olly wanted added to the contract. It had all come flooding back after reading the foreword, dear Michael Winner had kindly written for me for this book – and he had mentioned the king of hell raisers.

Due to my writing commitments – as Steve McQueen used to say – I had been off the sauce for five years. Mr Reed explained I would have to pass the driving test before I was even considered fit to become his biographer. The driving test, as I became aware, was a purpose built arena in a near-by barn connected to his house. There were around twenty low flung beams and each had been shaved flat in the centre to house a tot glass. The idea was a single measure of your choice – vodka, scotch, brandy, gin etc. which was previously placed on each beam – I suggested Pimps and I made him laugh. You then went monkey fashion swinging from beam to beam, one hand holding the joist, the other consuming the alcohol – manage them all and you have past – The Driving Test!

Despite everything, I was glad not to get the contract; if there was only half as many beams and I was drinking Red Bull - I still think I would have struggled.

I loved Reedy – after all I had grown up with him on film. He was every thing I wasn't and yet strangely he was everything I wanted to be.

There was an odd legacy with Oliver's life – that I wondered if he ever realised the irony? One evening I recognised Mark Reed, Olly's son from his first wife Kate Byrne, at some private party. I was going to introduce myself – but as I watched this educated, articulate gentleman, and in no way was it a criticism, he was a million miles away from his father. And then it dawned on me. There is a great movement towards rebellion against the parents who sired you – an in-built rejection to discard your nepotistic ancestors values and principles. For a brief second I saw the light and pondered the unfathonable. How the hell do you rebel if Oliver Reed's your father? Mark was going to be OK.

It appeared to be a great price to pay to avoid falling into the pit of failure. It was a random example of one, but are we not all random examples of one? In most cases are we not delicately forged at birth by two souls – ready to mould into shapes of all sizes and attitudes. Although we often reflect mannerisms given to use by ancestral entities that helped spawn us – we begin as blank pages – and life is an open book.

Life rotates and styles and trends can wait in the wings and be born-again by the so-called new-wave generation, as once again they re-invent the wheel. It is a recurring process that the fashion world has bottled since Mary Quant covered up young girls knees with plastic boots and the mini skirt that left nothing to the imagination.

I felt my life had revolved and stopped at an alarming point. It happened suddenly, while I was writing this book – and the barometer indices came in the unlikely shape of a sixties singer. With a thirty-three year gap I was back listening to Gilbert O'Sullivan songs! I originally bought my first O'Sullivan single, *Claire*, when I was 10. I played it none stop, shortly after *Kes* received its national praise, for the two weeks it was at number 1 – it was October 1972. I devoured every Gilbert hit for that year and then hated everything about him for well over three decades.

A few days ago I pulled up at the pelican crossing, waiting for a couple to cross, and the other car, windows down, was blasting out O'Sullivan's *Claire*. It took me back to that old plastic and baker-light box record player. Impatiently scraping the needle, as it spiralled towards the centre, to start the track off again. My parents would moan in disbelief, as Gilbert began to whistle the opening tune and break into *'Claire, the moment I met you I swear...'* If I could only whistle, sing and play the piano like him, I used to dream. Was Gilbert O'Sullivan my *Kes*? My escape? I even acquired a Gilbert O'Sullivan padded cap. Although when friends and family looked back at photographs of me I used to tell them the cap was influenced by Robert Blake in *Baretta* – which was on television at the time.

As the guy pulled away in his car, who was strangely around my age, *Claire* became fainter – and I knew then I must at all costs pick up a Gilbert O'Sullivan CD. Not in my small town of Bridgnorth, even if they should have one, the risk was far too big – it would be around the town in no time.

I logged onto ebay and nervously tapped out the artist's name. To my amazement there were several hits – either Gilbert O'Sullivan Live in Japan or the Berry Best Of Gilbert O'Sullivan. I opted for the latter – but was bewildered to find all the CD's fetching between £25 and £35. I had this vision of all these sad 43 year-olds sitting in front of their screens desperately trying to secure an album of their long lost leader. What was happening to me? Where was I going? Is this what it feels like to have a mid-life crisis? Are these the first signs – buying Gilbert O'Sullivan CD's?

Perhaps life is all swings and roundabouts – and we do not go anywhere. Are we not taught – what you lose on the swings you can gain on the roundabout? My personal escape from The Billy Casper Syndrome was my writing. I was never going to be the next Gilbert O'Sullivan, although I tried music. I tried many things, I was fortunate enough and privileged enough, for my parents to be in a financial position to grant my many artistic desires. There is something in all of us – if people only bother to look.

Kes was about a working class family, nearly 40 years ago. It was not an average family – probably not normal – but what is normal? Perhaps the word does not exist when describing families. If we are creating a higher number of Billy Caspers than we did back in the sixties – then we have got it wrong somewhere. The 15-minute culture is indicative of life as we live it now. We expect so much independence and maturity from our youngsters. Most of the praise directed at youth is about growing up and being more adult. We live our own lives so furiously because of the pressures placed upon us.

Young babies, who are yet to walk and talk, are placed in nurseries – their parents busy people who need a convenient safe haven for their offspring during the day. So in some cases the major influence of a child's waking moments are child carers and teachers. The Billy Casper Syndrome appears to be expanding to cover all social groups, not just working class mums like Mrs Casper.

The factory where they build and assemble young minds - is the learning centre – whether it is a nursery or school. The blank mould enters the factory on day one and a finished product, anything up to 16 years later, is squirted onto the street. Some will flourish and grow strong, others; late developers, come into their own in mature years – but there is still a worryingly high proportion with no ambition for life. We have not even given them the basic tools to help them unlock their mind – to the chant of *'anything is possible'* phrase. This is the case of the ever-decreasing circle and perhaps until we have an epidemic of Billy Caspers we will never change and dissect the system.

The government - the system or the establishment, are ultimately responsible for the treadmill of mediocrity. They are the guardians and bastions of our future – they certainly shape opportunity and give us all certain parameters to work within. I will not give up on Billy Casper's ghost and will back any revolt from within. May be in this case it is the teachers who are able to pick up the sword and fight?

During the time when *Kes* enjoyed a national release; Maria Callas said, *'That is the difference between good teachers and great teachers; good teachers make the best of a pupil's means; great teachers foresee a pupil's ends.'*

29

The Legacy – What was it all about?

To use one of Michael Caine's most famous phrases (great biography), *what was it all about?* Unlike most films this book was written and developed in chronological order. It was a voyage of discovery from start to finish. Although my original concept had no bearing on the finished product – I can thank my publisher and his team for sharing my organic experience. Without their input the novel would have been twice as long and half as good.

My personal journey, making friends along the way, during the two years of writing and editing, was a fascinating passage meeting the cast and crew. Everyone, without exception, had a story to tell – some sad, but mostly upbeat and often very funny. I adopted the town of Barnsley and the people never let me down.

The statistics for Barnsley make quite interesting reading. A few years ago an independent study named Barnsley Britain's favourite town, on average only 115 people a year leave - out of a population of almost 250,000. The seeds of youth were falling very close to the tree and there was little breeze. I began to understand the strong feelings and passions going back generations. Barnsley was a big house – the kids played in the back garden and in adulthood they returned home. When their mining heyday ceased and the last of the twenty pits closed down – the whole town was in mourning – like one large family. It affected everyone.

The nightclubs and many bars, in a five mile radius – it is impossible to visit them all in one night – but the community is cemented by time and tradition. The town, famous for the 3lb mutton Barnsley Chop, is larger than you think. It actually covers 127 square miles. The naked city holds many stories, but Barnsley had prestige, drama, loyalty and a great film that was a snapshot of their times.

The events that linked this extraordinary expedition, the meetings, the telephone calls, I often viewed in mixed order. On reflection, there was no underlying priority to my choices, no hidden agenda – conscious or sub-conscious.

A great image that enters my mind as I rewind experiences of the last two years, is being summoned, I do not think that is too strong a word, to the council offices nestling neatly in the heart of Barnsley. In fact the leader of Barnsley council, Steve Houghton, could easily be identified as the breathing, beating heart of the town.

Barnsley Town Hall is an imposing architectural structure, faced in Portland Stone. There are four stories, 140 rooms taking up nearly 35,000 square feet, with a central tower reaching 145ft above the street level. I thought if there was ever a revolution and the Town Hall was stormed, the challengers, out of respect, would knock before they entered the civic building.

I climbed the steps and swung the heavy door to be greeted by an elegant smiling lady. This concierge, come receptionist, come secretary, come PA, come whatever she wanted to be, knew who I was, what I was there for and probably knew my inside leg measurement.

My eventual introduction towards Steve Houghton's office was quite awe inspiring – it was a mixture of Georgian expertise meeting the Victorian gesture of confidence. I suppose I suspected all the ornatness, the pompous disregard for economic awareness – but of course this was similar to any city throughout Great Britain. The men and women that built, paid for and lived in these hulking structures of artistic obesity had long since gone.

I echoed down the hallway and was invited to take a seat in a building, connected to Councillor Houghton's main chamber. This inner office could have happily held the claustrophobics AGM.

After only a few minutes I was shown into the middle sanctum and was instantly greeted by a tall slim man, slightly older than myself. There was a twinkle in the eye, which I assumed opponents of Mike Tyson had witnessed before a big fight.

Once I had assured Head of Barnsley council; Steve Houghton that I was not about to attack his Borough, or as he put it; 'come Barnsley bashing', our chat was constructive and positive. This proud, lively Yorkshireman, with immense influence and power over his town explained his visions for the future. Some legacy of the poverty and unemployment had already been eradicated. 'It's 12 years since the last coal mine in Barnsley closed and the Town looks very different. The spoil heaps have gone, as have the pit headgear – replaced by shiny new business parks. New houses are being built and many of the old terrace blocks, which typified mining villages, have been pulled down.'

It was slowly becoming apparent, listening to this enthusiastic, softly spoken councilman, that although it may take time (about 10 years) and money (a billion) that if anyone could make it happen – Houghton was your man. *'Barnsley has - statistically at least - full employment, and communities, which were once plagued with crime and drugs, now enjoy the lowest crime rates in South Yorkshire. Teachers even call their students by their first names. The place is unrecognisable compared to the days of coal and certainly to the days of Kes.'*

Many mining towns suffered slow agonising deaths, as the people were strangled of employment resulting in the local population facing recession. *'It's easy to destroy communities but it takes time to rebuild them and even longer to change cultures. It took time to get over the loss of the mining industry. We went through a long period of mourning. Yet there is hope.'*

No amount of money can buy hope, and it is the people of Barnsley, not all, but huge proportions who will help and support the new way forward. *'We now have Remaking Barnsley,'* explains Steve. *'Inspired by Will Alsop, the International Architect, we've been through some serious thinking. Barnsley lost its purpose with the loss of coal mining. What are we as a Town to be about in the future? A Tuscan Hill Town, that's us. A Hill Town surrounded by a wall. Beautiful Barnsley. It always was and now the world will recognise it.'*

Like all bold ideas and visions, they may alter from other people's aspirations. A council dedicated to forward thinking, complemented by a community, although may not welcome change (who does?), was willing, in majority, to let the leaders paint their canvas. *'As you can imagine, Will's (Alsop) ideas took many people by surprise,'* explained, Steve. As he points out, comments such as, *'A wall to keep us in, and keep the others out,'* and *'Give him his petrol money and send him back down the M1,'* exclaimed one disgruntled writer to the Barnsley Chronicle.

'Barnsley bashing' was something all the press had engaged in at some time, but now Barnsley tried to get up off its feet, and stand erect, the uneducated hacks and unbelieving TV populace dipped their tongues and pens in poison and painted the town black. *'Some of the press and media wasted no time in making fun of us,'* says, Houghton. *'It was a difficult period – but we pressed on.'*

Steve Houghton believes that Barnsley will become The 21st Century Market Town. Not just for Yorkshire or England but the whole world. *'Too ambitious?'* he smiles, *'Remember in 1977 when Barnsley FC played in the Premier League? When we beat Manchester United in the FA Cup? Mr. Sugden wouldn't have believed it. But it happened and so will this. World class that's us from now on. Nothing less will do.'*

The councillor has the power and the energy to make things happen. *'Pride in our strength,'* says Steve, *'to overcome adversity will be replaced by pride in our success.'*

In *Kes* the kids sitting in front of the teacher had little or no opportunity for personal growth or occupational hopes beyond the pit, mill or dole. This bleak observation of schooling during the late sixties - probably accurately mirrored the times. *'A World class Barnsley has to have a World class education system,'* echoes Houghton. *'So we also have Remaking Learning. Schools in Barnsley are getting massive revenue and capital investment. We want our youngsters to compete with the best. We want every child to have a quality experience in their school years, irrespective of their abilities. We want each and every one of them to reach their full potential.'*

After talking with people – parents, teachers, kids – at the sharp end, Steve believes the council has some answers, *'We have to change the way we teach and the way they learn, and we have to create a learning for life culture. So new curriculums are being developed. Teachers and parents are being supported like never before. Schools will become full service schools supporting social and welfare needs as well as educational ones.'*

Although the concept may take time – it is brave and positive. Imagination is at work and the lessons of a bygone age are bought to the surface and dissected. New plans are hammered out – with egos and individual quests buried together with Billy's bird. *'Our Secondary Schools will be replaced by new Advanced Learning Centres celebrating both Vocational as well as Academic achievements for both young and old,'* explains, Steve. *'Centres at the heart of our communities where business and employers will be integrated into the learning process. Our brightest pupils will fly and every child will learn at a rate which suits them.'*

Steve Houghton's passion for Yorkshire and all things Barnsley, course threw every vein in his body, others, equally proud, may be concerned with the transformations. You may be giving up the past, at great expense, to build a future that nobody wants. Everyone knows that *change* can be a very disturbing word. All along the way questions have been answered, ideas have been modified, new problems have occurred – the whole project is gargantuan and exciting.

'Its fantastic – we're on our way – nothing can stop us,' comments Houghton, adding realistically, *'or can it? When Will Alsop displayed his visionary model of a future Barnsley in our Design Centre (the only one in the North of England by the way) two old ladies paid a visit. "Is*

this where we come to complain about the Alsop model?", they said to the attendant. "But you haven't seen it yet", was his reply. "Yes, but is this where we come to complain when we have?" Nothing can stop us - except perhaps ourselves. There's still work to do before Casper's ghost can be fully laid to rest!'

Kes flew high over the Barnsley countryside, drinking in the view. The same meadows, pastures, fields and hedge and tree lined walks, are still splashed amongst the houses and industry. New buildings are going up, ambitious future plans sit on architects drawing boards as visions are slowly translated into reality. Schools are ready for modification or re-location, ready to bring exciting new learning to our children – the real future of the Borough. Steve says, *'Barnsley will be a place where our children can dream and those dreams can come true.'*

The words from Steve Houghton stuck in my mind as I pulled out of the Council car park and headed towards the busy M1 on my way home. I wondered what I had dreamed about when I was a child? In a way I was living out my dream – being a professional writer. I wondered about other unfulfilled souls who had not been so fortunate?

As I am penning these words the England test team have just won the Ashes at the Oval. Their first victory over world champions Australia in 16 years. In fact cricket was suggested to me as a way out of the system. My way of escape. My hawk.

While at Haden Hill, I was around ten, Mr Wickfield – the PE teacher, a million miles away from Mr Sugden, suggested I have a trial for England's under 11 team. I had a good pedigree, as my father used to open the bowling for Dudley, in the Birmingham League, at age 16. He went on to play at a respected level until his early sixties. A few top professionals described him as the finest player not to have played for a county team. With his immense pace and accuracy a national career was hinted at.

I had all the promise but lacked that most important ingredient, where sport is concerned, determination. It was quite ironic really, my father had everything going for him to become a professional cricketer, but shied away from his ultimate passion due to the fact he had a young family – me, he chose to carve out a career in engineering and started up his own business (although he gives my mother all the credit). Professional sportsmen, even footballers, did not earn a great deal in the sixties. Here I was, handed it on a plate, and didn't really know what to do with it. I settled for being a big fish in a little pond and played for my school and local cricket team. I suppose when you find that special something, that passion, that gives you the drive and enthusiasm you need to succeed – everything can often just fall into place. I never spent a happy minute practising in the cricket nets, yet think nothing of 18 hour spells writing in my claustrophobic office.

Billy Casper found his passion in the kestrel – it was an escape from the drudgery of life. When *Kes* died so did a part of Billy. I had found writing and I could never imagine losing it.

Quite amazingly, as I near the end of this book, tapping out the last couple of pages, the telephone rings and it is Richard Hines. We have not spoken before and the call is completely out of the blue. Richard, Barry's brother, was technical advisor on *Kes*. In a way Richard had started it all off – as he reared and trained kestrels as a teenager. *'I actually climbed the same wall as Casper, Old Hall Farm* (renamed Monastery in the film) *in my teens, to get a fledgling Kestrel,'* explains Richard, laughing he adds, *'Only I was with my mate and we had a huge ladder.'* Barry's book *A Kestrel For a Knave* was actually dedicated to Richard.

I thought about the people I had dedicated this book to and thought of our daughter Summer, who is rapidly coming up to two and a half years old. Presently she goes to nursery twice a week. This may increase at Christmas, as we prepare her for full-time schooling. Step-children Oliver and Goldie, eight and ten respectively, are already in the system. Their individual folders are growing, especially as important tests (SATS) are collated by age seven. I do hope this information is used wisely and it is not turned against them when they reach double figures and enter senior school. Our young children, the ones that are not academic or even the late developers should never be written off like Casper was. We all have a responsibility to our youth, our future.

Everything in life has a beginning, for *Kes* it was probably Barry watching his brother fly his kestrel. For this book, *Life After Kes*, it was ex-Scaffold member John Gorman telling me about this publisher called Brian. I had worked with John on a couple of plays at the Theatre On The Steps, in Bridgnorth. John eventually left for the right reasons and I followed him. He was a fantastic writer, good friend and a great asset to the town. His move back to Liverpool is Bridgnorth's loss.

I pitched my book idea to Brian Davies at GET Publishing, and although the book resembles little from that first meeting two years ago, I prepare myself for publication.

It actually turned out all right for me. A few stops on the way, a few blind alleys, quite a few mistakes and here I am, living the dream. My dream. For me it came true.

I knew and still know quite a few Billy Caspers. Some have fallen by the way side and have made little for themselves. Others have plodded along contentedly, with their own family and security around them — enough to invalidate the system brandishing them failures. And of course, the odd one has done very well, owning property and land up and down the country. Off course, most of these don't know or recognise they are Caspers? Do you know any — are you one yourself? What can we do to change this most unfair system?

There are a few people who care. The Dickie Bird Foundation was established by Dickie in March 2004 with the aim of helping disadvantaged young people, nationwide, to participate in sport. This most important initiative will go a long way in giving underprivileged kids the chance to develop their sporting skills, in an arena not normally available to them. A few Billy Caspers may be able to show the world they are not write-offs, they only need someone to give them a chance.

I started daydreaming, it may have been the warm breeze of a late summer evening, it may have been England's cricket victory in the air, or even the call from Richard Hines. I wondered what had become of Billy Casper? I wondered where he was now — would he have left South Yorkshire?

After leaving school with no qualifications I was pretty sure Billy would not have ventured down the pit. *'I'm not goin' darn pit!'* Billy vehemently informs the youth employment officer. I also thought professional footballer, librarian, bookie, teacher or youth employment officer — were all out of the question — they all just got in Casper's way. He was interested in nature — may be farming or as Disney would have loved to place him — working in a zoo! But I think this all misses the point and underestimates Billy Casper's resourcefulness, dedication and determination. I personally think he would have made a million! It may not have been totally honest, not at first, but without the shackles of authority breathing down his skinny neck, he would have grown. Maybe not much in stature. If anyone could have worked the system it is Billy Casper. I don't think he would have ended up running the country — he wouldn't have wanted to (who does?), but I think he would have found his true worth. And as he told Mr Farthing, I think he would have got that Goshawk he had read about.

The call from Richard Hines really made me think. This was the original Billy Casper, not necessarily in the book, *A Kestrel For a Knave*; Richard was around eighteen when he started falconry. Barry Hines was teaching, and it is assumed he moulded Casper out of the young minds seated in front of him in class. But Richard had lived and breathed Billy's life and there is no doubt Barry absorbed this frustration before putting pen to paper.

Richard's life at eleven was spiralling downwards out of control. *'I mean Barry went to Grammar school,'* says Richard, *'I failed my eleven-plus and I was dumped – and it had a serious effect on me. I think it was that that sparked Barry off. A lot of it was based on my life. I couldn't believe I was written off like that. And then I became so obsessed with hawks and of course I was so good at it. I mean I think I was more academic than Billy.'*

He was living the day-to-day nightmare of Casper's world. *'I was wild, not when I first went to the secondary school, but I used to have stick every day.'* The badge of failure deeply effected Richard and it took time, together with his love of falconry, to turn his life around.

To try and make a difference, Richard knuckled down and entered Teacher Training College and qualified as a teacher. A few years later he was promoted and became Deputy Head of his school. *'One day I blew it all and went on a one year film course. Channel 4 was just starting and I put an idea into them – and they accepted it. It was about working class people who, like me, had failed the eleven-plus and how they had turned their lives around.'*

Eventually Richard Hines had turned the system around on its self. By using his experiences and cataloguing them, and people like him, he had exposed an unjust world, he realised he could make a difference as a filmmaker. It was a career, as writer and director, which spanned nearly fifteen years, making as many documentaries for main stream television. Richard was responsible for the first ever British broadcast showing the striking miners viewpoint for Channel 4.

Today Richard is a lecturer at Sheffield University. *'I now help all the students at university. I help a lot of working class lads and lasses.'*

Perhaps that is what Billy Casper is doing today. Helping people who, like himself, were written off by the system. Failures who society had turned their back on. We all have the power to make a difference. Maybe the best people to help are those most damaged by the Billy Casper Syndrome?

* * *

Although we have now reached the end of my narrative there are a few more things I would like to share with you.

Firstly, throughout my research I have received numerous emails and telephone calls from an array of celebrities who wished to share their thoughts of the film and its creators. A selection of these have been included to show the depth of feeling which Kes has generated.

Many of us have our favourite scenes which are fixed in our minds whenever we remember Kes, with thanks to www.ayup.co.uk I include a few examples.

Finally I have compiled a filmography and credits to show how the careers of many of those involved with Kes have gone on to become household names within the industry.

Good Night Billy.....................

The Peers – The Industry Salutes

I must admit my life changed slightly when I undertook to include this section. Through International Movie Database Pro and Spotlight – I tracked down most of the actors and actresses who had been a big part of my life for nearly 44 years. It was a surreal time receiving calls from people I had greatly admired from silver screen, television and stage.

From the very first call from Bryan Forbes, one Sunday afternoon, and we chatted about the movies he had made and the actors he had worked with. Bryan was a wonderful man and indulged my passion and answered questions, that had nothing to do with the this book, that had swam in my head from the first film I ever saw of Bryan's; *The League of Gentleman*. He kindly gave me full writes to quote from his wonderful biographies. I spoke with John Sessions about *Kes*, Geoffrey Palmer about *Cathy Come Home* and been told off by Glenda Jackson while cooking sausages. John Noakes, from *Blue Peter* fame, called me up from Majorca, he had heard; through the Spanish grape-vine, I was writing a book about *Kes* – and wanted Colin Welland's number. Bizarrely, John had worked with Welland in Rep and had met up years later in Spain, but had lost his address book on the roof of a car. We chatted about his career and I asked him what he was doing now? 'Well,' John pondered, '*on Sunday I am doing a car boot sale.*'

One evening, just before I was leaving to go out, I received a call and our young baby sitter answered and handed me the telephone, returning to watch *Coronation Street*. Unsure of who it was, I slowly realised it was someone I had contacted about the book. I explained I would take the call in my office; I work from home and placed the caller on hold. '*Who was it?*' I asked immediately? She looked up from the screen, it was the adverts, thought for a second and said '*er… something Stewart, I think.*' My short walk to my office I racked my brains… er something Stewart, James Stewart, no, not him. Rod… no, I didn't contact him. I nervously picked up the telephone not wanting to sound stupid by asking the person to repeat his name. '*Hello, I'm back,*' I said. I need not have worried, as soon as he started talking I knew who it was – the powerful, formulated voice was enchanting. I chatted for 30 minutes about *Kes* with Patrick Stewart. I have heard it said that certain people could read the telephone book and people would turn up to listen. Richard Burton was one and I believe Patrick Stewart is another. I was totally mesmerised by this eloquent, articulate Yorkshireman. Patrick never paused or hesitated. I had never heard such intelligence. My first mistake was I never recorded it onto mini disc – my normal procedure after asking permission.

My second mistake, the biggest one, I could not remember a tenth of the conversation. I was so wrapped up in the chat, like a child listening to Hans Christian Andersen or a great comic telling jokes – afterwards you often remember nothing.

I would never swap a second of my time chatting about *Kes* with some of the people who I especially admired. Some sent emails; others approached me by post, and most just called me up out of the blue.

David Jason – *Actor*
'A great film, by a great film maker.'

Willy Russell – *Writer*
'In any discussion of the film, Kes, honour has got to be paid to one of the greatest novels of the twentieth century. To go and see Kes and read Kes, and to have the whole of ones own life and times and class validated in that way; without it being, and what has happened subsequently in some of Ken's films, becoming politically conscious or the process being elevated above itself. I think personally it was the most political thing Ken ever did but it was subtly validated because he got it so right.'

John Lynch – *Actor*
'Kes both as a book, it was part of the curriculum, and then as a film had a profound effect on me as a boy growing up in Northern Ireland. I re-read the book only two years ago and was still moved by its power. Often films of books disappoint but in this case I think both complement each other perfectly. Ken Loach in the film captured beautifully the aching loneliness of the boy and the soaring freedom that his relationship with the Kestrel gave him. I remember tasting that freedom as I read the book. His work with the actors and his gritty refusal to over dramatise their world was beautifully realised. I think that both as a book and as a film Kes speaks to both the child and the Kestrel in us all.'

Geoffrey Palmer – *Actor*
'I though Kes was wonderful. I admire Ken (Loach) and admire his sticking to the truth. He is one of our wonderful filmmakers.'

John Sessions – *Actor, Writer*
'Ken Loach is a great filmmaker – I haven't seen Kes for thirty years, but I remember it being very good. I also remember the wee lad being wonderful and the late, great, lamented Brian Glover.'

Bob Brydon – *Actor and Writer*
'I saw Kes as a child and can still remember key scenes, "Hands off cocks and on with socks!", and the football match. It made an impression on me in as much as it seemed so different from my own childhood; it probably coloured my view of the North!'

Stephen Fry – *Actor and Writer*
Without doubt the quickest response I received was from Stephen – even his agent Jo Crocker was impressed, commenting, *'I think this is a record response from Stephen!'*
'Ken Loach is a reason to be proud of British film-making. Like many of my generation I was shown Kes at school and it blew my socks off. I think the extraordinary thing about any great film is how it works its moments. It's the tiniest details that stand out in Kes. The pullover, the hanging from the goalposts in that dreadful football game, the grass, the sky, the smoke from the chimneys. For all the symbol and sweep of the narrative it is the vivid, authentic and heart-wrenching detail that lives forever in the mind.'

Patrick Stewart – *Actor*
'Kes pleased me because someone had made a film about exactly the world I had grown up in and the longings of a young lad in that environment were very familiar to me.'

Bryan Forbes – *Director, Actor, Writer*
'Ken Loach occupies a unique position in contemporary British cinema. Never a compromiser, his canon of films reflects his burning and unwavering convictions about the society we live in. He has always clearly seen what lies beyond the evidence and applied his considerable visual talents to putting on the screen his individual view. I have always saluted his courage, his singleness of mind and his lasting contributions to an indigenous industry that often shamefully neglects true originals.'

Joanna Lumley - *Actress*
'I think he (Ken Loach) is terrific.'

Michael Aspel - *Presenter*
'It's interesting how an artist can produce a piece of work which will ensure that, whatever else he does, his name will never be forgotten. Ken Loach did it with Kes. The film was a landmark. I had spent the 60's with BBC TV News, and as a far from gritty southern working-class lad, appreciated the realism of the movie.'

Nick Ross – *Presenter*
'I am no expert on Ken Loach and have little recollection of Kes other than being moved by it. Ken's approach is so often described as "gritty realism" – a soubriquet that probably goes back to his days directing Up the Junction and Cathy Come Home – but he could be as heart-warming as he could be bleak.'

Alan Ayckbourn - *Writer*
'...I am a great admirer of his (Ken Loach) work and achievements - a truly committed filmmaker.'

Alan Parker - *Director*

'Most of my generation of British film makers has been influenced by him (Loach), without a doubt. We all ask the question and I personally always ask the question – how does he do it? How does he get that level of reality, such truth, such honesty? Ken would always answer "it's nothing to do with the how; it's always to do with the why?"'

Virginia McKenna - *Actress*

'...I thought the film *Kes* was particularly outstanding.'

Nell Dunn – *Writer*

Nell Dunn is famous for writing *Up The Junction*, *Steaming* and *Poor Cow* – all made into films. The latter was Ken Loach's first feature and *Up the Junction* (1965) was an early Wednesday Play for the BBC. When Nell Dunn contacted me about the book, she very kindly told me that she was not in that world any more, but said, '*I hold Ken Loach in the highest regard he is a wonderful and totally individual director.*'

Uri Geller - *Entertainer*

'The film works because the boy befriends a hawk — not a ferret or a Jack Russell or even a racing pigeon. As a boy growing up in Israel, my closest friend was my dog, Joker, and I'm a sucker for movies about lonely children with life-saving pets ('My Dog Skip' left me in buckets of tears... my wife Hanna started to worry I was having a breakdown!)'

'Kes is different. If you think it's a weepie about a boy and his pet, you're missing the point; if you think it's an allegory about soaring wings and freedom from drudgery, you're still missing the point. In Kes, Loach invokes the universal symbolism of the bird of prey, an image which resonates for people of every race and culture, and one which has stirred human souls for thousands of years. In Egyptian mythology, for instance, Horus the hawk-headed god is the ruler of light and law, the opponent of evil who watches over all of humanity.'

'Movie-goers don't need to know anything of ancient mythology to feel the power of the hawk image. It is hard-wired into our minds. We respond to the magnificent photography of the kestrel in flight with the same helpless awe that moves our spirits when we hear great religious music.'

Other people who just admired Ken Loach's work and let it be known to me... Ricky Tomlinson, Tim Roth, Jane Asher, Nigel Planner and Roger Lloyd Pack, but some just didn't want to play...

Of course it was not all a success story when contacting busy people often high up the movie ladder or hot television faces. I had some nice refusals, like the respected veteran writer, my ultimate hero, William

Goldman (*All The Presidents Men, Butch Cassidy* etc.) who made the effort to call and say he had not studied enough of Loach's work to offer an intelligent critique or the wonderful Richard Briers who told me he loved *Kes* but was ill-qualified to comment on Ken's other work, even the busy chef/presenter Jamie Oliver who had little time to contribute, personally wished me every success with my book, *Life After Kes*.

On the other side of the *village* Hayley Mills, when asked if she would give me a quote for my book – on Loach, *Kes* or child stardom, would only do so for a starting fee of £2,800, it wasn't the sort of quote I was after. If I paid everyone £2,800 for a comment or the equivalent in US Dollars, I may as well give up writing – I'd earn more money going pearl fishing off Wigan Pier. Oh and Ms Mills would not comment on child stardom. She would not hint to what I would get for my money – as I would have to pay first and hear afterwards. I decided to decline the offer. There are lots of things I stay awake worrying about – and Hayley Mills walking the streets penniless, is not one of them. I still thought she was fantastic in one of my favourite films; *The Family Way* (1966).

Another telephone call that came out of the blue, while I was cooking breakfast, was Glenda Jackson. A great hero of mine, especially after seeing her in Melvin Frank's *A Touch of Class* (1973). Actually John Cameron, the composer for *Kes*, also composed much of the music for the film - so I thought there may be some mutual ground. I was wrong. I left her a message on her answer-phone explaining that I was writing a book – would she be able to give me a quote on Ken Loach or *Kes* or both? Having called me back first thing the next day – I assumed I was on to a winner. I was wrong. Ms Jackson appeared to be a little icy. I called her Glenda, she froze. Ms Jackson asked me what exactly I wanted. I now felt like a rabbit trapped, at night on a narrow road, in the headlights of a speeding car – I froze. I repeated my request. Originally I thought I had been very clever in selecting Ms Jackson. For one she had been a great actress – she knew the movie business inside out; secondly she was now an MP for labour, possibly learning a little to the left – so I assumed a powerful politically aware film-maker like Ken Loach, who makes films for the people - would impress her? I was wrong. I really did think both party's were singing from the same song sheet or at least the same book. Firstly, Ms Jackson claimed not to know or have seen a single Ken Loach film and she had certainly not seen *Kes*. I offered to send her a copy of the dvd, like I did for Bryan Forbes; who graciously accepted. *'For what purpose?'* she asked – I felt sick. Every vowel was stamped out. I explained that she may then make a comment on it. It was a huge political football with all the issues iin *Kes* which I assumed she would delight in kicking through the window of the Houses of Parliament. Ms Jackson refused my offer, but gave me a curt good-bye. Good-bye Glenda, I said. The curtain came down. In the presence of such awesomeness I was forever going to be a support actor.

The Favourite Scenes – Compiled by www.ayup.co.uk

NOT WORKIN' DARN PIT!
(Dai Bradley – *Billy Casper* & Freddie Fletcher – *Jud Casper*)

Billy - *"Am not gonna' work darn pit!"*

Jud - *"No. 'An do 'av to tell you why? For one thing you've to be able to read and write 'fore they'll set you on, and for another they wouldn't 'av a weedy little twat like thee!"*

THE MILK FLOAT
(Dai Bradley – *Billy Casper* & Duggie Brown – *Milkman*)

Milkman - *"Ay'up young un' 'ow thee goin' on?"*

Billy - *"Not so bad."*

Milkman - *"Why don't ya get one of these though? This is better than walkin'."*

Billy - *"Aah, only just. 'A could go faster on a kids scooter."*

Milkman - *"What? Well tha knows what I always say?"*

Billy - *"What?"*

Milkman - *"Third class ridings better than first class walking anyday."*

Billy - *"Ya call that third class riding in that ransack?"*

Milkman - *"What d'ya mean ransack? This is one o' best models dairy's got. Cheeky young un' See thee tomorrow."*

Billy - *"It can only go twenty miles an 'our as it is!"*

THE SCHOOL REGISTER
(Dai Bradley – *Billy Casper*)

Form Teacher - *"Casper?"*

Billy - *"Sir!"*

Form Teacher - *"Clegg?"*

Clegg - *"Sir!"*

Form Teacher - *"Fisher?"*

Billy - *"German bite..."*

Form Teacher - (Pupils sniggering) *"Did you say something?"*

Billy – *"Yes sir. 'A didn't mean..."*

Form Teacher - *"Stand up! What did you say?"*

Billy - *"German bite sir."*
Form Teacher - *"German bite..."*
Other pupils - *"E's daft sir, e's mad sir."*
Form Teacher - *"Is this your idea of a joke?"*
Billy - *"No sir."*
Form Teacher - *"Well what is the idea then?"*
Billy - *"Well when you said Fisher sir..."*
Form Teacher - *"Well, what about it?"*
Billy - *"Just come out. Fisher, German bite, shippin' forecast sir. **Fisher,** German bite, Cromertee. A' like...'a like to hear it every night sir, a' like names."*
Form Teacher - *"So you thought you'd enlighten me and the rest of the class with your idiotic information...?"*
Billy - *"No sir."*
Form Teacher - *"...Blurting out and messing up my register."*
Billy - *"It just come out sir."*
Form Teacher - *"And so did you Casper, just come out from under a stone."*
(Pupils laughing)

DIRTY BOOKS
(Dai Bradley – *Billy Casper &* Zoë Sunderland - *Librarian*)

Librarian - (Billy tries to walk past library desk) *"Eh! Are you a member?"*
Billy - *"Wha....' what ya mean?"*
Librarian - *"Are you a member of the library?"*
Billy - *"Don't know about that. I only want a book on falconry, that's all."*
Librarian - *"Well you have to be a member to take a book out."*
Billy - *"A.a.a only want one."*
Librarian - *"Well have you filled one of these forms in?"*
Billy - (stares long and hard at the form) *"No."*
Librarian - *"Well you're not a member then. You'll have to take one of these home first for you're father to sign."*
Billy - *"Me dads away."*
Librarian - *"Well you can wait till he comes back home can't ya?"*
Billy - *"A' don't mean that, a' mean e's left 'ome."*
Librarian - *"Ooh I see. Well in that case your mother will have to sign it for you."*
Billy - *"Aye but she's at work an' she'll not be home till tea-time, an it's Sunday tomorrow."*
Librarian - *"There's no rush is there?"*
Billy - *"Av' never broke a book ya know, I 'ant tore it or..."*
Librarian - *"Well look at your hands, they're absolutely filthy. We'll end up with dirty books that way."*
Billy - *"A' don't read dirty books!"*
Librarian - (looking embarrassed) *"A' should hope you don't read dirty books, ya not old enough to read dirty books."*

265

Billy - *"Me mam knows one of people that works 'ere ya' know. That'll help wint it?"*

Librarian - *"No. That doesn't help at all. You still have to have the back signed. To be a member you have to have someone over twenty one who's on the borough electoral role to sign it for you."*

Billy - *"Aah well, am over twenty one."*

Librarian - *"You're not over twenty one!"*

Billy - *"Aaah but a vote."*

Librarian - *"You don't vote, you're not old enough to vote."*

Billy - *"A do, a' vote for me mam, she don't like votin' so I do it."*

MANCHESTER UNITED 1 SPURS 1
(Brian Glover – Mr Sugden)

(Games teacher Sugden running back to centre spot after scoring a penalty)

Sugden - *"An' that boys is 'ow' to take a penalty. Look one way kick it the other. Right, come on Tibbutt lad."* (to himself) *"And Bobby Charlton has equalized for Manchester United. The score is one goal each."*

A BLATANT FOUL
(Brian Glover – Mr Sugden & David Glover – Tibbutt)

(Sugden tackles pupil Tibbutt knocking him hard to the ground)

Tibbutt - *"YA FAT TWAT... E' wants bleedin' milkin'.... tha' big fat get!"*

Sugden - *"What did you say?"... What did you say?"*

Tibbutt - *"Nowt sir."*

Sugden - *"Right! Get off! In that changing room, get off!"*

Tibbutt - *"A' didn't say nowt sir!"*

Sugden - *"Off! I wont tolerate that on a football pitch."*

Other pupil - *"That's not fair sir. E's our captain."*

Sugden - *"I don't care who he is. We play this game like gentlemen."*

THE FILMOGRAPHY AND CREDITS (IMDbpro.com)

Kes – Cast & Crew

Directed by
Kenneth Loach

Writers
Tony Garnett
Barry Hines (Also novel A Kestrel For A Knave)
Kenneth Loach

Producers
Tony Garnett ... producer

Cast
David Bradley ... Billy Casper
Freddie Fletcher ... Jud Casper
Lynne Perrie ... Mrs Casper
Colin Welland ... Mr Farthing, English Teacher
Brian Glover ... Mr. Sugden, Games Teacher
Bob Bowes ... Mr Gryce, Headmaster
Bernard Atha ... Youth Employment Officer
Laurence Bould
Ted Carroll ... Man in Betting Shop
Agnes Drumgoon
Desmond Guthrie ... Billy's Friend
The 4D Jones – Band Playing at Pub
Joe Miller ... Reg, Mother's Friend
Julie Shakespeare ... Girl in Classroom
Geoffrey Banks ... Mathematics Teacher
Duggie Brown ... Milkman
Stephen Crossland ... Billy's Friend
David Glover ... Tibbutt
Martin Harley ... Innocent Boy who was Caned
Joey Kaye ... Comedian at Pub
Robert Naylor ... MacDowell
George Speed ... Billy's Friend
Zoe Sunderland ... Librarian
Eric Bolderson ... Farmer
Beryl Carroll ... Mrs MacDowell
Billy Dean ... Fish and Chip Shop Man
John Grayson ... Jud's Best Friend
Trevor Hesketh ... Mr Hesketh
Harry Markham ... Newsagent
Frank Norton ... Billy's Friend
Leslie Stringer ... Butcher

Rose MacLean ...Mrs Casper's Friend
Mary Southall – Boy's Mother – interview
Jean Palmer – Bible Reading
Julie Goodyear – Woman in betting shop

Original Music
John Cameron

Cinematographers
Chris Menges

Editors
Roy Watts

Art Directors
William McCrow

Production Managers
David Griffith ... production supervisor

Second Unit Directors or Assistant Directors
Keith Evans ... assistant director

Sound Department
Gerry Humphreys ... sound recordist
Tony Jackson ... sound recordist
Peter Pierce ... dubbing editor

Miscellaneous Crew
Peter Allchorne ... filmmaker
Michael Barnett ... filmmaker
Harry Bell ... filmmaker
John Cameron ... conductor
David Clarke ... gaffer
Harry Daly ... filmmaker
Daphne Dare ... wardrobe
Jim Duffy ... filmmaker
Michael English ... filmmaker
Arthur Evans ... filmmaker
Penny Eyles ... continuity
Jane Harris ... filmmaker
Richard Hines ... filmmaker
Paddy Holman ... filmmaker
Sean Hudson ... filmmaker
Terry Lewis ... filmmaker
John Matthews ... filmmaker
Robert Matthews ... filmmaker
Mike McDuffie ... filmmaker
Mick Messenger ... filmmaker
Ray Orton ... filmmaker
Bert Payne ... filmmaker

Eddie Price ... filmmaker
Edward Riley ... filmmaker
Anne Robinson ... filmmaker
Franco Rosso ... filmmaker
Fred Ruff ... filmmaker
Nicola Webber ... filmmaker
Eric Wicks ... filmmaker
John Williams ... filmmaker
Tony Woodcock ... filmmaker

Production Companies
Kestrel Films Ltd.
Woodfall Film Productions

Distributors
BFI Films (1999) (UK) (theatrical)
MGM Home Entertainment (Europe) Ltd. (2002) (UK) (DVD)
United Artists Corporation Ltd. (UK) (theatrical)
United Artists (1970) (USA)
Warner Home Video (U.K.) Limited (1987) (UK) (video)

Organisations/Companies
Barnsley Education Authority ... *special thanks*
Lee Lighting Ltd. ... grip and lighting equipment (as Lee Electrics)
Twickenham Studios Ltd.

KEN LOACH

Future Films (2 titles)
When the Wind Shakes the Barley - Director 2006
Ticket – Director 2005

Past Films & Videos (24 titles)
Fond Kiss..., - Director 2004
September 11 - Director (segment "United Kingdom"), Writer (segment United Kingdom) 2002
Sweet Sixteen – Director 2002
The Navigators – Director 2001
Bread and Roses – Director 2000
The Limey - Special Thanks 1999
My Name Is Joe – Director 1998
The Flickering Flame (documentary) – Director 1997
Carla's Song – Director 1996
A Contemporary Case for Common Ownership (documentary short) – Director 1995
Land and Freedom – Director 1995
Ladybird Ladybird – Director 1994
Raining Stones – Director 1993

Riff-Raff – Director 1990
Hidden Agenda – Director 1990
Singing the Blues in Red – Director 1986
Which Side Are You On? - Director, Producer 1984
Looks and Smiles - Director (as Kenneth Loach) 1981
The Gamekeeper - Director, Writer 1980
Black Jack - Director, Writer 1979
The Save the Children Fund Film – Director 1971
Family Life – Director 1971
Kes - Director (as Kenneth Loach), Writer (as Kenneth Loach) 1969
Poor Cow - Director, Writer 1967

Past Television (21 titles)
The View From the Woodpile (TV documentary) - Director, Producer 1989
Questions of Leadership (TV documentary) – Director 1983
The Red and the Blue: Impressions of Two Political Conferences - Autumn 1982
(TV documentary) – Director 1983
A Question of Leadership (TV documentary) - Director, Producer 1981
Auditions (TV documentary) - Director, Producer 1980
The Price of Coal (TV movie) – Director 1977
Days of Hope (TV mini-series) – Director 1975
A Misfortune (TV movie) - Director, Writer 1973
After a Lifetime (TV movie) – Director 1971
The Rank and the File (TV movie) – Director 1971
The Big Flame (TV movie) – Director 1969
The Golden Vision (TV movie) – Director 1968
In Two Minds (TV movie) – Director 1967
Cathy Come Home (TV movie) - Director (as Kenneth Loach) 1966
Coming Out Party (TV movie) – Director 1965
The End of Arthur's Marriage (TV movie) – Director 1965
Up the Junction (TV movie) – Director 1965
3 Clear Sundays (TV movie) – Director 1965
The Wednesday Play (TV series) – Director 1964
Diary of a Young Man (TV movie) – Director 1964
Z Cars (TV series) – Director 1962

Appearing As Himself (2 titles)
Ken Loach in Nicaragua (documentary short) – Actor 1996
Cinématon - Himself 1991

TV Guest Appearances (1 title)
The Buzz playing Himself, episode (#1.2), 11 October 2002

TONY GARNETT

Past Films & Videos (14 titles)
Beautiful Thing – Producer 1996
Fat Man and Little Boy – Producer 1989
Earth Girls Are Easy – Producer 1988

270

Sesame Street Presents Follow That Bird – Producer 1985
Deep in the Heart - Producer, Writer, Director 1983
Prostitute - Producer, Writer, Director 1980
Black Jack – Producer 1979
The Body (documentary) – Producer 1970
Kes - Producer, Writer 1969
The Sweet Body of Deborah – Producer 1969
Incident at Midnight – Brennan 1963
Rivals - Jimmy Vosier 1963
The Boys - Ginger Thompson 1962

Past Television (27 titles)
Attachments (TV series) - Executive Producer, Devised By 2000
Stanton Blues (TV series) - Executive Producer 1998
Hostile Waters (TV movie) – Producer 1997
This Life (TV series) - Executive Producer 1996
Ballykissangel (TV series) - Executive Producer 1996
Cardiac Arrest (TV series) – Producer 1994
Between the Lines (TV series) - Executive Producer 1992
Born Kicking (TV movie) – Producer 1992
The Staggering Stories of Ferdinand De Bargos (TV series) - Executive Producer 1989
The Five Minute Films (TV short) – Producer 1982
Law and Order (TV mini-series) – Producer 1978
The Spongers (TV movie) – Producer 1978
Days of Hope (TV mini-series) – Producer 1975
Hard Labour (TV movie) – Producer 1973
Arturo Ui (TV movie) – Producer 1972
The Big Flame (TV movie) – Producer 1969
The Golden Vision (TV movie) – Producer 1968
The Parachute (TV movie) – Producer 1968
An Officer of the Court (TV movie) – Producer 1967
In Two Minds (TV movie) – Producer 1967
The Lump (TV movie) – Producer 1967
Little Master Mind (TV movie) – Producer 1966
Cathy Come Home (TV movie) – Producer 1966
Vote, Vote, Vote for Nigel Barton (TV movie) - Story Editor 1965
Stand Up, Nigel Barton (TV movie) - Story Editor 1965
Up the Junction (TV movie) - Story Editor 1965
The Birth of a Private Man (TV movie) - Colin Waring 1963

TV Guest Appearances (1 title)
Studio Four playing Gianmaria Bargigli, episode "The Imbroglio" (#1.12), 16 April 1962

BARRY HINES

Past Films & Videos (4 titles)
Shooting Stars – Writer 1991
Looks and Smiles - Writer (novel) (screenplay) 1981
The Gamekeeper - Writer (novel) 1980
Kes - Writer (also novel A Kestrel For A Knave) 1969

Past Television (5 titles)
Born Kicking (TV movie) – Writer 1992
Threads (TV movie) – Writer 1984
The Price of Coal (TV movie) – Writer 1977
Speech Day (TV movie) – Writer 1973
Billy's Last Stand (TV movie) – Writer 1971

DAI (DAVID) BRADLEY

Past Films & Videos (5 titles)
Asylum - Father Michael 2003
Zulu Dawn - Pvt. Williams 1979
Absolution - Arthur Dyson (as Dai Bradley) 1978
Malachi's Cove – Barty 1974
Kes - Billy Casper 1969

Past Television (8 titles)
Station Jim (TV movie) – Elliot 2001
The World Cup: A Captain's Tale (TV movie) - Actor (as Dai Bradley) 1982
The Flame Trees of Thika (TV mini-series) - Alec Wilson 1981
All Quiet on the Western Front (TV movie) – Kropp 1979
Play for Today: Kisses at Fifty (TV movie) – Policeman 1973
The Jensen Code (TV series) - Terry Connor (as Dai Bradley) 1972
The Flaxton Boys (TV series) - Peter Weekes (1970) (as Dai Bradley) 1970
A Family at War (TV series) – Alfred 1970

FREDDIE FLETCHER

Past Films & Videos (6 titles)
Brothers in Trouble – Redway 1996
When Saturday Comes – Judd 1996
Some Kind of Life - Mr. Thompson 1995
The Nature of the Beast - Ned Coward 1988
Terror on the Britannic - 2nd Radio Officer 1974
Kes - Jud Casper 1969

Past Television (6 titles)
The Governor (TV series) - Arnie Franks 1996
G.B.H. (TV mini-series) - Poacher Vic 1991
Nearly a Happy Ending (TV movie) – Tim 1981
Clouds of Glory: William and Dorothy (TV movie) - Tom Hutchinson 1978
Another Sunday and Sweet F.A. (TV movie) - Albion Captain 1972
Queenie's Castle (TV series) - Raymond Shepherd 1970

TV Guest Appearances (4 titles)
Peak Practice playing George Milton, episode "Tender" (#3.2), 1995
Heartbeat playing Sam Carver, episode "Bitter Harvest" (#2.4), 9 May 1993
All Creatures Great and Small playing Bob Derrick, episode "Only One Woof" (#4.6), 21 February 1988
Bedtime Stories playing Liam, episode "The Water Maiden" (#1.2), 10 March 1974

COLIN WELLAND

Past Films & Videos (9 titles)
War of the Buttons – Writer 1994
A Dry White Season - Writer (screenplay) 1989
Twice in a Lifetime – Writer 1985
Chariots of Fire – Writer 1981
Yanks - Writer (story) 1979
Sweeney! - Frank Chadwick 1977
Straw Dogs - Reverend Barney Hood 1971
Villain - Tom Binney 1971
Kes - Mr Farthing, English Teacher 1969

Past Television (21 titles)
Bramwell: Loose Women (TV movie) - Mr. Barclay 1998
Bramwell: Our Brave Boys (TV movie) - Mr. Barclay 1998
Trial & Retribution (TV mini-series) – Mallory 1997
The Fix (TV movie) - Harry Catterick 1997
Bambino mio (TV movie) – Writer 1994
Femme Fatale (TV movie) - Martin Harty 1993
For the Greater Good (TV movie) - Sir David Whites 1991
The Secret Life of Ian Fleming (TV movie) - Reuters Editor 1990
Farmers Arms (TV movie) – Wally 1983
United Kingdom (TV movie) - Chief Constable James McBride 1981
Cowboys (TV series) – Geyser 1980
Blue Remembered Hills (TV movie) – Willie 1979
Machinegunner (TV movie) - Jack Bone 1976
Your Man From 6 Counties (TV movie) - Writer (play) 1976
The Wild West Show (TV series) – Actor 1975
Leeds United (TV movie) - Actor, Writer 1974
Jack Point (TV movie) – Writer 1973
Play for Today: Kisses at Fifty (TV movie) – Writer 1973

Roll on Four O'Clock (TV movie) - Lennie Brown, Writer 1970
The Hallelujah Handshake (TV movie) – Writer 1970
Z Cars (TV series) - PC David Graham (1963-1965) 1963

Appearing As Himself (1 title)
The 54th Annual Academy Awards (TV special) - Himself - Best Original Screenplay
Winner 1982

TV Guest Appearances (5 titles)
Stars Reunited playing Himself, episode "Z Cars" (#2.3), 7 January 2004
After They Were Famous playing Himself, episode "Z Cars", 23 December 2002
Z Cars playing Angry Northerner, episode "Pressure" (#12.13), 20 September 1978
The Sweeney playing Tober, episode "Faces" (#2.2), 8 September 1975
Fraud Squad playing Olly West, episode "Two Kinds of Crash" (#1.12), 5 August
1969

BRIAN GLOVER

Past Films & Videos (26 titles)
Stiff Upper Lips – Eric 1998
Up 'n' Under - Stan, Doreen's father 1998
Snow White: A Tale of Terror – Lars 1997
Bob's Weekend - The Boss 1996
Royal Deceipt - Caedman 1994
1942 A Love Story - General Douglas 1993
Leon the Pig Farmer - Brian Chadwick 1992
Alien³ - Andrews 1992
Kafka - Castle Henchman 1991
To Kill a Priest – Actor 1988
The McGuffin - Man in Brown 1985
Laughterhouse – Writer 1984
Ordeal by Innocence – Executioner 1984
The Company of Wolves - Amorous Boy's father 1984
Britannia Hospital – Painter 1982
An American Werewolf in London - Chess Player 1981
The Great Train Robbery - Captain Jimmy 1979
Absolution - First Policeman 1978
Joseph Andrews - Gaoler 1977
Jabberwocky – Armourer 1977
Sweeney! – Mac 1977
Dirty Knight's Work - Sidney Gore 1976
The Old Curiosity Shop – Furnaceman 1975
Brannigan - Jimmy the Bet 1975
O Lucky Man! - Plantation Foreman/Bassett (Power Station Guard) 1973
Kes - Mr. Sugden, Games Teacher 1969

Past Television (21 titles)

Rumble (TV series) - Johnny Pecs 1995
Anna Lee (TV series) - Selwyn Price 1993
The World of Eddie Weary (TV movie) - Strip Club MC 1990
Campion (TV series) - Magersfontein Lugg 1989
Lost Empires (TV mini-series) - Tommy Beamish 1986
South of the Border (TV series) - Edgar Rowley 1985
Bottle Boys (TV series) – Actor 1984
A Midsummer Night's Dream (TV movie) – Bottom 1981
Thicker Than Water (TV movie) - Actor, Writer 1980
Sounding Brass (TV series) - Horace Gilbert Bestwick 1980
The Wild Bunch (TV movie) – Writer 1977
Chester Mystery Cycle (TV movie) – Actor 1976
Melvyn's Marauders (TV movie) – Actor 1975
You'll Never Walk Alone (TV short) – Maurice 1974
Initiation (TV movie) – Actor 1974
Speech Day (TV movie) - Mr. Warboys 1973
Playthings (TV short) – Actor 1973
Sez Les (TV series) - Various Characters (Series 4-6) 1972
Joy (TV movie) – Actor 1972
A Day Out (TV movie) – Boothroyd 1972
Shakespeare Or Bust – Miner 1972
The Fishing Party - Miner 1972

Appearing As Himself (3 titles)

The Making of 'Alien 3' (TV documentary) – Himself 1992
The Modern World: Ten Great Writers (TV mini-series) - (Conrad segment) 1988
Don't Ask Me (TV series) – Actor 1974

TV Guest Appearances (23 titles)

The Bill playing Ken Farley, episode "Broken" (#9.73), 22 June 1993
Press Gang playing Dr. Threeways, episode "UnXpected" (#4.2), 14 January 1992
Bottom playing Mr. Rottweiler, episode "Gas" (#1.2), 24 September 1991
All Creatures Great and Small playing Mr. Dawson, episode "Here and There" (#6.1), 2 September 1989
Doctor Who playing Griffiths, episode "Attack of the Cybermen" (#22.1), 5 January 1985
Foxy Lady, episode (#2.3), 1 February 1984
Minder playing Yorkie, episode "The Beer Hunter" (#2.6), 16 October 1980
Hazell playing Harry the Ear, episode "Hazell and the Greasy Gunners" (#2.11), 28 June 1979
Return of the Saint playing Plackett, episode "Signal Stop" (#1.12), 26 November 1978
Target playing Labour Party Agent, episode "Queen's Pardon" (#2.3), 29 September 1978
The Famous Five playing Tiger Dan, episode "Five Go Off in a Caravan" (#1.6), 7 August 1978
Secret Army playing Crpl. Emil Schnorr, episode "Growing Up" (#1.6), 12 October 1977
Raffles playing Billy Purvis, episode "A Costume Piece" (#1.2), 4 March 1977
Quiller, episode "Any Last Request" (#1.3), 12 September 1975

Dixon of Dock Green playing Chuck Windell, episode "Baubles, Bangles and Beads" (#21.5), 15 March 1975
Not on Your Nellie playing Battling Bill, episode "Requiem for a Heavyweight" (#2.3), 7 February 1975
The Sweeney playing Moose, episode "Thin Ice" (#1.3), 16 January 1975
Porridge playing Heslop, episode "Men Without Women" (#1.6), 10 October 1974
Porridge playing Heslop, episode "The Hustler" (#1.2), 12 September 1974
Porridge playing Heslop, episode "New Faces, Old Hands" (#1.1), 5 September 1974
The Protectors playing Allen, episode "Quin" (#2.1), 21 September 1973
Whatever Happened to the Likely Lads? playing Flint, episode "No Hiding Place" (#1.7), 20 February 1973
Paul Temple playing Waites, episode "Party Piece" (#4.5), 7 July 1971

CHRIS MENGES

Future Films (3 titles)
Papa – Cinematographer 2005
The Three Burials of Melquiades - Cinematographer 2005
North Country – Cinematographer 2005
Ticket – Cinematographer 2005

Past Films & Videos (36 titles)
Criminal – Cinematographer 2004
The Good Thief – Cinematographer 2002
Dirty Pretty Things – Cinematographer 2002
The Pledge – Cinematographer 2001
The Lost Son – Director 1999
The Boxer – Cinematographer 1997
Michael Collins – Cinematographer 1996
Second Best – Director 1994
CrissCross – Director 1992
A World Apart – Director 1988
High Season – Cinematographer 1987
Shy People – Cinematographer 1987
The Mission – Cinematographer 1986
Singing the Blues in Red – Cinematographer 1986
Marie – Cinematographer 1985
Which Side Are You On? – Cinematographer 1984
Winter Flight – Cinematographer 1984
The Killing Fields – Cinematographer 1984
Comfort and Joy – Cinematographer 1984
Local Hero – Cinematographer 1983
Battletruck – Cinematographer 1982
Angel – Cinematographer 1982
East 103rd Street (documentary) - Cinematographer, Director, Producer 1981
Looks and Smiles – Cinematographer 1981
Babylon – Cinematographer 1980
The Gamekeeper – Cinematographer 1980

Star Wars: Episode V - The Empire Strikes Back - Director Of Photography (studio second unit) – 1980
Bloody Kids – Cinematographer 1979
A Sense of Freedom – Cinematographer 1979
Black Jack – Cinematographer 1979
Gumshoe – Cinematographer 1971
Black Beauty – Cinematographer 1971
Kes – Cinematographer 1969
Abel Gance: The Charm of Dynamite – Cinematographer 1968
If.... - Camera Operator 1968
Poor Cow - Camera Operator 1967

Past Television (7 titles)
The Concert for George (TV documentary) – Cinematographer 2003
Walter and June (TV movie) – Cinematographer 1983
The Red and the Blue: Impressions of Two Political Conferences - Autumn 1982 (TV documentary) – Cinematographer 1983
Made in Britain (TV movie) – Cinematographer 1982
Walter (TV movie) – Cinematographer 1982
A Question of Leadership (TV documentary) – Cinematographer 1981
Auditions (TV documentary) – Cinematographer 1980

JOHN CAMERON

Past Films & Videos (32 titles)
To End All Wars – Composer 2001
Driftwood – Composer 1997
Hawks – Composer 1998
The Jigsaw Man - Composer, Conductor 1983
Jimmy the Kid – Composer 1983
The Mirror Crack'd - Composer, Conductor 1980
The Omega Connection – Composer 1979
Sunburn – Composer 1979
Lost and Found – Composer 1979
The Bermuda Triangle – Composer 1979
The Stud - Conductor, Music Arranger 1978
Nasty Habits – Composer 1977
Come una rosa al naso – Composer 1976
Great Scout and Cathouse Thursday – Composer 1976
Made – Composer 1975
Whiffs – Composer 1975
Out of Season – Composer 1975
Moments – Composer 1974
The Bunny Caper – Composer 1974
Who? – Composer 1973
Scalawag – Composer 1973
A Touch of Class - Composer, Conductor 1973
Night Watch – Composer 1973
Charley One-Eye – Composer 1972
The Ruling Class - Composer, Musical Director 1972

The Strange Vengeance of Rosalie – Composer 1972
The Death Wheelers – Composer 1971
Black Beauty – Composer 1971
The Rise and Rise of Michael Rimmer – Composer 1970
Every Home Should Have One – Composer 1970
Kes - Composer, Conductor 1969
Poor Cow - Musical Director 1967

Past Television (13 titles)
Joseph and the Amazing Technicolor Dreamcoat (TV movie) – Orchestrator 1999
Hey, Mr Producer! The Musical World of Cameron Mackintosh (TV special) – Orchestrator 1998
Les Misérables in Concert (TV special) – Orchestrator 1995
Frankenstein (TV movie) – Composer 1993
Jekyll & Hyde (TV movie) – Composer 1990
Jack the Ripper (TV movie) - Composer, Conductor, Music Arranger 1988
The Secret Garden (TV movie) – Composer 1987
Philip Marlowe, Private Eye (TV series) – Composer 1983
Witness for the Prosecution (TV movie) - Composer, Conductor 1982
The Thief of Baghdad (TV movie) – Composer 1978
1990 (TV series) – Composer 1977
Spectre (TV movie) – Composer 1977
The Protectors (TV series) – Composer 1972

KES – Composed by John Cameron

Track listing

1. FRONT TITLES (02:49)
2. BILLY'S PAPER ROUND (00:17)
3. DAWN - BILLY SEES KES IN THE TOWER (03:45)
4. STEALING THE BOOK (01:18)
5. MIDNIGHT - BILLY CLIMBS AND CAPTURES KES (02:47)
6. TRAINING KES (00:59)
7. KES' FIRST FLIGHT (00:41)
8. JUD WALKS TO THE MINE (00:53)
9. KES FLIES FREE (01:01)
10. KES FLIES HIGHER (01:00)
11. BILLY ASLEEP IN THE BOILER ROOM (00:18)
12. FOREBODING (00:33)
13. LOOKING FOR KES (00:57)
14. REALISATION (00:39)
15. BURYING KES (00:40)

Total Duration: 00:18:37

Personnel: Harold McNair (Flute), Ronnie Ross (Bass Clarinet), Danny Moss (Clarinet), Tony Carr (Drums), David Snell (Harp). Engineered by Vic Smith. Recorded at Olympic Studios in 1969. LP produced by Jonny Trunk.

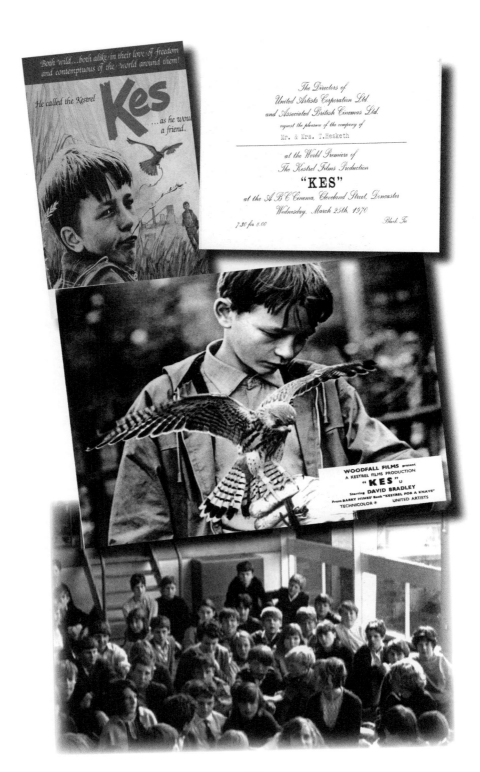

The early morning paper rounds proving too much for Billy

PE teacher Sugden picking his Manchester United team

Casper with Mr Farthing - *'Is it heck tame..........'*

The Festival
Committee
described it as
the outstanding
film of the year.

The bullies lair!

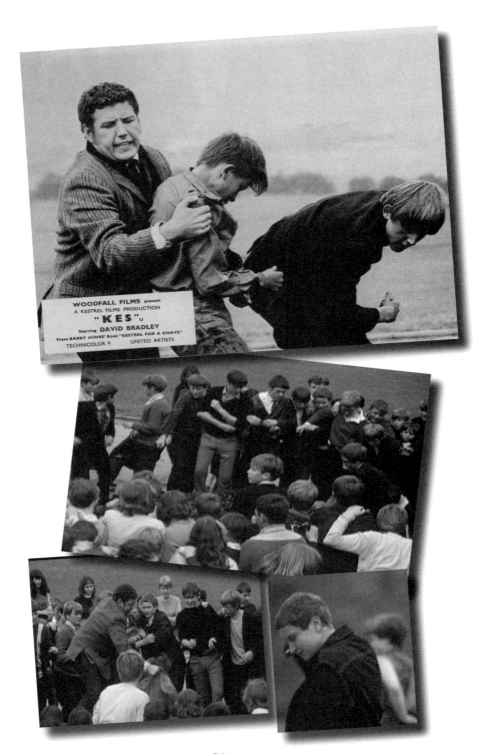

A day in the life of the Caspers

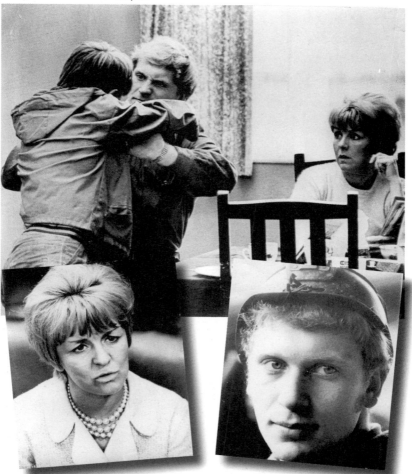

Lynne Perrie who played Mrs Casper   Freddie Fletcher who played Jud Casper

Dai Bradley who played Billy Casper wearing Mr Sugden's over-sized shorts

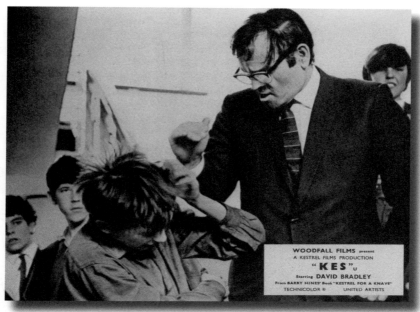

Headmaster, Gryce puddin' getting to grips with young Casper

Peter Clegg,
Cleggie in the film

Trevor Hesketh
who used his
own name in
Kes

George
Speed was
on Sugden's
team

Bernard Atha
who played the
Youth Employment
Officer

Acknowledgements

Special thanks to the cast and crew... Ken Loach, Tony Garnett, Barry Hines, Chris Menges, John Cameron, Dai (David) Bradley, Freddie Fletcher, Lynne Perrie, Colin Welland, David Glover, Bob (Robert) Naylor, Michael Joyce, Roy Turner, Martin Harley, Joey Kaye, John Grayson, Duggie Brown, Julie Shakespeare, George Speed, Zoe Sunderland, Eric Bolderson, Jim Ryder, Desmond Guthrie, Peter Clegg, Bernard Atha, Mike (Michael) Padgett, Trevor & Hazel Hesketh, Leslie Stringer, Jean Palmer, Julie Goodyear, Ann Goulding, Penny Eyles, Ray Orton, Mr Addy, Dennis and Eric Wicks, Tony Woodcock,
The 4D Jones Band - John Stenton, David Hargeaves, Les Stokes, Alan Lodge, Geoff Hollin.

Additional thanks to... Tara Glover; Camilla Bray and Alistair Griggs from Sixteen Films Ltd.; Iciar Bollain and Paul Laverty; Georgia; Jacob Leigh - The Cinema of Ken Loach; Garry Lammin; Melvin Bragg; Leon Garfield - author of Black Jack; Derek Malcolm; Penguin Books; David Robinson - The Financial Times; David Chell - Moviemakers at Work; Pete Redmond – Mojo; John Benton-Hughes – Trunk records; Jarvis Cocker; David Henderson - Carnegie College of Physical Education; Peter Crookston - The Sunday Times; Billy Bragg; Jean Renoir; Uri Geller; John Threlkeld - Morning Telegraph; Clarence Hirst – headmaster of St Helen's; Secrets of the Street by Blake Publishing Ltd.; Christy Welland; John Warrack – The Telegraph; Dave Burland; Vaughan Allen - The Big Issue; Nina Hibbin - Morning Star; Kathy Green; Jack Wild; Darryl Hickman; Jackie Cooper; Shirley Temple Black; Margaret O'Brien; Mark Lester; Adrian Hall; Roddy McDowall; Brian Forbes; David Jason; Willy Russell; John Lynch; Geffrey Palmer; John Sessions; Bob Brydon; Stephen Fry; Patrick Stewart; Paul Petersen; Joanna Lumley; Michael Aspel; Nick Ross; Uri Geller; Alan Ayckbourn; Alan Parker; Stephen Frears; Virginia McKenna; Nell Dunn; Eve Kenny - BECTU Membership Department; Ay Up. Friends Re-United; The Stage; Andrew Robinson - The Yorkshire Post; Ian Thompson - The Barnsley Chronicle; International Movie Database; Equity; Amanda Swanne - The Spotlight; The British Newspaper Library; Caroline De Wolfe; Lisa Palmer; Andrew Youdell & George Watson - British Film Institute; Avta - Phoenix Arts; Comics UK and especially founder Alan Notton; and web users Colin Nobel and Billy Hicks; Damien Royal; DC Thomson & Co Ltd – The Dandy; Steve Lee - The British Falconer's Club; Sandy Knight & Sarah Culverhouse - Not A Pushy Mum; A Minor Consideration; Walt, Mickey and Me - Confessions Of the First Ex-Mouseketeer – published by Dell; Sue Hamby & Carole Henshaw at Edward Sheerien School; Cllr Steve Houghton and Barnsley Council; Richard Hines; Dave Brown; Lula; Cynthia Dunne; Akin Ajumo – The Guardian; Don McCorkindale; Paul – Apollo security guard; Ethan Hardcastle - The Daily Mail; Nicky (Spilly) Blackman; John Cunningham – The Observer; Geoffrey Mather - Daily Express; Mike Tomkies - Show Page; Bel Mooney - Daily Mirror; Geoffrey Hilditch & Maurice Jagger; Malcolm Brown; Mr Peter Conder – former director of the Royal Society for the Protection of Birds; Margaret Hinxman - The Sunday Telegraph; Alexander Walker - Evening Standard; Patrick Allen; Patrick Gibbs - The Daily Telegraph; Howard Schumann; John Russell Taylor – The Times; Fergus Cashin – The Sun; Ian Sainsbury; Bill Tidy; Mr M. Young; Stefan Kanfer – Time Magazine; Jay Cocks; Wendy Middleton – Radio Sheffield; Carol Sarler - The Sunday Times.